BATTLE for

*A Memoir of Pain, Redemption
and Impossible Love*

**By Cynthia Toussaint
with Linden Gross**

Special Contributions by John Garrett

ISBN-13: 978-1482592047
ISBN-10: 1482592045

Cover photos: Coral von Zumwalt (front), Dana Patrick (back)

Cover & Interior design: Michael P. McHugh, DigitalFusion – Santa Monica, CA

Note to the Reader

While all people, companies and incidences described in this book are real, certain names
and, in some instances, other identifying characteristics have been changed. Whenever a
name is changed, an asterisk follows the name where it first appears.

WHAT THEY'RE SAYING...

"*Battle for Grace*—Cynthia's journey and story—is a true testament to the strength of the human spirit. Cynthia is at once honest, determined, raw and inspiring. You will find yourself rooting for her through the challenges and delighting in the victories."
>   — Beth Darnall, PhD, clinical associate professor, Division of Pain
>   Management, Stanford University

"Be forewarned: Reading Cynthia's memoir will break your heart. Yet despite her agony, she has not only survived, but thrived. She gives hope and courage to other women in pain."
>   — Cheryl England, editor/publisher, *Southern California Physician*

"Cynthia Toussaint's life is one of the most incredible stories I've ever heard. Her passion for life and for helping others—even in the face of seemingly insurmountable hardship and devastating pain—can inspire all of us. Her life story also sheds light on the shortcomings of a health system that too often fails to meet the needs of patients such as herself."
>   — David Olmos, former health editor of the *Los Angeles Times* and
>   Pulitzer Prize finalist

"I enjoyed *Battle for Grace* because it looks deeply not just at the person experiencing pain, but also at the caregiver who shares in the experience. I appreciate the degree to which the love between the two people in this story promotes their healing."
>   — Kevin Dobson, actor

"*Battle for Grace* shines a light on the plight of women in pain and the perseverance it takes to change the system. This is a story of hope and success. In a word, inspirational."
>   — California State Senator Carol Liu

"Cynthia's book depicts how life-changing pain can be and the importance of hope, courage and an openness to new treatments. Expressing pain in words can be remarkably healing as *Battle for Grace* reveals."
>   — Paul J. Christo, MD, MBA, host, *Aches and Gains* Radio Show, associate
>   professor, Division of Pain Medicine, Johns Hopkins University School of
>   Medicine, www.paulchristomd.com

"Loneliness...trapped...despair...fear. These are the reactions I hear from my chronic pain patients. This book is part of Ms. Toussaint's journey to get beyond her fear and despair. Her book will inspire, comfort and inject hope into the lives of my patients and their loved ones. I call it required reading for their healthcare providers!"

— Steven Richeimer, MD, chief, Division of Pain Medicine, University of Southern California

"Chronic pain's impact on society is enormous. More than anything else, we need champions who will speak to the millions whose lives have been devastated. *Battle for Grace* answers that call."

— Penney Cowan, executive director, American Chronic Pain Association

"Pain management is still an uncharted territory in medicine—ask anyone who has chronic pain. Cynthia's story is maddening, but provides hope for everyone who deals with pain and, like she, has learned to conquer an unseen enemy."

— Tiiu Leek, actress and former Los Angeles newscaster

"Undaunted by pain, disability or the tyranny rampant in our broken healthcare system, Cynthia tells it all in this book. She speaks with the authority of a survivor and the conviction of a saint. Purveyors of healthcare injustice beware."

— Don Schroeder, PhD, producer, *The Healthcare Solution: California OneCare*, founding chapter co-director, Health Care for All–California

"Despite her incredible hardships and struggles, there is a silver lining in Cynthia's life. She not only has a compelling story, she has that rare ability to tell it in ways that touch our hearts. She is a beautiful, engaging and loving woman who shines a bright light on issues that have lived in darkness for too long."

— Laura Morgan, former director of communications and chief media spokesperson, *Los Angeles Times*

"Cynthia's book speaks for all women in pain. Women who not only suffer physically, but who also struggle with finding the right doctors—doctors who take them seriously and don't brush them off with 'it's all in your head.'"

— Diane Hoffmann, law professor, University of Maryland and co-author of *The Girl Who Cried Pain: A Bias Against Women in the Treatment of Pain*

"It takes a remarkable and special individual to rise above a debilitating disease and dedicate her life to helping others. That's Cynthia Toussaint and this goes for her man, John, as well. His commitment to Cynthia and *Battle for Grace* is beautiful."

— **California State Senator Liz Figueroa**

"Several years ago, Cynthia spoke at Women In Government's annual conference, bringing a new, deeper understanding of pain to our membership of legislators. I was moved to tears, and felt especially blessed to have met Cynthia shortly after I started experiencing persistent pain. Her book comforts all of us."

— **Joy Newton, founder, Women In Government**

"It's been an honor to work with Cynthia Toussaint over the past three years to forge legislation that will improve access to care for people with pain. Cynthia's inspiring story moves the most thick-skinned legislators and brings hope and encouragement to everyone challenged by pain and difficulties."

— **U.S. Congressman Jared Huffman**

"*Battle for Grace* tells how Cynthia Toussaint's commitment to expose the HMO industry's wrongdoings helped move public opinion that created historic change here in California and beyond. Her courage took her own great misfortune at the hands of a failed healthcare system to give a voice to others trapped by these profit-driven corporations."

— **Jamie Court, president, Consumer Watchdog and co-author of** *Making A Killing: HMOs and the Threat to Your Health*

"Ms. Toussaint's testimony before the California Senate on the disparate treatment of women in pain was a pivotal event. She continues to be a strong advocate for change, particularly for a single payer system in California. Her book speaks volumes about this."

— **California State Senator Sheila Kuehl**

"Some stories have to be told. Cynthia Toussaint's is one of them. This story, this life, lets the world know that it's possible to live in pain and grow despite it."

— **Will Rowe, former executive director, American Pain Foundation**

For my mother

*who gave me the love, appreciation
and wisdom to find grace*

CONTENTS

INTRODUCTION

This is a book about my life. A life that has been molded by pain.

A battle for grace—told from the gut and so much from my heart. A second storyteller, John Garrett, the beautiful man in my life who has had as much to do with this story as I, also shares his life and struggle as a caregiver and lover of someone whose body deserted her.

I know, deeply, that I would not be telling this story now if John had not remained such a vital part of it.

One warning. This ride will get bumpy. We'll share some tears, fear, joy and laughter. And we'll arrive at a place that surprises even us.

Writing this memoir, for both of us, has been a journey from the pits of pain and despair to peaks of love and compassion. And, often, back again to the pits. Pits I can no longer imagine I allowed to happen.

It's also a journey that healed and lifted us into a peace and consciousness we never thought possible. And revealed to us the transformative power of suffering.

We hope our story and its life-empowering aspects will touch other lives threatened by physical and emotional pain that can go to depths few of us ever experience.

Welcome to our life.

Cynthia Toussaint
March 2013

ONE

THE FIRE WITHIN

The pain makes me feel like I've been doused with gasoline and lit on fire. My gut tells me I'm never going to get better. I'm never going to walk again. Worse, I'm never going to dance again.

I know it.

Still, I won't give up, even though I have more to fight than screaming pain and disability. Yet another doctor has told me this is all in my head. They've been saying the same thing since my initial injury 13 years ago. Their attitude used to make the suffering worse. Now it infuriates me and strengthens my resolve not to be a victim. How many others in pain do they refuse to believe? How many others are condemned to a life of torture that could have ended with belief and early treatment?

❧

It started that day at the barre at the University of California, Irvine. I faced the mirror, the ballerina's daily companion. I stretched, rehearsed and stretched some more. In this odd state of tranquil intensity, I watched my reflection, aware of my body as an instrument. I had just relaxed into the top of my stretch at the barre when my friend Meg shattered the moment.

"What would you do if you had to be in a wheelchair for the rest of your life?" she asked.

I shifted, uncharacteristically slipping out of my turnout to stare at her, then blurted it out.

"I'd kill myself."

It took just that moment to ponder—and reject—the unimaginable. Quite simply, it could never be. The world was waiting for me to star in the movie, dance the dance, sing the song. Being in a wheelchair, crippled, was not part of that picture. I wouldn't want to survive in that condition.

My life path had been set at age 7 when Mom took us kids to see *Funny Girl* at the old Hillcrest in Pleasant Hill, my hometown in the San Francisco Bay Area. I'd never been to a movie house before. Big green curtains veiled the giant screen until after the overture. When they opened and the screen lit up, I saw the back of a woman draped in a leopard fur coat and matching hat, collar raised, walking toward a theater with a glowing marquee. Her high heels clicked on the pavement. Finally, she turned to a backstage mirror, pulled the collar away from her face exposing eyes accented with heavy liner and purred, "Hello, Gorgeous." That was *it* for me. I couldn't take my eyes off the screen. She was the most beautiful woman I had ever seen. I wanted to be just like her.

The Ziegfeld Follies number captivated me even more. All the stunning women in their make-up, feathers and rhinestones, long, slender legs in fishnets walking up and down a massive staircase, bookended with glittering sets. I'd never seen anything like this. I was so overwhelmed, tears streamed down my cheeks. I turned to my mother. "I don't want it to ever end." Mom smiled and held me tight.

By the time it did end, I knew exactly what I was going to do for the rest of my life and I couldn't wait to get started. As we walked to the car, I saw a glamour-filled future in which I sang, danced and made people laugh, all splashed on the big screen and stage. I knew I would be famous.

I enrolled in a ballet class, and was soon contriving reasons to stay home from school so I could choreograph my own musicals. I would decide on a character to play for the day, and then dive into my wardrobe department of Halloween holdovers—boxes in the garage full of Mom's old prom and homecoming queen dresses along with big-hair wigs, gigantic boobs and thick make-up rescued from the Goodwill. Each time I'd use a new voice and accent, always over the top. When Mom came home, I performed using her grand piano as a show-stopping prop. Unfailingly, my acts made her beam.

David, who was 6 and the youngest of my three brothers, often teamed up with me to crank out carefully choreographed song and dance numbers from the great musicals. From early on, David and I were the two closest siblings. We just got each other and shared a love for performing. Using screwdrivers as mikes, we improvised, playing off each other like Lewis and Martin, except that both of us were Jerry. Then I'd start singing Marie Osmond, vamping "I'm a Little Bit Country," exaggerating all that was over the top about her, and David would jump in as a bigger-than-life Donnie. Our living room became Carnegie Hall, the Grand Ole Opry and a Hollywood sound stage almost every night.

In my mid teens, my productions with David began to grow. We went all out for *Chicago's* "He Had It Coming"—costumes, choreography, a ton of rehearsal. This was our showstopper. When David eventually tired and quit for the day, I begged him to do the number just one more time, then carried on by myself for hours. I never tired of performing my repertoire and making the kids from the neighborhood, with parents in tow, peal with laugher. They'd burst into applause each time I exploded in *A Chorus Line* kick or spoofed Streisand.

My polished acts also included imitations of everyone I knew. Neighborhood kids, teachers and stars like Tippi Hedren, Liza Minelli, Morgan Fairchild. You name 'em, I could do 'em.

"I can't believe how many you can pull off," said my sister Beth, who I loved to mimic. "It never ends." My favorite number from

Gypsy said it all: "Let Me Entertain You." I was addicted to the high of it. I loved the adrenaline of grabbing people's attention and stirring them up. I was good, and my little 9-year-old self flat out knew it.

Ironically, at school I was painfully shy. I never raised my hand and barely let out a peep. I didn't have many friends, so I usually ate lunch alone and spent recesses in the library. After a teacher's conference, Mom remarked with a giggle, "I can't believe you're the retiring girl they just told me about!" I didn't fit in. I didn't like the cliquey-ness of it, and the kids couldn't understand why I was always shooting off to ballet class.

As much as I loved all types of performing, in those days I lived for ballet. My first teacher, Lily, told me I could become a professional ballerina. Each day, I counted the minutes until the final bell. I couldn't wait to get to the studio. That's where I was comfortable and could really be me. With ballet, you're either right or you're wrong. And my body was slowly evolving to a point where I rarely hit a bad note.

I no longer wanted to dance. I *had* to. I'd tap dance all the time, scuffing up Mom's parquet floors. Then I'd grab our family friend—burly, eager Vince—to be my ballet partner. I'd teach him intricate lifts to *Don Quixote's pas de deux* while *en pointe*.

As Mom did dishes in the kitchen, she would think, "I'm the luckiest person in the world." She had dreamed of being an accomplished ballerina, but her mother wouldn't allow a single lesson. By the time she had started dancing in her late 30s, no amount of hard work would compensate for the lost time. Now she was watching her oldest daughter live her dream.

Though ballet had become my nutrient, as natural and necessary as the air I breathed, I wasn't exclusive. I also wanted to be in front of the cameras. I studied the women in TV commercials and soon was doing my own. I was one of the early hyphenates:

writer-director-actor. I delighted in practicing the commercials I wrote. I'd balance a bottle of Mom's Prell on my shoulder and do the perfect pitch. I knew instinctively which words to use and emphasize. Plus I knew how important it was to be likeable, charismatic and effective. Little did I know I was grooming myself for a sales pitch light years away from *any* commercial.

I often talked to Mom about my dream of stardom on the screen and stage. She was always there for me, but I never felt she shared my belief that this would happen. Nonetheless, she always supported my pursuit of this dream. Strangely enough, show business was already in the family. Her dad, Grandpa Haering, played in the John Phillips Sousa Band and often shouted, "Once you get showbiz in your blood, you can never get it out." I'm Exhibit A to prove that one.

A week after Meg asked me the unthinkable question, I dressed for a full day of classes and rehearsals, then skipped off to my favorite UCI ballet class. Wearing my black knitted bodysuit pulled down just below my waist, I hit the barre and soon warmed up to a delicious coat of sweat. After the 45-minute barre work, we stretched before going centre floor just as we did every day. But this time, my favorite teacher, Larry Rosenberg, said, "You're such high level dancers. When you pull your body up from your knee, stretch your back out. Enjoy it."

So I did. And then it happened. *Pop!* Like a guitar string being plucked, something snapped in the back of my right leg.

My body dropped and I impulsively held my leg just above and behind my knee. I looked up and was stunned to see the other dancers finishing their stretches and moving center floor as if the entire universe hadn't abruptly changed.

I took a few moments to assess the damage. Up until then, I'd suffered an unusually low number of injuries and had even looked down on hurt dancers. Despite the occasional pulled muscle or tendonitis, I never let weakness slow me down. Never.

I was determined to keep going this time as well. I got up, but instead of moving to my usual spot front and center, or as close to it as possible, I gingerly took a position in the back. I tried to do the *tendu* and *dégagé* combinations, but my right leg wouldn't react. I limped to the side of the studio, cheeks flushed with fear and shame, picked up my green duffle bag and beelined to UCI's dance trainer.

I liked Rick. He was kind, professional and caring. He knew exactly what he was doing. I felt safer right away despite the news.

"You've torn your right lateral hamstring just above the knee. That's where the muscle connects with the tendon," he said.

"What's a hamstring?"

Rick shook his head. "You dancers! You can do anything with your bodies, but you don't know where anything's at."

"Hey, man, I passed kinesiology. Doesn't that count for something?" I asked with a crooked smile. He pulled out a diagram of the human body and pointed to the crisscrossing bundle of muscle that was the culprit.

"Listen, Cynthia, hamstring tears are bad. You're going to have to do physical therapy here three times a week, and swim on the alternate days. You might not be able to dance for up to eight weeks."

Eight weeks? "Rick, I can't do that. I'm in rehearsals. I've got classes every day. And finals are coming. I can't take the time off."

"You don't have a choice."

As much as I respected Rick's expertise, I knew I wouldn't wait that long. I'd double up the physical therapy and get back on my toes. I didn't want *anything* to do with this injury crap. It just wasn't me.

After an hour of weights and whirlpool, Rick carefully Ace bandaged my right leg and I hobbled off to my campus apartment. The gnawing pain pulled at my knee. That loss of control left me confused and disoriented. Before long, I heard a pack of screaming girls in a car pull up next to me.

"Hey, Cynth. Wanna catch a ride? And why aren't you in class, Miss Ballerina?" scolded Melissa* who was wedged between her sorority sisters.

I didn't smile back. "I got a leg injury in class today. It hurts like hell to walk, but I'm almost there."

Melissa crinkled her brow with concern. "Okay, doll. See you at home. And you get off that leg quick, ya hear? Want me to pick you up something at Big Bob's?"

I waved her off.

When I got to the apartment, no one was there. I dropped down on my bed in the room I shared with Anna Marie. My side was pristine clean; hers was draped in clothes, papers and books. I'd always been a neat freak and had driven my family nutty with my tidying tendencies. The joke was that I'd pick up and clean the tableware before they finished eating. Okay, they had a point. For once, however, I didn't care about the mess. I lay there for a long time, eventually turning to my side and cradling myself. *It's going to be okay*, I told myself. *It's going to be okay*. Peering at Baryshnikov's image on my white wall, I whispered, "What would you do, Misha?"

I woke to my roommates chattering about the chicken dish Kelly was whipping up. These gals I adored were making a special dinner in honor of me surviving the day. Lifted and wanting to get out there to share in the mirth, I headed to the bathroom, almost forgetting the pain. The moment I sat down on the toilet, I screamed in agony. It felt like a lightning bolt was firing both ways from my hamstring up to my right buttocks and all the way down to my foot. The girls rushed in, looking confused and helpless.

"What's going on?" Melissa asked. "I mean, it shouldn't be this bad, should it?"

"I don't know, Melissa," I said, the tears starting to pool. "I don't understand. But the trainer says I'm going to be okay. He says the physical therapy will fix me."

After dinner, pain still stinging my leg, I called Mom on my rotary telephone. She became so alarmed that I tried to reassure her. "It's just a simple injury, Mom. Ballerinas get this stuff all the time, right? Now it's my turn. I'm really going to be fine."

I was trying to calm myself, too. My leg was telling me everything was not okay. My star was dimming, my future not so sure.

Over the next few weeks, I fell into a different routine. My early morning swims in freezing water were painful, but also familiar since I'd swum competitively during my childhood. Often I had the pool to myself. I felt loneliness completely foreign to me. Each day I sat through every one of my dance classes among a pile of dancer bags and toss-offs. I'd write notes about the movement and choreography in order to maintain my grade. Incapacitated for the first time ever, it was hard not to feel like a failure.

No one seemed to understand my sense of devastation, including John Garrett, my boyfriend and fellow performer. John, who I fell for at first sight, had been a vital part of my life for two years when my hamstring popped. But despite his entrenched sensitivity, he surprised me with his initial blasé attitude. He actually had a gas playing around with my crutches. That kind of playfulness was not new. From early on, whenever John and I first saw each other, he'd immediately pick me up and turn me upside down. "She's light as a feather, no bigger than a postage stamp," he'd say with a laugh. I loved it. But now some of his clowning was tougher to take. He'd been cast as a kamikaze commander in an environmental theater piece and used my crutches to play-act a wounded soldier, complete with yelps from the battlefield. He was pretty good and even looked the part with his new Marine buzz-cut, but my amusement was tainted with a sense of loss because he didn't seem to get just how much my injury hurt and how deeply it frightened me. I could only focus on trying to appease the throbbing that had started to control my life.

During the evenings, I sat through rehearsals for an original ballet, *Space Odyssey*. Before I'd been hurt, Corrine Calamaro, another top ballerina at Irvine, had asked me to perform in the piece. Instead, I had to watch the choreography as the dancers rehearsed. Capturing it in my head, I used my hands, flicking sharp and quick, to mimic the movement—a ballerina's trick to learn intricate footwork. As I watched the dancers, my muscle "memory" let me feel the high of it. I longed to be on that stage sweating, gasping hard, extending my legs and arms to their limits and fiercely floating.

The only time I felt normal and anything like my old cheerful self was when I was with John. Even though I wasn't mending as quickly as I'd hoped, he remained unconcerned and upbeat, certain this was just a passing setback, a small bump on the road to stardom. He told me about the ballplayers he'd followed since he was a kid. They'd pull a muscle or tear a ligament, hobble a bit, rest, get a cortisone shot and *voilà*, they were back on the field of dreams no worse for the wear. I, too, would be there again—and soon.

"Babe, it'll take just a bit more time," he'd say with a peck on my forehead. "Then you'll be kicking it up again."

I'm not sure I believed him. But eating dinner in the Commons with many of the performers who resided in Prado, the theater dorm, lifted my spirits. Those meals, with all the jokes, improvisations of various injuries, and play-acted scenes with doctors, nurses and spilling bedpans, helped me forget reality. For a blink, I was one of them again.

After five weeks of rest and physical therapy, I returned to class. Back in the studio, I felt like I was home. The pain was still there, which scared me, but I was in control of my body again. Despite the pain that we ballerinas are taught to smile through, I did a beautiful, high-level barre. To be safe, I joined dancers two levels below my ability. Aside from avoiding front center, no one would have known that I was way off my game or how much that performance cost me. I overheard other girls whispering, "That's the girl in Ballet IV who's so good. Can you believe her technique?" I pushed myself to meet their expectations and to satisfy my ego, and left a puddle of sweat to prove it.

Itching to get back to speed, I attended my advanced ballet class the next morning. I wanted to be working with high-level dancers again no matter what. My friend Dan joined me while I carefully warmed up my right leg.

"This is great, Cynthia! Hallelujah, you're back. What knocked you out for so long?"

"I tore my hamstring, Dan" I confided sheepishly. "It still isn't right."

"Bummer," he said. "I tore my hamstring two years ago. You have to know it'll never be the same. But it won't show in your dancing. You're just going to feel it." He paused as he watched me. "I always warm up my bad leg with extra care. You should too."

Comforted to have a kindred soul, I asked anxiously, "So your leg always hurts, too?"

A quizzical look crossed his face. "No. Mine's still tight and I don't always get the extension I had before. But the pain eased up pretty quick after the injury."

Dan's response sent a chill through me. Something's really wrong. This isn't normal.

John's Take

It's just a matter of time and healing before we'll put all this hamstring nonsense behind us. Cynthia knows what she wants and she's going for it. I marvel at this dedication. For her, it's Manifest Destiny.

I can't believe this incredible, talented and determined woman is in love with me. She's compelled me to finally escape from my almost unshakeable hang-ups about commitment. I love her that much. It's a once-in-a-lifetime with Cynthia. She is something special. Her warmth, her kindness, her decency and humanity. If I'm ever going to take this plunge, this is the girl. At first, I put up my defense shields. Hid behind the smoke and mirrors of being a man of the theater. Aloof, cerebral. Bullshit. She cut through it like a surgeon, going straight for the heart. She took this terrified man-child by the hand and led me to paradise. She gave me reason to trust. Her blue eyes and soft touch made me stop running away. She is Pachelbel's Canon in D personified. Flowing full of grace and light, lifting me to a place where I am free. No more hiding. No more shame. I am loved. And I love.

That being said, I'm convinced that at any moment she'll come to her senses and give me my walking papers. I'll be yesterday's news. I'm not chopped liver, but I know when I'm out of my league.

Professionally, I see myself as a bit above average, a dime a dozen at the casting calls. Maybe a character lead, maybe a supporting player. An Italian thug. A cop with a few lines. The lead's best friend. But if I can make a living at acting—any living—that would be just dandy with me.

Cynthia has a different design. She operates the way she dances. So sure. So focused. She just needs some rest and physical therapy and we'll get on with our lives. The lyrics of that Top 40 song echo in my head: "The future's so bright, I gotta wear shades."

Really, I'm not worried. Hell, it's not like her leg is about to fall off. Cynth's as tough as they come. But why won't this damn pain let up?

TWO

OUT OF SYNC

Floundering.

Suddenly, for the first time ever, that's where I was. It began the moment I felt my pain wasn't a normal hamstring injury. I grasped for straws like I was being pulled in three directions. I'd process my ideas, choice by choice, embrace one strongly, then realize it was either impractical or didn't make sense. I was drowning in this kaleidoscope of crazy-makers that ran my life as much as my ever increasing pain.

I initially chose to ignore the pain, even though I truly couldn't. Because I was in my senior year at UCI, the only things standing between me and the stardom I wanted were a little more time to get my diploma and the pain in my leg. This led me to search my copy of *Dramalog* for auditions, many of which were not suited to someone with a leg injury. Testing the waters without an agent, I submitted my headshots and resumes anyway.

The phone started ringing, and more often than not I came home from class to my three screaming-with-excitement room-mates. They'd be huddled in my doorway with messages from Paramount, Fox and the like. Hollywood was calling, and I was still stuck in school with a messed up leg. My goal had been to be famous by the time I was 17. I was now four years past my expiration date with fear and uncertainty growing every day.

Then suddenly, success called. "You need to be at Paramount this afternoon to interview for the producers of *Fame*," said the hit show's casting director. They were casting a new female lead.

Double wow! All those years of laser-beam focus and sweat were about to pay off. No agent, no union card, just me limping a tad with sparks flying, adorned in a lavender jumpsuit and matching high-heeled Candies.

My one-on-one chat with the producers felt great to me, and I knew they'd be in touch. I envisioned signing the contract, learning lines, joking with my costars and seeing my name in the opening credits. It was a matter of when, not if.

That night I lay awake, my head buzzing with uncertainties and possibilities. I couldn't wait to take the first steps to stardom. But I also couldn't wait to get my diploma. I'd wanted that piece of paper since I was a kid. Almost everyone who was important to me had one. This, of course, triggered a major conflict. It was impossible to get both at the same time. I stewed a lot, but eventually convinced myself I would find a way to have it all.

For me it was fame or bust, and bust was not an option. So I returned to dance class, still waiting to hear from *Fame*. Despite the pain, my footwork was precise and I nailed each combination. My balance *en pointe* was still flawless. Damn it, I was going to hang on to my dance technique no matter how much my leg hurt.

With each class, my whole being honed into ballet to the exclusion of everything else. Once again I felt the joy of being immersed in the movement, instructions, piano music and combinations, until a *grand battement en face* sent me crashing back to reality. My hamstring snapped again, this time with a sickening familiarity. My leg dropped and I immediately limped off through the crowded class. Feeling beaten for the first time, I sat on the floor and cradled my leg, tears flooding my face. *No, no, no. Not again. I was supposed to be okay.*

Paula, a dancer and trainer who was keenly aware of my injury, rushed over. "How bad is it?" she asked. My head dropped and I sobbed my answer. She ran out and brought back a bag of chipped ice. I put it on my leg, but the fear in my eyes must have told her that ice wouldn't fix it.

The next morning, at Paula's urging, I hobbled to the Student Health clinic to see a doctor. Low on hope, I smiled back at the nurse who took my vitals and handed me a gown. Dr. Patterson, slight, middle-aged and kind in demeanor, listened carefully. He tried to reassure me, drawing a healthy hamstring on a blackboard, then explaining that mine had partially torn.

He said that with rest and physical therapy I'd be better before I knew it, which was scary because the trainer had said the same thing. He brushed off my question about the burning pain I'd felt since the initial injury.

"You're a dancer, Cynthia. And like every dancer, you're acutely aware of each inch of your body. It's a huge challenge, but I urge you," he paused and looked into my eyes, "don't pay too much attention to that pain."

I knew Patterson was sincere and very much in my corner. But I also knew he was missing the boat. I had already begun to read my body better than virtually any doctor I ever saw.

I returned to classes and rehearsals with just my Ace bandage for company, only now I had to sit through them again instead of participating. To my surprise, the other dancers seemed less friendly, avoiding conversations and no longer asking how I was.

Internationally known dance teacher and choreographer Israel "El" Gabriel provided another surprise. Earlier in the year, he had advised me to leave school. For good. "You're too talented to stay," he told me. "You can do anything you want in the professional world."

After my injury, he told me to go home for a different reason. "Heal up, then come back," he said bluntly, waving his arms toward the door. First I was too good. Now I was too broken.

He was right about one thing. If I couldn't dance, I no longer wanted to be there. But I still had a tiny glimmer of hope. I belonged to the huge healthcare system, Kaiser Permanente, which had a compound in the Bay Area near my hometown. They would make it right. The Student Health clinic with its single doctor had to be limited compared to Kaiser's staff and facilities. Kaiser's doctors had to fix people who were seriously injured. I'd just bide my time until Christmas break when I'd be back home.

I remember that day at Kaiser so clearly. As soon as I hit the Bay Area, I drove my Honda Civic to the Urgent Care clinic in Walnut Creek. Rod Stewart blared from my car's stereo and electric pain seared through my leg. As I limped to the clinic on a foot so red hot I thought it would explode, I had strong hopes that Kaiser would have the answer. My family's experience with Kaiser and my lifelong belief in the healing power of doctors were heightened by the imposing facilities.

I learned something important that day; namely, how completely my hope could be shattered in just 15 minutes. I can't recall the doctor's name, but I can still see his dismissive expression. He barely looked at me and most certainly didn't listen. Inching toward the door, he rattled off something about how I had nothing to worry about, I would be fine.

He ignored my questions about why my leg felt like it was being carved from the inside out with a razor, hot coals lumped on for good measure, and why the pain never responded to rest, ice or physical therapy. He didn't order *any* tests and offered no diagnosis, prescription, prognosis or follow-up visit. I sat there alone, my leg pulsating and turning purple, as it was apt to do.

Back at school, my feeling of hopelessness increased again when the *Fame* casting director sent a telegram urging me to get in touch. I returned to reality and brokenheartedly put the telegram in my top desk drawer. I knew I couldn't pull off a round of dance auditioning and, God forbid, the show's long season with its grueling rehearsals.

I spent afternoons alone in my apartment while everyone else bustled along with their lives. I needed a new plan of action, and quick. Since for me living meant performing, I revisited *Dramalog* and again submitted my headshot and resume for any role or show I thought I could handle. It didn't matter that I did this sitting on the floor of the living room, my right leg folded uselessly underneath me and my left leg naturally extended out to the side, arched toes pointed.

A short time later, I got a call from illusionist Mark Kalin, who had just seen my submission. The casting call specified that Kalin was looking for an illusionist's assistant who moved well onstage, which sounded splendidly low impact. *Okay, sign me up.* Following my trainer's advice, I didn't say a peep about the injury.

Mark explained that the girl who got the job would have a short, show-stopping, eye-popping jazz dance solo twice a night at the Reno Hilton. "She'll start right away," he said, before adding that he'd technically hired someone for the job, but she hadn't yet signed a contract. Would I audition for him at a dance studio in Pasadena the next morning before he flew back to Reno?

My heart plummeted. I couldn't handle my dance classes at school and was only taking the academic classes required for my diploma. *I want this so badly, but how can I ever pull it off?* Feeling I had no choice, I told Mark that I had to complete my studies and couldn't take a job until summer.

Upset, I limped over to John's apartment for some comfort. John being John told me to go for it.

"But I can't dance, John. Not even a short solo. And I couldn't bear to be in Reno without you."

He smiled. "Sweetie, it's simple. You go to Reno now, and I'll hop up there right after graduation. It's just a couple of months." Then he paused. "Anyhoo, you don't have to worry about the dancing. You're never going to get the gig. They're looking for Amazon women for those shows."

Alternately reassured and terrified that I'd missed my chance, I made a beeline for my phone. *Oh my God, what if he's already flown back?* Mark picked up and I shouted, "I've changed my mind. I want the audition tomorrow."

Because I'm the world's biggest direction idiot, John, as always, customized a map with yellow highlights and big, fat arrows. His directions were usually foolproof, but not this time. On the way to the studio the next day, I got turned around and had to call Mark's choreographer, Jennifer, from a pay phone. Not once, but twice. I felt like a total dweeb upon meeting her, but she immediately bailed me out. "Everyone gets lost," she said winking.

I quickly shed my street clothes and told her about my injury.

"Do I dare keep my plastic pants on to keep the leg warm?" I asked.

"No, never," she said definitively. I sensed she was pulling for me, especially when she re-choreographed the solo so I could do all of the high kicks with my left leg. *Yes!* I could have kissed Jennifer. *This is how I'll fake my way through.*

"This is perfect for you, Cynthia," she said. "The dancing's light and it'll give you time to rest your bad leg."

When Mark arrived with Armando, who I later learned was a world-class magician, I already glistened with a thin layer of sweat. I was down to my matching light blue tights, leotard and jazz shoes, accented by a hot pink boa Jennifer had supplied for punch. I felt ripe, just right for a knockout audition. After meeting Mark and Armando, we got down to business, adrenaline muting the pain.

Jennifer poked the button on the cassette player, and an upbeat, vaudeville-like striptease number spilled out. I bumped, grinded and kicked. "The audience has been watching the big production numbers," Mark announced. "Now it's just you downstage. I want you to seduce the audience with your face as well as, er, everything else." I felt I was inches from landing the job and I played to the studio mirror like a hungry lover.

After my number, I toweled off. The minutes ticked by as Mark and Jennifer remained huddled. I made some small talk with Armando, nerves rattling, until they came back and asked me to sit down. Mark grinned. "Basically, the job's yours, Cynthia, if you want it." I don't remember my response because I was stunned silly. I knew I'd nailed the audition, but that often doesn't bring home the bacon. Now, I'd just been offered the whole hog.

"I need to talk with my family first," I said after I'd composed myself. "And I have to think long and hard about leaving college."

Jennifer chimed in. "Cynthia, school will always be there. You'll learn more working professionally for four months than you'll learn in four years at college. Trust me on this."

Mark gave me one day to make a decision. By the time I put the key in my Honda, I already knew. I was heading for the bright lights of The Biggest Little City in the World.

John's face turned from stunned disbelief to eyes twinkling with the excitement of what was to come. I felt on top of the world. Deciding to brush up on my jazz dance and to test my abilities, I took class the next day with Kenny, a phenomenal jazz dancer and Irvine's best. After telling my friends Steve and Carla about the job, I assumed my old, familiar spot front and center.

Kenny liked me, but was forever tough because I was a ballerina. Usually he loved to needle me, nicknaming me "Bun Head." But when Kenny called roll on this day, he yelled, "Toussaint! I heard about the job." There was a long pause. "Congratulations, Toussaint."

The whole class buzzed at the news. I mean, no one ever really got a job like this. Even better, it was a solo. Man, I was proud, and

I wasn't going to disappoint Kenny, the class, or anyone else—including myself.

I danced hard, loving the choreography I was certain Kenny used in my honor. My long, lean body made it look like sweet butter. I felt that even the master Bob Fosse would have given me a second glance that day. Down and in, then back arched into a high kick and dropping into the splits on the floor. Sweat rained as I sprung back up, high kicking with the other leg leading to a bent knee, *jeté* jump. I was flying. I was in heaven.

I didn't know it, didn't have a clue. But that would be the last time I would dance full out ever again.

John's Take

For the life of me, I can't figure out why she wants to stick around for that diploma. I mean, what's it going to do for her? She's got all the stuff to make it in Hollywood. Let's go, baby! Time's a tickin'. This town is cruel to women and the longer you wait, the older you get. The younger versions of you start getting the parts you would have or should have gotten. Then the baby happens and next thing you know, you're a late 30s-something actress for whom they don't write roles.

Maybe the injury's a good thing. Maybe it's a wake-up call to move on down the line. Maybe Cynthia, the thoroughbred, has been at the starting gate too long. That's why she threw the shoe. The body's too tight, too tense getting ready for the Big What's Next. Screw that piece of paper. Run, run, my beauty. Let your strawberry blonde hair flare like a meteor shower in the night.

Ah, hell, what do I know? I just know I love her and I want the best for her. All things in good time. But that pain's starting to make me squirrelly. This is supposed to be a simple hamstring tear, right? I don't know squat about pain that doesn't quit. People get injuries, then they get better.

Don't they?

THREE

PUSHING THROUGH THE PAIN

Bathed in the thrill of getting the Reno job and all the congratulations, I headed back to the apartment. Then it hit like a blowtorch. My right leg could barely move forward as pain seized it far worse than ever before. With each step, dread and despair rolled in. *Why this time? What in hell am I going to do?*

By the time I saw Dr. Patterson the next day, my purple, sweaty leg was twitching uncontrollably. This time he was concerned because my pain was so much worse. When I told him I had to be well enough for Reno in a week, he urged me to turn the job down and move back into my mother's home. With that, he handed me a pair of crutches.

I spent the next week on the living room couch moaning intermittently due to the pain that now radiated up the right side of my back. As my roommates took turns caring for me, excited dancers stopped by to offer their congratulations. What a bizarre time.

Even John was sky high with excitement, making plans for our new life in the Sierra. He didn't realize something was going wrong big time until our spat over canned corn. I'd asked him to get me some from the kitchen. That would be dinner since I couldn't go grocery shopping. "Just get it yourself," he said, not moving an inch. I finally hopped to the kitchen and sat on a stool, moaning and eating the corn. My feeling of helplessness quickly turned to anger.

"I can't do it!" I shouted. "I can't even walk on this leg. How can I be a soloist in Reno?" I broke into tears, and John held me. "It's going to be okay," he murmured. "You'll get rest doing this show. It's going to be the time of our lives. We'll make this happen."

When I finally told Mark about the injury, I fudged and said it had just happened that week in class. I knew he might cut me loose, but I didn't have a choice. I was in too much pain to fake it. Instead of firing me, Mark gave me the rehearsal schedule and instructions to pick up the custom-made jazz shoes he'd ordered for me. That nailed it. Though the pain never let up and I wasn't sleeping much, I would damn well go for it.

John packed all my belongings, and Anna Marie went to the Hall of Administration to dis-enroll me. I got ready for my brother Paul's wedding in Santa Barbara which I'd attend the day before flying out to Reno. I'd been so excited he was marrying Tracy, especially since it would be the first wedding in our family. Now, the event terrified me because my pain was constant. Still, I picked the perfect outfit—a short, ruffled gray dress with a big pink bow tie around the waist, stunning gray pumps and a beaded purse. The drive up the coast with John, however, proved sheer torture. I was no longer moaning. Now I was screaming.

By the time we got to the hotel where my family was staying, I was hysterical. Leaning heavily on John's arm, I struggled my way to their suite. They greeted us with big smiles, but I couldn't be Cynthia. When Kazuko, a close friend from Japan who'd flown in for the wedding, got up to hug me, I broke down in sobs. Feeling embarrassed and guilty, I hobbled into the bathroom and lay on the cold tile. Mom followed me, and I cried in her arms. The rest of my family came in one at a time, hugging me as I lay on the floor. Their love helped me rally. Beth took off my make-up and quickly applied a new coat, while Kazuko found me a pair of slippers to match my dress. The pumps were out.

At the wedding, I steeled myself. A single tear would fall occasionally, betraying my agony. The worst pain came when I posed for the family wedding photos. I stood on my left leg, since the right one couldn't bear the weight or even straighten, and faked a smile for what felt like hours. To this day, I can't bear to look at those photos because all I see is the torture.

On the plane to Reno the next day, the gum-popping lady with two-foot high white hair sitting to my side made me panic about the move. *What, is Reno the trailer trash capital of the U.S.?* But I felt a familiar comfort when I saw Mark at the gate. We had quickly become friends because of our shared self-deprecating humor. This was exactly the medicine I needed.

It got better from there. Driving to Mark's townhouse in his Mazda RX-7 with tinted windows, I fell in love with Reno. It was spring. The Sierra, covered with snow, lay to the west. To the east, wild mustangs spotted flat desert. A dreamy place to live, and I hadn't even seen the city.

Early that evening, Mark drove me to work. The thousands of lights and Razzle Dazzle marquee were too glamorous to be true. Mark's assistant, Scott, escorted me backstage, a city in itself, and a dynamic new world opened up for me. Gorgeous girls, feathers and rhinestones everywhere. The "boys" in their G-strings—no one was shy around here. Racks of costumes that were pure glamour and spectacle. This was several notches up from Mom's stash. I met Bombay, the tiger in the act, on the stage with its beautiful, three-story-high glittering stairways. A phenomenal juggler, Dick Franco, shot eight ping-pong balls in and out of his mouth as he extended his hand to greet me without missing a ball. The Bogie Brothers, a three-man acrobatic team from Italy, changed a stage light bulb without a ladder by simply jumping on each other's shoulders. I learned later that some of these performers were in *The Guinness Book of World Records.*

My face must have defined the word *awe.* I'd never had a clue that this universe existed. Now I was the newcomer, plunked smack dab in the middle of an insanely talented circus. Nothing was going to pull me away from this life.

After catching a peek at the six-foot showgirls carefully applying make-up over their breast augmentation scars in their cramped dressing room, I was led to a spacious suite I'd share with flaming red-head sex kitten and co-star Scarlett*. There were neatly hung costumes, rows of fake eyelashes and mirrors bordered with dozens of lights. We even had a private phone and a couch that was the envy of the other girls. An intercom cued us to the happenings onstage. Apparently it paid to be in the headlining act. This was complete magic in my book. And I hadn't even seen the magic yet.

Mark took me to the lighting booth to meet the guys and sat me down to watch the show while he readied the costumes and props. When the music started and the curtains opened, I again felt like that 7-year-old watching the Ziegfeld Follies. Only better. The topless showgirls, draped in sequins and crowned with pink feathers, descended a huge staircase on skates—*wow, it's an ice show too*—and glided gracefully below. There couldn't have been a more dream-like job. I had to be the luckiest person in the world. Even my pain paled.

At last I heard it. The drum roll. A light tech behind me whispered, "This is the act, Cynthia." Scarlett, a knockout in her blue sequined G-string and slender matching push-up top, lit a fireball from her palm as Mark entered stage left. Then the curtains parted and Mark made an empty acrylic globe, draped with a cloth, fly on a cushion of billowing smoke. Once in the air, Mark snatched away the cloth and suddenly, impossibly, a smiling Lisa (the woman I would replace) now filled the globe. As it slowly floated down, Lisa kicked her way out and jumped into a huge "ta-da," arms stretching to the sky. The audience went nuts.

The next 12 minutes wowed me. Scarlett was impaled on a sword suspended in the air. In the striptease solo—*there's that pink boa!*— Lisa tempted Mark with a sultry dance. She shed her costume behind a curtain and tossed out her last silver shoe before disappearing stage right. She then immediately reappeared stage left, fully dressed, boa in hand, from an empty crystal box. It was all so impossible and wonderful. After more fire, a snarling Bombay closed the act, swiping his claws through the bars of the cage.

Rehearsals started the following morning. I quickly discovered how much grueling work is required to make people disappear. I'll never reveal the secrets behind the tricks, but I will say that I had to get in and out of tiny traps quickly, something only a flexible and nimble person can do. I also learned to breathe so shallowly that no one in the audience—we played to 2,000 people twice nightly, six nights a week—would spot a movement when I "disappeared." It was always about getting faster, hitting the cues and working as a team.

Everyone in the act, including tiger trainer Don, was involved with each illusion. We depended on each other like an athletic team. One wrong turn could expose a trick or, worse yet, hurt someone. I was surprised at how dangerous the show was. Most of what made this intricate act possible originated backstage. We're talking fire, hydraulic lifts, tricky traps, quick changes and a fully loaded tiger. This was a sprint beyond anything I'd ever experienced. We even had an oxygen tank ready for anyone not yet acclimated to Reno's high altitude.

By my opening night, my body was black and blue. I later learned every new girl looks like she's been through 15 rounds. It's a rite of passage.

Surprisingly, my leg was holding up. I wrapped it in cellophane—a ballerina's trick—to keep it warm and supported as I traveled to and from the theatre. I iced it with frozen peas as often as possible. Because everyone in the act knew about the injury, they wanted to assist. Before my first dress rehearsal, Scarlett helped me slip into my skimpy, sparkling G-string and matching bikini top after I'd managed to don my fishnets and jazz shoes.

When I caught a glimpse of myself in the mirror, I burst out laughing. I was basically wearing nothing. That itty-bitty number made me look better than when I was naked!

Setting foot onstage for the first time where everyone could see my bum, not to mention everything else, mortified me. But I was a hit. Mark quickly got me into the entire act, which was as wonderful as it was scary. The audience's explosions of *oohs* and *aahs* sparked my courage and gave this adrenaline junkie her fix.

I lived with Mark in his gorgeous townhouse and he drove me to the hotel each night. It took only a beat for backstage gossip to link us romantically. In truth, Mark and I had become close and shared most everything. He made dinner for me when we returned at 3 a.m., knowing I couldn't manage standing any longer. He played his Moody Blues records, opening the sliding glass door for the snow to softly drift in as we talked for hours.

Mark was courting me and I knew it. At just 23, he was a star by Reno standards, making over $5,000 a week. Like me, he was a risk-taker who reached for the stars. And he didn't blend in. Witness his pets—a grown cougar and a talkative macaw. He was talented and daring, and he came close to sweeping me off my feet.

But I didn't stray from John, counting instead the days until his arrival. When he drove up to Mark's place in his silver Honda Civic packed with our stuff from college, it felt like I was seeing him for the first time—young and fresh, untouched by the showbiz world that had captured me. We moved into our own apartment and made it a love nest. Soon, Mark hired John to replace Scott, the assistant who was moving to Hollywood. John, like me, was knocked out by the glitz and glamour. The topless girls didn't hurt, either. In fact, I giggled as I watched him try to maintain eye contact with these six-foot goddesses in three-inch heels. John is 5'11". You do the math.

I'll never forget John's frazzled nerves before his first show. He pushed the wrong button and mistakenly sent me tumbling from my Space Capsule before the curtain opened. The scene apparently looked like a car wreck. I must have passed out, because I only remember a stagehand yelling, "Cynthia, are you okay?" while I staggered around holding my head. Somehow we finished the act. And despite this flub that became legendary, John and I loved everything about the show.

But I paid a heavy price for the dream life we shared.

My leg pain escalated so much I wasn't sure I could continue in the act. Though I gritted it out each time, the following day I had to crawl around our apartment to get myself back on that stage. John did all the cooking, cleaning and grocery shopping, which made me feel helpless. But I was determined to stay under those lights. I knew in my gut that if I quit, my stage career would be finished.

John's mother, Betty, who was a nurse, suggested a new miracle topical called DMSO (dimethyl sulfoxide), an organic by-product of wood pulp processing reputed to relieve pain and inflammation. I slathered it on my leg, but, yikes, it gave me garlic breath. That sent Mark into phony fainting spells while unfortunately offering no relief. In between shows, I iced my hamstring with popsicles made from Dixie Cups, which I alternated with a heating pad. Still, during some nights the pain trumped the adrenaline. A few times before going onstage, I was certain I'd crumple and the paramedics would haul me off.

With nowhere else to turn, John got me an appointment at Kaiser's facility in Sacramento. Because my leg was so much worse and I was now a professional dancer, I hoped that I'd be taken seriously. But Kaiser's Urgent Care doctor dismissed me within minutes. When I begged him for some kind of pain relief, he prescribed a muscle relaxant.

As we feared, the medication didn't work, but it was all I had during the now-tortuous nights at the theatre. When my prescription ran out, I resorted to popping two to three aspirins every couple of hours. Before long, my ears started ringing and severe abdominal pain set in. I landed in the emergency room. I had overdosed on the aspirin and the doctors were afraid I was hemorrhaging. Even then, all I could feel was my right leg burning from the inside out. Clearly, this was no ordinary ballet injury.

After 10 months, the act's contract with the Reno Hilton ended. Mark was waiting to find out if we were going to the Lido in Paris or the Flamingo Hilton in Vegas. So John and I headed back to the Bay Area to live with our parents and rest my leg.

The rest, however, didn't help, and the inactivity drove me nuts. I was thrilled when Mark finally called, telling us to pack our bags and head to the Flamingo. I couldn't wait. I'd never been to Vegas. Everyone had told me it was the sexiest place in the world. It blew my mind that we were about to headline in Bugsy Segal's original gaming house in the desert.

John and I flew to Los Angeles to rehearse in illusionist Harry Blackstone Jr.'s huge warehouse. In a trick called "The Spiker," neon spikes would seemingly impale me before I disappeared. Dave Mendoza, the maker of Mark's and most every other successful illusionist's props, was there to supervise. The new illusions were bigger and flashier, especially our opening motorcycle trick, complete with blazing flash pots (fire made from flash paper and gun powder that shot into the air) and all. This was Vegas, baby, and if you don't do it big, hell, don't do it at all. I'll never forget Dave's huge grin the first time he saw the motorcycle turn into a blaze, followed by Scarlett and me appearing from nowhere, wearing nothing but white sparkly G-strings.

Of course, I called Mom later and recounted every detail. She wondered out loud if I'd "ever come back to little Pleasant Hill after all the glamour." I told her I'd never come back for good, but that my roots were there. Pleasant Hill was the launching pad for everything I was and would do. And what a start I got.

As far back as I can remember, every kid wanted to live at the Toussaint's. Mom, being an artist, had decorated our house in eclectic, contemporary style, mixed with her antiques. She plugged in skylights throughout the house and adorned hardwood floors with oriental rugs way before this was the rage. She added softness with big pillows, cushions and red beanbag chairs accented by ferns hung from macramé hangers. Mom's gigantic oil paintings and pen-and-ink drawings spattered most every room with bold colors. She also hung black and white photos of us kids throughout the house and adorned the bookshelves and refrigerator with our school art projects.

Just as our home didn't look like the other suburban houses, Mom wasn't like the other mothers, which explains why all the kids also wanted my mom to be theirs. In fact, most of them called her by her first name. "Leona doesn't make uptight rules" or "Leona is so much fun." Mom had grown up with an abusive mother. No Christmas tree. No birthday parties. No visitors. No fun. When she was a little girl, she thought about how very different her home would be.

With her kids and our friends alike, she encouraged every interest and had our backs, especially when teachers and the like played their power games. Instead of being a disciplinarian, she lived her Midwestern values and led by example. As a result, all us siblings respected and didn't want to disappoint her. That created deep trust within our family, and a code that promoted kindness, compassion, tolerance and community. We were in this together.

The fun that ran rampant with the Toussaint clan amplified that love. Laughter was as abundant as Mom's boat-sized lasagnas and as expansive as our menagerie. Our beloved lab, Blacky, had joined us as a puppy before baby brother David was born. Next my big brothers, Paul and Jon, brought in rats and snakes. I was responsible for the birds, hamsters, ducks and geese that followed. And as best I remember, my younger sister Beth added the roosters and chickens that popped out their eggs in big wired pens. When we tired of that crowd, we regularly collected bullfrogs from the creek and piled them in the tub. Luckily the boys turned them loose after each big neighborhood bullfrog race, which meant that in addition to living out our homespun version of *Born Free*, I could take a bath again.

After Mom announced "No more pets!" Paul, who had a hard time hearing anything he didn't like, brought home Flopsy and started a flood of bunnies that became legend. Hundreds followed in her wake, including Thumper, Skynerd, Jolie, Sparkle Plenty, Groucho (minus the mustache and cigar), Zepplin and, yes, the late, great Kuzako, named after our friend from Japan. White, black, spotted, Dutch and Lops. You name 'em, we had 'em. While some lived the highlife in the hutches, others camped under the living room deck. We rotated them in and out and, when free, they did what came naturally. Thus the furry flood.

Not yet satisfied with our brood, Beth and I pleaded, begged and needled Mom for a horse. When she refused, we didn't let up until she cut us a deal. "If you girls earn the money, you can buy one!" Knowing she'd made her point, she brushed aside the horse problem. In fact, she'd done the opposite. This was our shot. Beth and I babysat all the kids in the neighborhood and saved every dime. With $750 in hand, we bought a beautiful young Arabian sorrel with a white blaze, along with one blue and one brown eye. Mom drove us out to Rancho De Los Pueblos in Martinez where Cinnamon was boarded. In response to our call, our new horse came running from the pasture hill at full speed. Even Mom fell for our biggest critter yet.

We loved riding Cinnamon along the seven-mile stretch of Re-liez Valley Road to our backyard where we'd hitch her to one of our enormous eucalyptus stumps. One day we took a different route, walking her through the house. Naturally, we stopped at the kitchen counter. Everyone laughed except for Mom's guests. Her best friend Carmie had recently married a stuffy doctor whom none of us liked. During our detour, Cinnamon presented the couple with a late wedding gift. She lifted her tail and pooped. Right there. In the kitchen. Splat.

As kids, much of our free time was spent in the creek that ran through our backyard. It was a place for adventure. Most of the neighborhood kids joined in the fort-building, pollywog-catching and panning for gold. We loved the gigantic rope swing that the boys had hitched up from the oak tree most. Cuts and scrapes were badges of honor. Our outdoor fun included hide-and-go-seek, freeze tag, tennis in the street and handball against the chipped, green garage door. We played until we couldn't see the badminton birdie or the ball. At dinnertime, Mom rang the famous Toussaint cowbell that had hung around the neck of her dad's favorite cow on their dairy farm in Minnesota. As its sound reverberated, our friends called out in unison, "Time for the Toussaints to go home."

Though I had started life as a sensitive girl who needed Mom's protection from her more assertive siblings, I clearly outgrew that. Mom joked that she could hear me coming from a block away because I was so hyped about my latest passion. Of course, the one that topped them all, even my treasured piano, singing and flute, remained dance. That had always been *the* thing for me, one that took me away from my dearly loved home base. It now had me in Las Vegas, which was even more exciting than Reno.

We performed two shows a night, seven nights a week. I even got to bow with a baby tiger that had joined the big striped boy for the Vegas show. Most miraculously, my leg was finally feeling better. Maybe the desert heat or dry climate helped. Whatever, I was convinced it was finally healing.

In between shows, fun and frolic reigned. Water-balloon fights and Ms. Pac-Man tournaments dominated the two-hour breaks, and Mark and I constantly tried to one-up each other with backstage pranks. He won the night he loaded my G-string with gobs of Vaseline. I was mightily pissed, but boy that show went smooth.

Before long, though, the pain reared up again. "John of Arc," so nicknamed by the cast, was ever by my side. He helped me get around, set my props, anything to save me a few torturous steps. To be extra cautious, I stretched twice now before going onstage. One night I was warming up in my dressing room when, unbelievably, I felt a snap in my left leg, almost identical to the one in the right leg that started this nightmare. Oh God, I now had fire up and down *both* legs.

Ballet injuries don't spread, I thought with a growing sense of terror. Unable to pretend that I didn't feel the pain, I cried before the curtain went up. I knew this was the end. I had to quit the show, but John would stay to honor the agreement we'd made with Mark not to leave together.

I don't know how I survived the two weeks it took to train a replacement girl. Mark offered more money, more stage time, anything for me to reconsider leaving. He couldn't really understand. I had no choice.

John's Take

My God, she's suffering so much. I want to pick her up and carry her away from all this hurt. In the wings before going onstage, she's looking at me like, "How in hell am I going to do this?"

It breaks my heart seeing the thing she loves give her so much pain. I know she lives for the stage, the lights. But her pain is so intense. Somehow, after wrapping her leg in cellophane and doing the frozen pea thing, she still goes out there.

Watching the person I love in this much pain breaks something inside me. I'm scared. I want to protect her, convince her to go home and get some rest so she can heal. I need her to get out of this suffering. Let's check this off as our one nightmare. Everyone goes through a trial by fire. You either make it or it breaks you. I ain't going nowhere. Let's get past this shit and move on to our dreams.

As she packs to go home, conflicting feelings bang around inside me. We're so close and I'm going to miss her so much. She's my everything. I love cooking for her, washing her clothes, kissing and stroking her leg until the throbbing stops. In some ways, this pain has brought us closer. It's made me grow up. We've been together for over three years now, and I'm already at the stage where I don't know what I'd do without her.

I guess they call that love.

Battle for Grace

FOUR

NIGHTMARE FROM HELL

Being in constant pain is murder. Literally. Your old self is replaced with a screaming lunatic neither you nor anyone else can recognize. Even so, John's homecomings—which I lived for—brought real joy. Once again working with the act that had moved back to Reno, he'd floor his Honda out of the Sierra in the middle of the night to spend each Monday—his one day off—with me.

At about 4 a.m. he'd crawl through the window like he had in our courtship years. That bedroom window had been our secret lover's portal. Early on, he left love notes and poems there. As our relationship deepened, he would climb through the window bearing flowers and brochures about Paris. We had both studied French in school, and he always promised to take me there. It was exquisitely romantic when John, hair disheveled, tumbled out the window into our hydrangeas to make his early morning exit. Mom wasn't thrilled about boys staying over, but her bottom line reflected her true self. "If my girls are going to have sex, I want to know they're safe. Better here than in a car somewhere."

For John and me, it wasn't just about the sex. Not by a long shot. I needed John. I needed to feel safe and I needed a committed partner to share my life. Maybe that's because I had lost my father at age 8. Whatever the reason, I've always wanted the secure love I had with John, which he made known to me so often, so tenderly. I was the center of his universe.

From the first, we flowed together deep in our souls. Four years later that had remained the same, even though my circumstances had totally changed our lives.

"I'm home, baby," John whispered each weekend after his record-breaking drives from Reno to my bedside.

"I'm here, sweetie. I'm here," I answered in the pitch black as I felt his love and closeness. "Just keep walking toward my voice."

A moment later I'd feel his touch, his safe embrace. "I said out loud that you'd be here when I opened my eyes. And here you are."

John, his lips close to my ear, murmured, "What took me so long?"

Cradled together, we'd try to make up for lost time and push back our nightmare for a few hours.

Even during these periods of complete connection, the pain dragon would flare up again and I'd wind up begging no one in particular for relief. Soon I could hardly walk. I was sure I had gangrene and my right leg would be amputated. What else could possibly hurt as much and discolor a limb?

With my mobility so limited, I mostly camped out in Mom's studio. My bedroom at the other end of the house was too lonely. Mom set up a mattress bed, and I spent whole days moaning and writhing as I lay there. I could only get up and limp a few feet, maybe two or three times each day. Nights brought no relief and little or no sleep.

Then, unbelievably, my condition got worse. Much worse. One warm, summer day, my close girlfriend Sarah* sat chatting with me on Mom's front porch. She could see my suffering and had taken her best shot at bringing back a bit of the good old times. But I couldn't laugh much. That's when a praying mantis—my only freaking phobia—leaped out of the bushes toward us. We were both startled. Sarah ran inside. I got up slowly and strained to follow her. When my green nemesis jumped closer yet, I stiffened and my right leg jammed into the brick patio. Within hours, I could no longer straighten that leg and the pain worsened a hundredfold.

It remained so severe that I finally told Mom I couldn't walk to the bathroom anymore. She summoned my brother Jon whose room was next to her studio. He tried several times to lift me, but that just made me scream. Finally, they wrapped me in a bed sheet and pulled me down the hall so I could relieve myself.

At least I didn't have to use a cripple's chair, I told myself. That's what I called it. Avoiding a wheelchair made me feel like I was winning, even though Mom and Jon pinballed me off the walls each time they dragged me on our weathered hardwood floors. As I lay back in the sheet, I'd stare at Mom's ceilings—bare and simple, nothing like the rest of her home—trying not to think about the indignity of this bumpy ride. Sometimes I'd be dumped out of the sheet when Jon lost his grip. Grunting and yelling orders, they'd re-wrap me like a mummy, the sheet's clean smell of Tide detergent tempering the insult.

Jon soon began to develop back problems. This clearly wouldn't work in the long run. Even though I'd fought it with everything I had, I finally okayed renting a wheelchair. But I wasn't going to let anyone in Pleasant *Hell*, as I now called it, see the one-time toast of Powell Avenue not even able to walk. Most everyone still thought I was hitting it big in Vegas. So I crawled around the house like a turtle, even resorting to thick, athletic kneepads. Anything *not* to be in that chair. If that God-awful, light-blue, sterile thing that belonged in a hospital with the decaying and dying had a scent, it would smell like the pile of dog crap, full of maggots and covered with flies, that my best childhood friend Kim Morrow and I had spotted in her front yard years before. And if I gave into it now, I'd be in this shit for the rest of my life, guaranteed. Or so I thought.

Days and nights disappeared into the fire of my pain. Only a few activities—including reading classics like *Jane Eyre*, given to me by David with the inscription "A classic for my classic sister," and hot baths during which I shifted nonstop to find a moment of ease—interrupted the relentless agony.

When I was able to sit up, I returned to an old friend, Grandpa's gorgeous grand piano. Years before, our family had built its living room around this wondrous instrument. The room followed Mom's design and included antique windows and doors that she'd collected. As a kid, I hated the fact there always seemed to be another antique store around the corner. But she loved stained glass and kept searching for more of it.

Mom had hired a contractor to frame and sheet rock the new space with Paul and Jon functioning as assistants. Beth and I "helped out" by pounding a few nails and holding up some boards. But mostly we played in our skipper skirts adorned with giant flowers, jumping rope and hopscotching between the two-by-fours alongside Blacky. At night, before the roof went on, we kids slept out on our cement patio in mummy bags, counting the shooting stars and spooking each other with stories about the Zodiac Killer until we dozed off.

I now took up residence at the piano and spent hours losing myself in its music. Whatever I played, Bach or Billy Joel, the piano whisked me away. Though I sat awkwardly, my right leg folded underneath me and my left leg free to cheat with the pedal, I disappeared into the notes, briefly flying above the agony, which had now become mental as well as physical.

As weeks and months ticked off, the ugly crisis phase downshifted into an acceptable "normalcy" for my family and, quite depressingly, sometimes for me. Less and less notice was taken of me writhing in bed or of my crying jags. A new image of Cynthia was taking hold in the family and neighborhood—one of a sickly young woman quickly running out of luck. Terror consumed me as I watched other people getting on with their lives.

I was out of moves, and the pit of my stomach told me my life was slipping away. If I couldn't convince John and my family to help fix me now, I'd be stuck in this nightmare forever. It was as though I were on the side of a freeway having survived a head-on collision, my face caked with blood. I waved and screamed, but nobody saw me.

Even the joy that was John and Cynthia was being swallowed by my traumatized body. John wasn't my lover anymore. Sex had dropped off the radar a year prior. He was now a human crutch, a means to move from one place to another.

If John was becoming a sad piece of medical equipment, I was turning into a cold, inanimate object. Eating was, at best, optional. I had no desire to get outside and soak up the sun. What the hell for? To come back and spend another night in bed, balled up in torture?

Pain and fear became the essence of my existence. Soon they began intruding on my one place of escape—the precious, little sleep I managed to get. I began to have a recurring nightmare. Each night, a mysterious, black-hooded ghoul chased me. I ran and ran, scrambling to escape certain destruction, but it always caught me. I fought back, repeatedly stabbing the ghoul with an ice pick. *I won't let it get me again*, I told myself. But my ghoul never died.

One night the dream woke me in a panic. Hyperventilating, I jerked into a sitting position while John lay asleep. My head spun with anger and fear. *I'm not getting better. Nobody gets it and nobody's listening. I'm losing my life, damn it, and I'm not going to let it just slip away without a fight.* Hysteria and a boiling rage overwhelmed me. Putting on my kneepads, I inched my way to the bathroom and hoisted myself onto the vanity chair. I stared at the almost unrecognizable face in the mirror. She looked distorted, like a frighteningly clownish reflection in a funhouse mirror. But instead of a smile, a painful grimace pushed deep wrinkles across her forehead. Her lifeless, tear-rimmed eyes telegraphed defeat and sadness. My rage mushroomed and I let out a blood-curdling scream. My arms swung out wildly, sending everything on the vanity flying. I punched that terrible face in the mirror, over and over, as I screamed my hate at her.

Certain I was being attacked, Beth flew in from her bedroom just as John reached the door. She stared at my bloodied hands, then held me tight as we sobbed together into the dark night.

John just stood there. Silent. Aghast. Helpless.

John's Take

I realize one day just how sick she really is. We're in the backyard of her mom's house like we'd been a thousand times before. But this time she's in that damn wheelchair. We're talking about what we'll do to fix this and all of a sudden she spies Lumpy, a rabbit so named because she was deformed by a dog attack when she was a baby. Lumpy had been missing and the family worried she'd been poisoned by one of the neighbors. But here she is.

"Round her up," Cynthia yells frantically. I look at her like she's nuts. I don't know how to chase down a rabbit. You're the pro, you've been doing it for years, I say to myself. But she can't do it. She can't walk. She can't get out of that chair. It hits me like a Mack truck. Maybe this is the way it's always going to be. Maybe whatever she's got won't go away. Maybe I'm going to have to be her legs. Like chasing down Lumpy.

I freeze at the thought until Cynthia's shrieks snap me back. I jump up and run toward the white and black fur ball by the shed. Lumpy makes a dash for the creek, but I lunge, just catching her hind legs. I wrestle her to my chest, squeezing hard. She starts screaming the high-pitched squeal that rabbits make when they're terrified. The sound makes my blood run cold. I realize that's the sound inside my head. Screaming, terrified, trapped.

And I don't have a clue what will happen next.

FIVE

AT WAR WITH KAISER

Despite my two recent failed experiences with it in the Bay Area and Sacramento, I still felt hope, based on my family's experiences, that Kaiser would come to my rescue. When we Toussaints got sick, we went to Kaiser and they made us better. Poof! Like magic. As a kid, their friendly doctors made me feel special, and after each visit, Mom treated me to a double scoop of Baskin Robbins ice cream. I got chocolate chip mint on the bottom and orange sherbet on top, all carefully balanced on a sugar cone. Best of all, a trip to Kaiser meant special time with Mom. When you battled four siblings for attention, that was frosting on the ice cream.

Daddy took all us kids to Kaiser to see our new brother when Mom gave birth to David. One of my all-time favorite memories was watching the nursery carousel loaded up with babies going round and round. "There's David," Daddy would yell each time the newest Toussaint swung by.

Most importantly, Kaiser had helped keep me alive. At 12, I wanted to be the very best dancer at the ballet studio. Since being thinnest would give me the edge, I stopped eating. Before long I was skin and bones, weighing just 80 pounds at a height of 5'6". I got so weak I could barely stand. My family intervened and hauled me kicking and screaming to Kaiser.

Dr. Diller, our family's pediatrician for many years, hospitalized me for six weeks, during which time I was forced to eat. I rebelled at first, but finally succumbed to the lure of increased privileges, including goodies like phone calls, family visits and eventually home visits as I gained weight. By recognizing that I had anorexia nervosa and treating me aggressively, Dr. Diller saved my life.

I needed the same kind of insight and dedication for my hamstring injury. But Kaiser was now radically different. Even getting an appointment with a doctor was a challenge. When I finally saw an Urgent Care doctor, I wasn't referred to a specialist. Instead, my problem was routinely dismissed with the suggestion that I simply needed "more bed rest for a resolving hamstring injury."

I wasn't about to take this run-around lying down, even though I was literally doing just that. I launched the first of what would be many campaigns. Finally, after intense letter writing and many aggressive phone calls, a different Urgent Care doctor referred me to Kaiser's physical therapy center. My hope that someone might take me seriously quickly evaporated. The over-burdened therapists looked at my leg, did a little ultrasound, had me soak in the whirlpool and zipped off to their next patient. A few visits later, they cut me loose because I wasn't improving.

"You need to change your career," one of the physical therapists told me when I pleaded for help upon my discharge. I had already figured that out. In my mind, my aspiration to continue dancing professionally was long gone. I just wanted to walk again and move on to acting.

Desperate for medical care from a specialist, I asked John's mother if she could help. Betty had been an operating room nurse with Kaiser for many years, and, as a favor to her, a neurologist there agreed to see me. "To get you in, I had to pretend you were John's fiancée," Betty said.

That angered me. Why did I need to pull strings to get the medical care I paid for? I gave myself the simple answer. I couldn't get in any other way. When I finally saw Dr. Pierce* he ignored my complaints of never-ending pain and my plea for help. Instead, he quickly assessed there was nothing wrong with me. Worse yet, he had the gall to congratulate me on recovering so well from my injury. Devastated, I felt every door around me closing. Logic was quickly fleeing my corner of the world.

An orthopedic specialist, Dr. Lockwood*, our next Kaiser stonewaller, brushed aside Mom's "foolish" notion that sports medicine was something special or necessary. "Where did you get your medical degree?" he asked mockingly, pointing out that Kaiser had "everything for Cynthia right here." The unbelievable sameness of these physicians was taking on a life of its own. Unfortunately, this never changed.

Each visit made my suffering that much scarier for John and me and for my family. John didn't share his fears with me. I tried my hardest to control mine by peppering Kaiser with more letters. I still believed I was dealing with rational, caring people who were just making a mistake. Once they really heard me, they'd jump into action. This was an emergency.

When it became too painful to sit and type, my mother picked up the campaign, sending almost daily letters to administrators whom she referred to as "evil leeches." My family jokes that no one can type faster than Mom, even on her beaten up manual Smith-Corona. And when someone has wronged her or one of her kids, watch out!

Growing up, my siblings and I routinely watched Mom do battle. She wrote to Congress people, city council members, teachers, school counselors and administrators—any and all who abused her brood with their authority.

When Jon was editor of his high school paper, he wrote an article in the mid-'70s proposing a smoking section at his school so people who didn't smoke wouldn't be exposed. He was way ahead of his time, but the principal, Mr. Bellowamanie, bawled him out. "You're a very naïve young man," he concluded. Uh-oh. The moment Mom heard this one, she pulled out the Corona and began typing like mad. I never read the letter, but Bellowamanie left Jon alone after that and, lo and behold, roped off a smoking section at school.

Now that typewriter's rapid fire from behind the wooden shutter doors was the music of our lives. Mom's look of determination told us she was on the warpath. *Hmm, wonder where I get my "feisty" from?*

Her letters to Kaiser charged that I was receiving little treatment and had dangerous symptoms. The occasional response restated the myth of Kaiser's wondrous care and rejected our requests for outside specialists. It was madness.

Kaiser finally agreed to one of Mom's demands. An orthopedist, Carlton Sprague*, would coordinate my care. At last, some hope. My first appointment with Sprague went extremely well. He was a quirky gentleman of Norwegian descent, polished in manner while rumpled in dress. He projected true empathy, and we got along smashingly. I appreciated his honesty when he frankly stated, "I fix bones. I don't fix dancers." He went on to tell me I needed to find someone outside of Kaiser who could help me—and that Kaiser would send me to that person. For the first time in months, I stopped believing that amputation would be my answer.

The next appointment with Sprague crushed my hope and my spirit. Though I provided all the information he'd requested, he immediately denied me outside care. The charm and concern I felt during our first meeting was gone. Instead, he parroted Dr. Lockwood and suggested that sports medicine was just a "fancy term." Kaiser, he now believed, had everything I required.

I suspected Sprague had been "set straight," another confirmation that Kaiser no longer took the high road. But what was motivating these doctors and administrators to keep me suffering and unwell? It took a while for us to get it. Money. Some five-letter words are as dirty as their four-letter cousins.

After several weeks and more letters, Sprague relented. I would have an appointment with Kaiser's sports medicine expert, Dr. Thomas Buskirk*. Mom wheeled me into Buskirk's office, where he pointed to all his framed certificates of achievement on the wall. "Do you have a gun?" he asked in what seemed to me a casual manner. "Are you considering suicide?"

Stunned and frightened by his words as much as his behavior, I murmured that I didn't. I wanted to flee. But when he instructed Mom to take me into his examination room, I was so frantic that I agreed.

Virtually ignoring my cold, purple legs, Buskirk's examination was limited to checking my reflexes. His treatment plan was equally truncated and boiled down to me flexing and pointing my right foot every hour for three weeks. Then he suggested I might join his therapy group. On the way out, we saw this "sports medicine" group—20 elderly, what I perceived to be incapacitated stroke victims in their chairs. Mom, near crazed, raced my chair toward the exit, shouting, "You're not coming back here." I didn't quibble.

But Buskirk wasn't finished with me. He called the next morning in attack mode. "I've gone over your records, and I believe you have stage fright." He asked if I had a "big dark secret," referring to a prior appointment with another Kaiser doctor who had said my ballet injury not healing had sparked my anxiety. By all appearances, Buskirk used this to prove *his* diagnosis of the stage fright, one that eliminated any need for care. He had cherry-picked my records to make up—and support—his story.

I shot back a letter to Buskirk asking, "Will my future illnesses and/or injuries now be diagnosed as psychosomatic?" That question, unfortunately, proved prophetic. The Kaiser saga was becoming as tragic as the pain itself.

To ease my suffering, Mom suggested I make my fight to get well a full-time job. So I read anything I could find about dance injuries. We even paid out of pocket for a visit to St. Francis Memorial Hospital's Dance Medicine Center. Once there, we discovered a totally new world. At St. Francis, light filtered in from every nook and cranny. Caring doctors and physical therapists emphasized strengthening injuries so a dancer could continue to work. Each exercise, along with its specific purpose, was explained in detail. This allowed me to do the rehab at home, keeping my visits—and charges—to a minimum.

The reprieve, however, lasted for only four visits, since that's all Mom could afford. Then I returned to my impossibly unproductive struggles with Kaiser. Only after Mom threatened to sue did the doctors take notice of my disintegrating condition. Sprague approved an evaluation with Dr. James Garrick, the director at St. Francis Dance Medicine, so he might devise a treatment plan, which simply cost too much for us to have commissioned.

Dr. Garrick, who I hadn't seen during previous visits, was an angel. He examined me thoroughly, understanding my body as that of a ballerina's. He also noted I was depressed, a condition he deemed reasonable given the loss I'd suffered. When he carefully stretched my turned out right leg, replicating my movement as a ballerina, it almost touched my head. I cried with relief. I still had the stuff, and I couldn't stop smiling. That's what hope can do for a battered soul.

I knew this was the man to treat me. In his evaluation to Sprague, Garrick wrote, "She presents an exceedingly difficult problem out of proportion to what we'd expect with a normal hamstring strain." There it was. The first doctor to say I had something far worse than a common injury.

Sprague accepted the evaluation, but insisted I be treated in the Kaiser hospital by Kaiser physical therapists rather than at St. Francis. Mom, John and I agreed only because we felt this was Kaiser's last shot. If it failed, they'd have to send me elsewhere.

We arrived at the hospital early on a hazy morning in late November. When they said they had no beds, a dreadful "same old, same old" feeling sank in. I waited with Mom in a corner for five and a half hours. Then they put me on a gurney, and deposited me in an ambulance. No one told me why. They drove me to a facility across the street that looked like a retirement home. Finally, they told me I was being admitted into Kaiser's hospice because the hospital was overcrowded.

The hospice was a long, single-story cinderblock building with beige walls, stark rooms and the smell of bleach laced with urine. I was frightened. I was surrounded by elderly, dying people whose moans filled the air. Not the place for a 23-year-old woman with a ballet injury. The next morning, I was awakened and served breakfast by a young woman with whom I had gone to high school. I gasped in mortification, wanting to hide under my sterile sheets. How in God's name had I gone from performing in front of two thousand people to landing in this pit?

A few hours later I met my physical therapist, Maggie*, a stout, sharp-featured brunette. When she talked, her husky voice and her apparent lack of experience scared the hell out of me.

"I've looked over your records, Cynthia. They intimidate me." She paused. "You're a professional dancer. You've seen sports medicine people. I'll try my best, but I don't think I can compete with them. Since I don't really know what to do, let's just experiment together."

Any sliver of hope I was still holding expired.

I was imprisoned in *Midnight Express* meets *Cuckoo's Nest*. None of the doctors or physical therapists knew what was wrong with me. The food was so awful I couldn't eat much, and I began to shed weight I couldn't afford to lose. My bed was right in front of the bathroom, so the parade of nurses assisting elderly patients was in full view. The air-conditioning ran 24/7. I'm almost always cold, but now I couldn't stop shivering, and my pain hit the ceiling.

Mom panicked and grabbed some hospital blankets, but they were too thin. She then raced home for my heating blanket, but my nurse—I labeled her Nurse Ratchet—wouldn't have it. "Not allowed," she barked. Space heaters were also forbidden. Eventually, Mom brought me a down comforter, and we cheated with the heating blanket when Ratchet wasn't on the prowl.

At night, the moaning intensified. "I want to die. I want to die," a woman across the hall yelled as I tried to sleep. A male patient next door became irate and screamed that the nurses didn't let him get any rest. I had to agree. They'd wake me every few hours to take my temperature and blood pressure and ask about my bowel movements. They routinely switched my roommates, generally a two-hour process in the wee hours of the morning.

It was a place devoted to care, manned by people seemingly incapable of giving it. I fought to maintain my dignity, which Ratchet and company were dead set on stripping away. When she caught me crawling to the bathroom, she actually bawled me out for not doing my best. "I'm going to tell Dr. Sprague on you," she scolded, her finger wagging as if I were a 5-year-old who had just spilled the finger paint.

Mom arrived first thing each morning to help me bathe, sparing me from being hosed down on a shower chair. I refused to wear the standard hospital gown, which represented death to me. Instead, Mom dressed me in something pretty and colorful each day. I applied my make-up and with her help even curled my hair. I was still among the living and wasn't going to look sick and dying.

When he was in town, John generally took the afternoon shift with a parade of family and friends who filled my room with candy, flowers and stuffed animals. Home-cooked raviolis, meatballs and gnocchi, courtesy of John's Italian mama, helped me relish eating once again.

After hours, Beth often sneaked in through my sliding glass door. We watched TV and gossiped as she exercised in the middle of the floor in her red sweats and huge raccoon slippers. When Mom left for Hawaii, courtesy of us kids, Beth took over the morning shift. Her loving care bolstered me as much as her defiant in-your-face attitude that I'd always admired.

Even with this support, however, I couldn't bear the almost unspeakable horrors of the hospice, starting with Maggie's well-intentioned experiments that worsened my pain. Painful splints, ice and exercises on parallel bars left me screaming. As the setbacks piled up, Maggie shrugged her shoulders. She didn't seem to know what to do with me and didn't seem to care. Next came the Continuous Passive Motion Machine (CPMM), a thinly veiled torture device for my right leg, which was becoming more bent I suspect due to Maggie's flawed therapy. The strap-on device extended my leg as far as it would go, then folded it back. This was sheer hell.

A steady barrage of sexual harassment also added to my pain and degradation. This wasn't the first time I'd had to deal with such abuse at Kaiser. A young male physician before I'd gone to the hospice had told me my hamstring was very tight. "I like my women that way," he added, which instantly sent me out the door in my summer shorts. The doctor yelled after me, "I've got your prescription. Take care of those gorgeous legs."

The sexual abuse worsened in the hospice. Most of all, I dreaded Mack*, who was a physical therapy aide under Maggie. He continually flirted in a suggestive and seductive tone. "Cynthia, can you still get on your hands and knees?" he asked. Horrified and hoping I was misreading him, I affirmed that I could. "Well, that's all that's important," he said smacking his lips. When I reported this to Sprague, he told me I was getting what I deserved. I assumed he was pleased when I got similar comments from all sides. A string of creeps.

Speaking of creeps, Sprague's morning rounds always started my days negatively. While the nursing crew regularly sucked up to him, Sprague appeared to become increasingly angry with me. It was my fault I wasn't getting better. It was also my fault that we Toussaints didn't deify him like everyone else.

In what seemed an attempt at humiliation, he repeatedly walked in while I was taking a bath. Each time, my mom frantically grabbed washcloths to cover me. Finally, he waved dismissively at a glamorous photograph of me in Vegas, which had mesmerized him upon my admittance to the hospice. "You've got to give up this foolish nonsense of dancing and be what you're meant to be," he said as he headed to the door. Then he paused and added, "A housewife and a mother!" He was gone before I could open my shocked mouth.

To keep my sanity and let the chauvinist know he wasn't my boss, I made sure he saw the cover of the book I was reading— *MALe PRACTICE*—at every visit. Written by Robert S. Mendelsohn, the exposé reveals how male physicians victimize female patients in healthcare settings. This book was a savior for me, helping to make some sense of the madness to which I was being subjected. Coupled with my Kaiser hospice experience, it planted the seeds for my advocacy work many years later—a work of love I might never have found otherwise.

As a patient, I was failing. But as a student of health-care-for-profit in America, I was working my way up to the Dean's list. Nonetheless, Sprague broke me down one day. He brought Maggie into my room and closed the door. He stared at me for several moments.

"I know you, Cynthia Toussaint. You're not working hard enough. Maybe because your mother's too protective. Or maybe because you were afraid you'd flunk out of that dancing school," he hammered at me. Maggie, who'd done virtually nothing except make me worse, just stood there silently. Humiliated, beaten down and traumatized by the hospice, I dropped my head and sobbed so hard that saliva dripped on my lap. Sprague smiled and walked out.

Surprisingly, several days later Sprague agreed to let me go home for my birthday on New Year's Eve. I couldn't wait. However, Ratchet and her minions turned down my request to take the CPMM with me. An understandable rule, I suppose. But as much as the machine had been torturous in the beginning, my right leg now seemed dependent on it. The darn thing still hurt like hell, but the pain was even worse without it.

It was really a lose-lose situation until the partygoers came up with a solution. We would "steal" the contraption for one night only. Two close friends, a gay couple with whom I'd done community theater, joined my team. In broad daylight no less, Tom picked up the heavy machine and hoisted it over the back fence to Stephen. To cover their tracks, they put bundles of towels under my bed sheets to make Ratchet think the CPMM was safe and sound. I felt like part of a prison break, and we laughed all the way home.

Our New Year's ritual was always a high for me. The prior year, on my 23rd birthday, dozens of wild theater folks streamed in and out of the house, eating, dancing, laughing and singing like a band of gypsies. And, of course, we had the usual accoutrements—confetti, blowers, hats, kisses, hugs and "Auld Lang Syne." When asked to give a birthday speech, I got as far as "I want to thank all the little people..." before being playfully heckled by the mob. Dressed in a short, daring red kimono with black pumps, my hair newly permed, I had danced with John as best I could into 1984, despite the pain nipping at me.

As usual, the Toussaints had laughed that night about Mom's annual oyster stew. No matter how much we detested that wretched concoction, it always made an appearance on New Year's Eve. Paul generally slurped it just to make the crowd sick, while Beth and her friends poked at it. Frankly, I'd given it up when I was a wee one. *Yuck.*

After dinner, everyone howled when Mom sat down at the piano to play her magnum opus—two songs she had memorized as a child and the *only* two she ever played. Somehow, some way, "Sunrise Serenade" led into "White Christmas." This woman, who couldn't read a musical note, played both like a Carnegie Hall virtuoso.

Life didn't get any better than that. This year, however, I lay on the living room bed, the pain in my leg torturing me. Mercifully, the agony leveled off once my atrophied leg was returned to the CPMM rhythm on which it now depended.

Finally able to enjoy the party, I relished watching Beth's excitement as she tore into the slew of gifts I'd received. I tried to open them, but just pulling off the wrapping paper hurt too much. Sporting her casual model-off-the-clock look—no make-up, long brown hair tied tight in a high pony tail, a "Frankie Say RELAX" T-shirt and red classic Reeboks—Beth barely looked at one unveiled gift before ripping into the next.

When the pain returned later that night, I didn't want to moan and bring down the crowd, so I signaled John who picked me up and carried me through the party. Many of the guests reached out to stroke me and tell how much they loved me. I had no way of knowing this was the last time I'd feel cherished by so many.

I was back in the hospice the next day, barely able to eat due to my elderly roommate's increased coughing and spitting. I wasn't getting better and didn't want to watch people die anymore.

A few days later when I'd hit week six of my stay, I asked Sprague to release me. I'd spent enough time in this hellhole to prove that Kaiser was unable to ease my pain or diagnose me. I'd played their game at my physical and emotional expense. It was time for them to send me outside for real care.

But Sprague had another card up his sleeve. He sent a physical therapist to my home twice a week. My first impression of Jake* was that he was pretty cool. He hailed originally from L.A., drove a vintage Alfa Romeo and seemed kind and patient. But like Maggie, he appeared to be out of his league. Jake quickly become frustrated, chiding me for not trying hard enough when he didn't make me feel better. I could barely limp to our hallway and back. When he casually instructed me to walk outside, down the driveway to get the mail and come back, I realized his notions about my capabilities had nothing to do with reality.

Just two years earlier, I had been a high-level ballerina. Now I couldn't make it to the mailbox. Except for a few pathetic crawls to the bathroom, I was completely bedridden. I hurt more because of Jake's treatments and the loss of my CPMM. Almost anything—a light breeze, a loud noise, something barely brushing against me—hurt terribly. Yet I was still living without pain medication because none had been prescribed.

That I survived with such minimal care still astounds me. Except for the blue moon prescription of Tylenol III, I went 15 years with nothing. I was as helpless as I was desperate. Often the pain was so severe, I lost all sense of where I was. *How did I get here?* I wondered when the pain finally eased.

By then my mother's fury was matched only by her anguish at watching me suffer. Although Sprague refused to talk to her by phone, she made an appointment to discuss his treatment plan for me. I couldn't go since I was confined to my bed, but John, who had quit the act, would participate in a doctor showdown for the first time. That made me feel safe.

I was excited when I heard their car returning. Maybe the horror show at the hospice had been worth it. I saw the bad news written all over Mom's face as soon as she came in. I'd never seen such rage in her eyes. John couldn't even look at me. Instead, he stared off like he was in shock. Mom blurted it out. "Sprague says your problems are all in your head. That you need a psychiatrist. He says he knew from the very start that you never wanted to get well."

I burst into sobs, overwhelmed that a doctor would think I had faked the pain that was destroying me. Sprague and I had our differences, but I'd believed his goal was to make me well. Now I felt raped and violated. John held me tenderly, while Mom shared the ugly details. "Sprague sat behind his big desk. Just a little into the conversation, his eyes bounced back and forth and he slyly pulled out the letters I'd written. He threw them down hard on the desk, then yelled, 'I don't like your letters. Why don't you get health insurance somewhere else?'"

Try that one with a preexisting condition.

After his "Cynthia is nuts" speech, Sprague tried to *prove* his case. He said that Maggie had spoken with a physical therapist at St. Francis who mentioned that during a psychological evaluation, I had supposedly paused at the word *death*. "He was downright smug after he said that," Mom told me.

Sprague's words made my head swim. I had never been evaluated psychologically at St. Francis, only physically. Moreover, none of us understood how his story, even if it were true, would show that my condition was "all in my head." Maybe this verdict stemmed, at least in part, from his negative feelings about his lack of success in treating me. To keep his job, he clearly needed to dump his Hippocratic Oath, which in his memory I renamed "The Hypocrite's Oath."

The next morning, Mom wrote to Dr. Garrick recapping Sprague's report as it pertained to St. Francis. In short order, she received a letter stating that no psych evaluation had been conducted on me. That same morning, I phoned Kaiser's Oakland psychiatric department, which I'd heard was good. Psychologist Sandra Seligson, quite surprisingly, was kind, logical and more than willing to listen.

"Dr. Sprague wants me to see a psychiatrist," I told her. At the end of a two-hour talk, she said there was no reason for me to come in. "There's nothing psychologically wrong with you. But there's definitely something wrong with your healthcare." I pinched myself to make sure I wasn't dreaming.

She insisted I do two things. First, go outside of Kaiser to get treatment for my legs. And second, hire an attorney to fight Kaiser with everything I had. We quickly learned that suing Kaiser was not an option. "You have no chance of winning a case," an attorney, Nicholas Willbrand, advised us. "Let this be your Kaiser horror story and move on with your life."

The problem was, I couldn't. Not without a diagnosis and care. So our existing insurance was our only card. Sprague's pronouncement that I was a head case made everything that much harder. Although I suspected he was using this new excuse as his cover, I tried to believe I was crazy. If I *were* crazy, then by my standards he wouldn't be an unethical son of a bitch. I wouldn't feel that he had abandoned me. But this delusion was shattered by my pain. I knew I couldn't be making up all this torture.

Still, Sprague's inventions appeared to be seeping into other areas of my care. When my physical therapist Jake's treatment felt increasingly unkind, I finally asked, "Have you been talking to Sprague?"

He stammered, "Well, ah, ah, no. Not recently."

I could tell he was lying. Months later, Mom said that Jake had phoned her with an almost verbatim head case assessment. That nailed it. Kaiser doctors and their healthcare providers operate as a twisted fraternity that rewards the rationing of patient care. I wasn't the only one suffering. Taking care of me 24/7 had cost

Mom physically. Here she was, a woman in her 50s with severe, aching varicose veins, pushing me in that heavy wheelchair, hoisting me in and out of the bed, chair and car. Worse yet, she now had heart problems, which ironically her Kaiser doctors attributed to the stress of being my caregiver.

Emotionally, she was barely hanging on and financially even the $5 co-pay set her off. She paid a personal price as well. Once we kids had all left home, she had planned to finally move to New York to pursue her passion for performance. But her life had come to a screeching halt as she played caregiver to me with no end in sight.

Finally, a bigger truth dawned on us. The Kaiser system was designed, quite effectively, to beat down, demoralize and exhaust both patient *and* caregiver so they would go away. A well-designed plan to move the sick ones out. Nonetheless, Mom fought for and finally got another appointment with Sprague. We were eager to confront him with Garrick's letter and Seligson's psych evaluation. On the appointment day, Mom loaded me into the car, then listened to my cries of pain at every road bump. She secured a disabled parking space in front of the office, lifted out and assembled the wheelchair, and went inside to check me in.

"You don't have an appointment today," Sprague's heavy-set, salt-and-pepper haired nurse and ever-loyal gatekeeper said smugly. "Nope, not in the appointment book." A mistake? We'll never know. But it certainly saved my nemesis from a difficult situation.

Mom's head snapped with anger as she walked back to the car. She spat out the news. "They don't have an appointment for you." She quickly turned to the chair, presumably to store it in the trunk. Instead, with superhuman and anger-driven strength, she hoisted my 50-pound wheelchair and smashed it into her car. As I screamed in fear for my mother, she continued to bash the chair into the car again and again.

"They don't care about my daughter," she screamed out to everyone in that parking lot and the universe at large. "She's dying. They're killing my daughter!"

John's Take

No matter how I try to wrap my head around what's happening, I just can't make any sense out of it. I thought the doctors would take care of Cynthia. I thought they'd give her some pills, get her walking again since dancing was clearly out, and bring the pain down to a decent level so she could have a normal life. Never once have I doubted that she's in terrible pain. Despite the doctor's conclusion, there's no way this is some kind of charade to put off adulthood or to avoid performing or anything else. This woman has always just chomped at the bit. Why would she crap out on life now when everything I've experienced before tells me she wants to go, go, go?

I can't make sense of this surreal, Kafkaesque disaster. I lie next to her, my head on her stomach and cry. "I'm going to get you out of this mess," I promise. "We're going to figure out what's wrong, get you back on those beautiful legs and move to Los Angeles to slay the world."

But another voice spews God-awful nonsense as fear and loathing seep in. One look at that comet-like woman now squirming in agony, helplessly prone, needing comfort and someone to ease her pain, and I'm horrified. Hey, I didn't sign on for this, I think. I'm just 23 years old, too. This isn't in our contract. I don't remember any small print about hanging in there if the gates of hell swing wide open. Is this a test? If it is, fuck it. Sometimes love isn't enough.

SIX

SOCIAL PARIAH

As the pain intensified and I remained bedridden, people began avoiding me. These departures weren't my first experience with abandonment. When I was 8, Uncle Bill told us kids that our dad had gone away and wasn't coming back. I knew my dad was dead. The police had found his car empty on the bridge and his body in the Carquinez Straits. I would figure out in my mid-teens that he had taken his life.

The day Dad killed himself, Uncle Bill led us into the living room where my grandparents and Mom were sitting silently. Mom took one look at the five of us and began sobbing hysterically, physically recoiling from us on the couch. Four-year-old David kept repeating, "I don't understand why everyone's crying. He's going to come back." Eleven-year-old Paul's prepubescent, high-pitched cries left a permanent hole in my heart.

"I want you kids to know Daddy loved you very much," Mom said later that night as we ate vanilla ice cream. What an odd comment that seemed at the time. It never occurred to me that Daddy didn't love us.

For months after he died, I stood out on the front lawn whenever I heard a car coming and prayed real hard, face in my hands, eyes shut tight, to make it be my daddy. I missed him. I still miss him. To this day, a whiff of the cream soda he used to drink makes me cry.

Mom and Dad had been divorced for two years when he died. After they split up, he'd see Beth and me one weekend, John and Paul the next. David, the baby, always stayed home with Mom. On our weekends with Dad, we often took excursions. He gave us the choice of going to SeaWorld or Fairyland. We almost always chose Fairyland where he bought us packages of pink popcorn. He liked Fairyland almost as much as we did. I loved how it made him smile and laugh. It reminded me of when he got excited about spotting bears in Yosemite. And how he loved to play a game he invented—"the mosquitoes are out"—in which he'd pinch one of us as we sat on his lap. He was just a big kid. I remember him returning from business trips, bags filled with gifts and candy. Our favorite was the snot-nosed doll with a yellow balloon that came out of one nostril when you squeezed her tummy. Daddy, a man who'd earned his PhD in Economics at MIT, howled right along with us.

But there was the other Daddy, often preoccupied and staring off as if he were miles away. Once when I was 6, I brought him an egg my duck Jill had laid. I was excited to surprise him and expected he'd fry it up for breakfast. Instead, he put the egg in the refrigerator and without a glance in my direction went back to the chore of making breakfast. When he was deep in thought, he didn't see or hear me. I sometimes felt hurt and worried he wouldn't come back when his mind drifted off like that.

His behavior often disturbed me. What was he thinking, what did he want? One day I watched him in the bathtub, his eyes glassy and unfocused. He was standing in the water, carefully drying his body, including both feet. Instead of stepping out of the tub, he placed each dry foot back in the water before stepping from the bath with wet feet.

As an adult, Mom told me about the angry, violent Dad. How he would beat her, even when she was pregnant. How she feared for her life. She also described his frantic attempts to escape from people he thought were following him.

I now believe my father was a paranoid schizophrenic who directed much insane jealousy at my mother. Still, he harbored wisdom. When I was living at home, again bedridden, Mom finally shared his suicide note. With perfect grammar and punctuation, he told each of us kids to discover what we loved to do in life and to live that passion.

To this day, I feel a rush of sadness whenever I cross the Martinez-Benicia Bridge he jumped from. My 8-year-old self wonders where he was on that bridge and what he was thinking. He killed himself the day before Neil Armstrong's historic walk on the moon on July 19, 1969. I remember thinking that my dad must have really wanted to die if he didn't wait to see the first man walk on the moon. I wonder whether I had been in his mind when he decided to leave me and the rest of the world forever.

He was the first to desert me, but certainly not the last. Consumed with my own pain, I had no clue how my illness was impacting those close to me. I now know that my family and friends were frightened and disturbed by my transformation. They also resented the strain it put on Mom and the fact that I took up so much of her time. Nearly a decade after my pain began, Beth bolted from a rendezvous with my mother. "I need a mother too!" she shouted. Until that point, it hadn't dawned on me that I'd taken Mom away from my siblings.

I didn't mean to monopolize her attention, but like always, I needed her so badly. From the get-go, Mom and I were close. As a toddler, I never strayed, always wanting a cuddle, never causing any trouble. That's why she panicked the day I disappeared. It was a beautiful sunny day at a street festival in Ann Arbor, where Beth and I were born and Dad taught at the University of Michigan. Mom was pushing Beth in an English buggy and I was walking alongside. A moment later, I was gone. Mom frantically got a cop and they found me on a street corner in my yellow-checkered gingham dress, thumb in my mouth. Just waiting. I knew she'd come.

Looking back, this closeness mirrored the deepest feelings inside of me. I trusted her completely. I loved her fiercely. Growing up, there was nothing I didn't share with Mom. Her calm, wise words always steadied me. To this day I joke that if you want to get to know my mother, just open the dictionary. She is the definition of "love" and "goodness."

The rest of my family had completed that safe, loving world. We'd all been so close. Each summer, Mom took the five of us on delicious excursions around the country and once into Canada. Our trips involved boats, trains, planes and miles of walking with our suitcases in hot pursuit of a cheap hotel. Money was tight, but Mom pushed hard to help us experience something different from sunny, safe Pleasant Hill. In addition to visiting relatives in Minnesota and North Carolina, we saw the city lights of D.C. as well as Beantown and the Big Apple. When all of us lined up from the tallest to shortest, hand in hand, people would stare wide-eyed as they grinned and pointed. We were a risk-taking tribe that didn't fit the norm.

Whether on the road or at home, I helped our fun-loving and sometimes volatile family run smoothly. Being a middle child, I was a natural at making sure everyone got fed, had what they needed and got along. I simply did what it took to bring our warring crew back into harmony or at the very least keep them from harming each other. After one particularly long-running altercation, Jon came after Beth with a big kitchen knife. I put my body in between them and talked reason to him while Beth escaped through a bedroom door.

"We've just got to keep this family together," I frequently told Mom. And we did—up till I got sick and the "glue" broke.

I now know that people were upset, frustrated and often angry with me because I'd gotten ill and by all appearances wouldn't get better. The magical Cynthia was gone, never to return. That proved too much for most of my family and friends.

Some of my dancer friends left first, as if my injury might prove contagious. Scarlett, who had worked with me in the illusion act, called out of the blue one day when she was in town and wanted to see me. She mentioned having all the great Vegas tapes in her car trunk.

"Cynthia, I've got everything. You can have whatever you want," she said. I was excited. We made a dinner date, lasagna at the Toussaint's. She insisted on treating me to a movie after dinner.

"Oh, no, Scarlett, I'm sorry. I can't get into a movie theater. I can't walk."

There was an immediate change in her tone. "I thought you were done with all that, Cynthia."

Mom whipped up the meal, but Scarlett was a no show. I never heard from her again. I was devastated as I assumed her real-life disappearing act was due to my ongoing pain.

Most of my college friends and some of my closest girlfriends vanished as well. Even my grandparents on Dad's side pushed me away. Pre-injury, they'd been proud and boastful of their "little ballerina" and had paid for my college tuition. But when the pain didn't stop, they quit responding to my letters. I heard later from David that they peppered him with questions. "So just how bad is it with Cynthia, anyway? I mean, in a wheelchair and everything." They passed away without ever speaking with me again.

My brother Jon and I are close now, but he left early on. When I asked him why, he said, "It was just so dark, Cynthia. You never got better and all the doctors said you were nuts." His admission helped me understand that some people actually bought the doctors' lies. Jon is about the smartest cat in the world, but even he got lost in their deceit.

I believe that everyone close to me mourned my "death." Some still do. Several years ago, John and I headed east to visit a close family friend, Claire*. From the start, the dream trip turned into a nightmare. She contradicted my every word and criticized every move. This was not the Claire I knew. When her behavior showed no sign of letting up, we cut short our trip.

I called her after returning home. "Claire, what happened? Why don't you like me anymore?"

She broke down. "It's just that Cynthia was our little ballerina," she said through her tears. "You were never supposed to get sick."

It couldn't have been easy to watch me morph from happy-go-lucky Cynthia into this new, always-in-pain lady afflicted with a mysterious disease.

Some likely left because they didn't love me enough, others because they loved me too much. Any way you cut it, they became the collateral victims of Kaiser's abuse. By the time I received the diagnosis I hoped would fix this mess, it was too late. Too much damage had been done. Most of my loved ones did not return. With those family members who did, the relationships never fully recovered.

As I watched people leave, I slipped into a depression that would last, off and on, for years. But I did not go quietly into that dark night. For the first time since my injury, I raged against the circumstances of my life.

My anger was fierce and destructive. I hated everyone and everything. I couldn't see any way to recapture my life. The slightest thing would set off what was now a hair-trigger temper. If I wasn't acknowledged, I took it as a slight. I'd rip the "insensitive" speaker or storm out of the room, even if I had to crawl.

Hell, if there were an Olympic competition for verbal abuse—or better yet, cutting a person's self-esteem to shreds—I'd have won the gold medal. Mom and John could have used those padded suits they wear in the military when defusing bombs, because I was a land mine.

It didn't matter if I was busting up someone else's good time. It was all about me and my hate. Time and again, it all surged up. Whether it was the middle of the night or day, I often let out blood-curdling screams and thrashed my body around on my bed, arms and legs flung out. As family members and John tried to restrain me, I could see the fear in their eyes. After every outrage, I sobbed uncontrollably. "It's all so ugly," I told myself again and again. "I'm so ugly."

As terrible as this rage was, I had no notion of the degree to which it would grow and explode. Throwing things became commonplace for me, and my swearing made Joe Pesci sound like a choirboy. I threw a chicken drumstick at one of my brother Jon's friends due to a perceived slight, then left the dinner table after telling him to fuck off. At a soup and salad joint, I countered a waitress' snide remark made under her breath by hurling my salad, plate and all, against the wall. "You bitch!" I yelled. She returned the compliment, while John sat dumbfounded. He often looked this way when I ran my atom bomb act.

Mom got it one afternoon when she took exception to a sharp remark I'd made. As usual, I reacted before weighing the consequences. I fast-balled the frozen pea package I was using to ice my leg hitting her square in the belly. As she let out a guttural moan, I plummeted to an all-time low and called her a cunt. It was the most awful thing I could say to a person I love. I'll never forget the pain this brought to Mom's eyes before she rushed up, whacking me with the peas over and over, as I curled my body in self-protection.

No wonder people turned and ran instead of sticking by me. Though many fled because they couldn't cope with my illness, I drove others out of my life. Then I mourned their loss.

One of the most painful departures was when my sister Beth pulled away. Growing up just a year and a half apart, we swiped figs off the neighbor's tree, hula-hooped and swooned in unison when David Cassidy sang on *The Partridge Family*. We even wore identical outfits that Mom made for us when we were little.

Being so similar in looks, we'd always been compared. The constant barrage of "who's prettiest?" or "who's most popular?" meant that there was always a winner and a loser. In grade school, kids cruelly teased Beth with, "How come you're so ugly when your sister's so beautiful?" In high school, the shoe was on the other foot. She was a hit with the popular girls. I was the fish out of water.

"That's Beth Toussaint's sister," I'd overhear the cheerleaders whisper in the hallway with a giggle.

"No way! I've never even noticed her."

When Beth was 19 and I was at UCI, I encouraged her to model. She was stunning, but had never expressed to me any interest in show business. Beth always wanted a house with the white picket fence and three kids. But to my joy, she got an agent in San Francisco and began working. Her career blossomed just as mine crashed and burned.

Everything was upside down. After all of my early successes, here I was back at 209 Powell Avenue, living in a bedroom across from Beth just as I had when we were younger. But this time I was in pain that brought my life and dreams to a halt. And it didn't look like it was going to get any better. One night, David found me curled up in my closet sobbing. "I'm afraid I'm never going to get well," I wailed. He disagreed. I asked him why and I've always remembered his simple answer. "I can see it in your eyes. You want to get well so much."

My hell took on a new dimension when Beth began living the life I thought was going to be mine. Here I was, lying in bed and watching my future slip away, as my stunning sister was becoming an international model. Neighbors called to share their excitement about seeing her in a magazine or on television. Her phone rang constantly. It was almost always an agent with a booking or "go see." But I mostly just laid in bed sobbing quietly to myself.

Each day when Beth left and I heard the front door close, I felt the door to my life slamming shut. She became more successful, scoring numerous commercials, music videos and full-page magazine ads. Every time I went to a doctor's appointment in San Francisco, I passed "her" billboard. I don't remember what she was selling, but there she was towering above me. I couldn't get away from her.

Then she started acting. The better she did, the less she seemed to notice me. One day, after reading lines with a friend for a soap opera audition, she told Mom that Michael J. Fox had flirted with her. The feeling that she didn't acknowledge me lying corpse-like in my bed turned jealousy into fury. How could she not see me?

In time, I've come to realize that Beth's non-reaction was likely caused by an experience with Jon several years earlier when he suffered mysterious pain after a fall from a ladder that left him unable to walk for five years. Jon's experience taxed my family's fortitude and proved an ever-present, dark cloud on our psyches. During that period, I was constantly aware of the strain on Mom. My gal bud, Sarah, and I tried doggedly to pull Jon out of his bed and back onto his feet. It got scarier when he had to crawl. I suspect the ordeal especially troubled Beth.

As my condition worsened, I felt that Beth just couldn't handle another family illness. She seemed to distance herself both physically and emotionally as much as she could. In hindsight, it wasn't all black and white. Sure, we'd been close growing up, but now there was this different me. Angry. Hating almost everything. And sometimes violent. I snapped one afternoon. With trembling rage, I crawled into our hallway with its beautifully framed family pictures. On one side were photographs of me dancing and an unframed poster of Beth. Just her lips. Lots of lips, like a Warhol painting. I despised her gorgeous lips. From my knees, I ripped the poster down and tore it to shreds. Then with adrenaline and rage pumping, I grabbed other huge photos and sent them crashing to the floor. As glass shards flew, my screams reverberated down the hall. Mom and Jon raced to the scene, but by then I'd shattered everything.

Beth and I became even more separated when she moved to Hollywood in the summer of 1985, almost three years after I'd been injured. I wanted—no, needed—her to go away so I could survive. We didn't speak for several years after her departure, and no one in the house mentioned her name. Then she landed a lead opposite Patrick Duffy on the TV nighttime soap *Dallas*. Instantly, she was famous. The divide between us widened even further with the inevitable comparisons. Even Arsenio Hall jumped on the "which sister is prettiest?" bandwagon, calling Mom for that answer while taping a show with Beth.

So I was shocked when she phoned one day from L.A. "Cynthia, come stay with me." She said, "I'm making a lot of money now, and I can get you to better doctors."

I snapped. Years of jealousy and perceived dismissal poisoned my thinking. I felt certain that my sister thought she was so far above me that she could only offer her charity. How had I become someone to be pitied? Blinded with envy, I spewed, "Don't ever call me again. You're not my sister anymore." She begged me not to say such a horrible thing, sobbing uncontrollably. I hung up on her and felt infinitely better. Now I could just hate her and that hate would save me.

From that time on, whenever Beth visited, I was never home. Still, I couldn't escape her success. While I remained mostly bedridden, people knocked at our door, hoping to get a glimpse of Beth and an autograph. How could I ever catch up?

Even John, who had never believed in his viability as a pro, was back in the act and doing well, again as the illusionist's onstage assistant. I had to battle my jealousy over his exciting life as he worked with the likes of Donald O'Connor and Peggy Fleming, two of my all-time favorites. Adding insult to injury, he told me the act was moving to South Africa for two months to play before audiences of 6,000 each night. Begrudgingly, I gave him my blessing.

Years prior, John had been at my house when he got the lead in *The Importance of Being Earnest*. I was so happy and proud. He was such a talented actor. In fact, the UCI drama dean would later compare him to a young Brando. I was in awe of John's ability to get his head into a character and become someone else. He was confident, even a bit cocky. Once he mooned a casting notice because he hadn't gotten the lead. At the same time, he was quite modest.

It was a perfect combination in my book. We were 19 and life couldn't have been better. We shared a passion to perform. We supported each other and celebrated our growth. But that was then. *Now look at me*, I thought bitterly. I'd lost the joy I used to have in his successes.

I certainly didn't want to hold John back. Still, I felt insane jealousy, not only of him, but also of everyone in the act. There would be a huge media splash, and Trish, the girl who had replaced me, would be the toast of the town. There was nothing in the world I would rather have been doing.

The morning John left, his mother Betty delivered a basket of yellow and white carnations from him. This bouquet felt like my floral consolation prize. *He's on a plane to Africa with my job. My life has been stolen from me!*

Betty intruded on my pity party. "You know, John wanted me to get you a dozen long-stem red roses. I couldn't believe what they wanted for them. It was highway robbery. So I chose the carnations instead. They were less expensive and just as nice."

That did it. As soon as she left, I grabbed the basket, trembling with rage, and somehow hobbled my way to the backyard. With tears stinging my face, I threw the basket of beautiful flowers over our back fence and into the creek. But instead of easing my anger, I felt sorrow, like I had just thrown John and our love into the muddy water.

John's Take

No one can write this nightmare. If it were fiction, it would be too contrived. A woman whose life has been all about getting to the lights of Hollywood watches her sister live in those lights while she wastes away. The tension when the two are in the same room is unbearable. They dance around each other like snakes ready to strike. A single word, a misspoken syllable, the wrong inflection sparks the hate and spite. Leona and I try to keep the peace by redirecting conversation, by reinterpreting hurtful words. But we're just applying a dollop of antibiotic on a gaping wound. The resentment, spite and malice run way too deep.

Try to understand your sister, I want to tell Cynthia. She's got a right to live her life. It's not her fault that something took yours away. She didn't snap your hamstring. She didn't get the doctors to lie about you. She's trying to make sense of this shit just like everyone else. Yeah, she's not perfect. Hell, neither are you. Neither am I. Neither is anyone. Let's not make this worse than it already is. I literally shake, waiting for the next unintentional insult. A neighbor comes knocking at the door wanting an autograph. The well-to-do sister drives up in a new BMW. These reminders are a lot like Chinese water torture.

When Beth comes home for a few days, we flee to Carmel or Napa to escape. It will just be a mess if we stay. People will get hurt, Cynth will storm off. Then silence. There'll be an awkward attempt to avoid entering the same room. Pale small talk to cover the simmering contempt. A door will slam. Words shouted out that I try to muffle with my hand over her mouth. "Just stay cool, Cynth. She'll be gone soon. Just no more yelling tonight. Please, I need to sleep." Sometimes my pleas hold. But most times not.

I guarantee Cynth we'll get out of this. We'll be back in L.A. soon and there's still time to claim what's ours. She's the star and the cream eventually rises to the top. I half believe it. I've got to. How else can I make sense of this madness as I stroke her burning legs? So I can sleep. So I can rise the next day to keep the lid on our boiling pot. As I lie in bed thinking of the new hurt and harm that will capture us today, I turn to look at her. Her eyes are wide open, a single tear trickling down her cheek. Dread fills my heart.

The Animal's rock anthem runs through my head. "I gotta get out of this place if it's the last thing I ever do." It's all decay and hate, pain and loss, disappointment and dead ends. The doctors don't know what's going on. They loathe her and just want us to go away.

These are my prime years. I've got to spring myself out of this suburban dead zone and see the world if I can. "I'm sorry, baby," I think to myself. There's no sense in me sticking around for more of the same. Maybe I'm part of the problem. Maybe I'm coddling too much. Maybe if there's no one around, you'll have to move, stand, walk. Function. Maybe your body and nerves will respond and take you back to square one.

I can't stand seeing your 10,000 expressions of pain. The howling, the endless tears. The pleading for relief. It's killing me. They feel like a cavalcade of arrows hitting me from all sides. I'm so tired. Every day it's like this. Even the short periods when the pain eases don't provide relief anymore. I need sleep. Up all night with you, whispering, stroking, begging God.

South Africa. I think that's going to be far enough away. Half a world away. Eight weeks of separation. Respite for the weary. I think I'm a cold-hearted asshole for splitting. But, man, it's either this or I take a run to the desert and just keep running. I'd run until

the past was gone and the miles that help me escape stretch forever.
Black and empty.

SEVEN

HOPELESS

I felt more lost than ever with John halfway around the world and out of communication. All my family and friends were moving on with their lives, and I couldn't bear living—if you could call it that—in sleepy Pleasant Hill. *I'm not supposed to be here. Only losers return to their little hometowns.* I've always been the quintessential city girl; I feed on its excitement, the worldly people and frenetic energy. But I couldn't make my way back.

My unsuccessful battle against pain was old news to me and everyone else. I was exhausted from trying to find a diagnosis and medical help. I knew dance was long gone. Worse yet, I felt the movie career, which was now my *raison d'être*, might never happen either. Depression set in big time. I was light-years away from the strong, capable person who had suffered that injury. Sure, I'd had my share of blows, but I always bounced back. This was different. Everything I loved to do was out of reach. I felt stripped of my dignity and life force.

Parts of me were literally wasting away. My right leg had almost completely atrophied with muscles as shriveled as my dreams. I avoided wearing shorts after a troubling encounter with a neighbor. "My God, Cynthia, do you realize your bad leg's half the size of the other one?" asked Mike, an ex-cop dealing with constant neck pain himself. I hadn't realized it was that obvious.

I rarely showered or dressed as it wasn't worth the pain and effort. I no longer wore make-up or jewelry. For whom, for what? People rarely came to visit me except for Sarah, one of the few friends who hadn't fled. She showed up every Wednesday evening with Baskin Robbins ice cream to watch *Dynasty*. I appreciated her attempt to perk me up, but I had no interest in watching a TV soap. What I really needed was a strong, supportive friend with whom to process my mental chaos.

One night when Sarah jumped up to leave during the show's closing credits, like she did every week, I stopped her. I voiced my fear that I might not walk again. Sarah brushed it off as silliness. Eyes rolling, she chided, "I can't believe you said that. But next time you get a ballet injury, you're going to get off it right away so we never have to go through this again." *Okay, so this is my fault now.* Soon after, she stopped coming by for our dates.

Then Mom dropped a bomb. She was moving to Manhattan like she'd planned for years. In toto, she moved back and forth several times. She never sold our house in Pleasant Hill, so it continued to be her home base.

She was in her mid-50s, and all the "kids" (except me) had flown the coop. The news devastated me. *Now Mom's leaving, too.* I had always believed she'd stay by my side until we found an answer. When my anger over her abandonment spilled out, she countered, "This doesn't mean that I'm not backing you up anymore. That'll never change. But maybe there's something good in this. Maybe you'll become more independent. You know, do more things on your own."

Even she thought my disability was somehow voluntary. I shot back, spitting fire, "What, like now you've forgotten that I'm the most independent person you've ever known? Hello. It's me, Mom. Remember, Cynthia?"

When nearby, John had deflected some of the insults thrown at me. Now I sensed people doubted that my devoted partner would ever return.

For the first time in my life, I felt utterly alone.

Smelling my vulnerability and seeing my physical limitations, many uncaring people emerged from the woodwork. Over the years, I have learned that the chronically ill, especially those of us who use wheelchairs, are public domain for inappropriateness. Often people ignore me altogether, asking John simple things like "What's her name?" as if my legs not working have also impaired my ability to hear and speak. "It's so good that folks like you have the courage to come out," people I've never met routinely tell me.

Much of this—and worse—came from people we knew. An acquaintance of Mom's put it this way, "Geoffrey and I, we've done a lot of talking. We see how the rest of your life will be useless. The way we feel, if we were you, we'd kill ourselves." A so-called friend of Jon's asked, "Are you the type of person who crawls into a hole before you die?"

Freaks or heroes, that's how we disabled folks are often assessed by the temporarily able-bodied world. In America, the chronically ill have little or no value and are blatant symbols of mortality. We're feared because we're different. Unfortunately, what people fear they frequently demonize or demoralize. I got equal doses of both.

Thankfully, John remained the exception to that rule. After eight weeks in South Africa and a few more months in Atlantic City, he left the act for good. I was surprised when he broke down soon after his return.

"I just couldn't be away anymore," he said, unable to restrain his tears. "I stayed in the act because I couldn't handle what was happening here. But then I knew, finally, that I have to be home. Home with you."

I took his hand. "Yes, but you need a life too. My death sentence shouldn't be yours. I'm rotting away here. I can't keep doing this."

"No, no, no." he said. "I know there's an answer out there. Someone, somewhere, has what you have. We're going to find that person and get you diagnosed. I need you here with me." He cupped my face in his hands. "We'll do this together."

While he held me, I shared my feelings of hopelessness. He pleaded for me to let him move the mountains and help. He was crying hard now. "I promise. I'll never leave you again."

With that commitment and Mom's move to New York, John became my full-time caregiver. I was afraid he had no real idea of how to take care of me. He'd done some of it during our Reno and Vegas days, but that was a lifetime ago when I was a lot healthier. Caregivers and recipients have a rhythm, but John and I weren't in sync. Mom knew my every move, sound, look—and what it all meant. Plus, she's the woman who cared for me as a child. I mean, how could a man do that for a mostly bedridden woman in constant, severe pain? Who was going to buy my Kotex? My panties and bras? Little did I know then, but this guy of mine would get damn good at all of it. He especially liked it when Kotex added the wings. *Ain't love wonderful!*

John knew that being my caregiver meant not pursuing his acting passion. And he'd been around long enough to know there wouldn't be any social life. The bustling, joyful house of my youth had become a morgue. No one visited anymore, the phone never rang and I barely got outside. He'd be tied to the strings of my condition. But John reminded me daily that this was temporary. He still believed I'd get well.

Often he tried, without much success, to break the monotony of the pain and isolation. Occasionally, he'd carry me to the car for a drive. But the car door closing, no matter how gently, and the bumps on the road, shot my pain too high to continue. Car trips were out.

The nights were worse. I still had that recurring nightmare—when the pain allowed me to sleep—and the ghoul always woke me in a cold sweat. Before long, anxiety attacks added more stress to my life. Everything looked and sounded distorted, scary and unreal. Often I couldn't even look at John or the TV. Everyone seemed to be moving and speaking in slow motion, as if submerged in water. I spent most of my time in bed facing the wall, staring at the pale cream paint. I memorized the drywall cracks. At least *they* looked real.

Eventually, John was compelled to take an entry-level marketing job at the local Sun Valley Mall to pay the bills. Each day, he stood for hours with a clipboard, interviewing suburban housewives about their preferred snack cracker. I thought lots about how his dreams had been shattered just like mine. He had become my nursemaid instead of the star he deserved to be. He even had to bring a bowl to my bed so I could pee. So much for the UCI couple voted "most likely to succeed."

It's difficult to describe, but I felt like the living dead. Pain and loneliness ran my life. I was being buried one shovelful at a time. The despair was so awful I sometimes banged my head on the floor hoping to black out the misery even for a moment. I wanted the fire to go away. I wanted to stop seeing my sister's face when I turned on the TV. I wanted to stop destroying John's life. I wanted to fall asleep and never wake up.

I had to get out.

I came up with a plan for my suicide, a perfect "crime." I located a motel nearby that, with enough grit, I could drive to on my own. Room 23 would be easiest. I would take pills. I had stashed a month's supply from a previous prescription mix-up with Kaiser—enough to do the job. It would be horrible for the cleaning woman who found me in the morning. But I'd slip away into the night, killing everything I hated and giving John's life back to him.

I was certain I'd carry out my plan. In hindsight, I'm probably the last person who would ever commit suicide. I have too much respect for myself. True, I did know it was impossible for me to sing or dance again. But I had experienced so much joy in my life during the good times that part of me wanted to hang around to see what was next. Still, I was standing on the edge.

It took me 25 years to step back. I thought about taking my life for that long. *I'll do it tomorrow,* I'd tell myself. It was my fantasy. It was my coping mechanism. It meant I had a way out. And having a way out tomorrow gave me the strength to survive today.

John's Take

When things were fine early in our relationship, I was okay with being the only man around. I even relished in it in an Alpha Male sort of way. But as things came unglued for Cynth, I felt I didn't have the necessary juice. Now I need her dad around to take charge. To kick some ass. To tell those asshole doctors to treat his daughter with respect. To fight for her and give her a sense of possibility.

I'd never felt a strong sense of protection in my family. Mom and Dad were the types to bury things and let us kids sort out our own problems. Not a lot of hand holding or talking at the Garretts. I love my folks, but they came up short in the take-charge department. Sometimes I wasn't even sure of their love. As a result, I grew up feeling nervous and timid, afraid of confrontation. I chewed on my nails starting at age five and never stopped. I don't know how to stand up for myself. And I sure as hell don't know how to back someone I love.

Leona is doing her best trying to protect her daughter. But these chauvinistic Kaiser thugs just toy with her, stonewalling her every attempt to make them do right. She is just a woman after all—one who doesn't have the sense to bow in their presence. I'm the one who needs to step up and let the testosterone roll. Mano a mano. I can't do it. These guys have MDs and lab coats and that air of confidence that I can only play-act. After eviscerating the mother, they look to me to return their volley. But there's nothing in my guns. I sit there, mouth shut, trying to find a hole that will hide me from the shit storm that's raining down.

I can barely look in Cynthia's eyes. I'm failing her. I wish her old man was around to pull an Atticus Finch. I wish her old man was *around to pull my sorry example of being a man out of the fire. I find myself wishing he'd kept driving on the bridge that day. Maybe things wouldn't be coming apart.*

EIGHT

NOW YOU SEE IT, NOW YOU DON'T

If I wasn't going to kill myself, I had to find a way to make life tolerable.

I got a couple of big breaks. A doctor diagnosed me with an anxiety disorder, which studies have shown is not uncommon for people living with pain diseases. Within days of starting the anti-seizure medication, Klonopin, my anxiety was down to almost nil. Perhaps more miraculous, my pain steadily declined to the point where I experienced a partial healing. I felt on top of the world. For the first time in the five years since my injury, I could hope again.

I'd recently won a hard fought Social Security disability claim and had been awarded a significant back payment. At the same time, I became eligible for Medi-Cal, California's version of Medicaid. That gave us the means to get quality care. In short order, a dance therapist, Penny McCowan, hooked me up with a doctor who treated the San Francisco 49ers. He referred me to Dr. Eric Bailey*, a wonderful physiatrist at Stanford who told me that physiatrists treat athletes who are going to get better. *Get better.* That rang through my head nonstop.

Bailey, a saint of a man, was the first doctor since St. Francis who didn't think I was cuckoo. In fact, during my initial evaluation, I told him that the doctors at Kaiser had said I was crazy. I was floored by his response. "That's what they tell everyone at Kaiser. That doesn't get in our way here." I felt like doing cartwheels.

I became involved in a series of studies. Someone was finally really, truly checking out my body! A nerve-conduction test showed nerve damage in both my legs and an MRI exposed a bulging disc in my back. Dr. Bailey shared his evaluation. It sounded better than Tchaikovsky's second act of *Swan Lake.*

"The bulging disc probably isn't a big deal, Cynthia. Many ballerinas have them. But it could be causing some of your pain, so we'll give traction a try. But the nerve damage *is* a big problem. Your hamstring injuries gave you all kinds of scar tissue that's knotted up and pressing against the nerves. This is where most of your pain is coming from."

I could barely wait to ask it. "So what do we do?"

"We'll start with intensive physical therapy. I want to strengthen the muscles surrounding the nerve damage in your legs and your whole body. There's so much atrophy, we need to rebuild those ballerina legs." Bailey grinned. "If the physical therapy doesn't work, we're looking at surgery, in which case I'll remove the scar tissue."

Even though I didn't have a clue how we'd pay for surgery if it came to that, I couldn't imagine better news. I wanted to kiss Bailey right on top of his beautiful bald head.

Overjoyed, I jumped into physical therapy at the non-Kaiser clinic where Dr. Bailey had referred me. I loved Bob, my physical therapist. He was a pro who was nearly as motivated as I. When I could no longer pay him, he hooked me up with a gym and met me there to make sure my PT regimen was exact.

Traction was a trip. Bob's capable assistants trussed me up in mountain boots with hooks, a gladiator belt and chains. They told me to take a deep breath, then with one swoop they swung me upside down. It was better than an E ticket ride at Disneyland. Hanging like that stretched my body out, giving me a high I hadn't felt since the ballet studio. How my body yearned for this. Quickly dubbed "The Upside Down Ballerina," I playfully begged Bob at every session to leave me up longer. The half hour always passed too quickly.

I was getting ultrasound and doing stretching exercises as well. I worked out on the weight machines, and they had me go up and down a set of faux steps. For balance, I used a seesaw-like saucer. I only lasted a few moments, as standing was still my biggest problem, but I could feel my legs getting stronger. Bob pushed me to work my upper body with the weights, and I was crunching 5,000 (really!) sit-ups each day. *Hey, give me a red cape and I'll stand in for Wonder Woman.*

I also did Pilates. Today it's all the rage, but in the mid-'80s mostly injured dancers used this weight-bearing therapy, which focuses on strengthening core muscles for proper alignment and support. Pilates' main apparatus, the Reformer, freed me to do turned-out, ballet movements from a prone position. My joy was boundless. But no matter how strong and flexible my body became, I still couldn't stand without feeling like bone was grinding on bone.

Even so, I was antsy to get back to my essence—performing. I'd never stopped thinking about show business, no matter how bleak my condition. I had to get back onstage or in front of a camera. I still wanted to be a star and fast, since I'd lost so many years. I got a subscription to *Backstage*, the Bay Area's *Dramalog*, and leafed through it to find an acting coach.

After several chats with instructors, I got Verna Winters on the line. A Berkeley resident, she was a fiery ball of positive, creative energy. We resonated immediately. After talking at length, I realized I could confide in Verna. She seemed to really understand me—where I'd been, where I was, where I wanted to go. I shared my concern that if I joined an acting class, my scene partners might feel ripped off working with an actress who couldn't stand and move with them. We decided I'd take private classes to start.

Verna, as the newspaper headline on her bulletin board read, truly ran a "Winters' Wonderland." My God, this woman could teach anything. Voice, dance, piano, acting, speech. Her talents seemed endless. After a long career in show business, teaching was now her passion. The acting studio was located in her home, an old Victorian with charm to burn. I especially loved her grand piano adorned with pink bromeliads. In between acting exercises, I watched from her second floor picture window as Verna collected chicken eggs while the sun set. Even through the dimming light, I could see her broad smile and twinkling green eyes.

I loved the classes as much as I loved Verna. Because my focus was to be a film actress, she always put me on camera. "You're a director's dream," Verna said even though my acting was initially too big due to my years of working onstage. "The camera loves you and your energy is so juiced. That's okay. It's easy to tone down an actress. The ones who lack fire are those who never hit it."

Verna not only encouraged my acting aspirations, she helped me to accept the scariest reality of all. I was disabled. I'd plateaued with my rehab, and Bob had said my right leg would never straighten again. I had to forge ahead with what I had left. Verna's logic, love and total support of my passion to be an actress enabled me to live with that. Most importantly, she helped me realize that accepting my truth—and making accommodations for it—would move my career forward.

One afternoon I spoke with Verna about changing the time of my class because it was so painful to drive home in heavy traffic. The clutch was killing my leg. She responded that I should get an automatic no matter how much I loved my car. She also suggested a disabled placard. For Verna, there was always a solution. Inspired by her matter-of-fact attitude, for the first time since my hamstring injury I was able to use the word "disabled" in reference to myself and feel dignity. That contributed hugely to my inner peace, a rare event for me back then.

After a couple months of classes, I auditioned for a San Francisco acting/modeling agency called Runway*. The craziness of the office thrilled me. Their phones rang madly and papers were strewn everywhere. Whole walls were covered with headshots. I nailed the monologue I had prepped, then the interview. They signed me on the spot and tacked my new headshot smack dab in the center to trumpet their find. Then I spilled the news to Kate*, Runway's lead agent.

"There's one thing I haven't mentioned. I'm still dealing with an old ballet injury, and I can't stand for long."

Kate's brow furled. "That's awful, but I know you dancers beat the hell out of yourselves. Like you're all insane," she punctuated with a kidding laugh. "When will you be better? We want to send you out pronto. You're gonna work like crazy."

"I've been fighting it for years now. My body's in really good shape and…"

Kate interrupted. "I know. Your look is phenomenal."

We went back and forth a bit until I said. "I still can't stand for more than 30 seconds." When she hesitated, I went for it. "Look, Kate, you love my monologue. You love my look. I just want to work, and I can't if I'm not totally honest with you. I can't do standing jobs."

She smiled. I'm sure she was having a chat with herself, but her agent instincts kicked in. "Listen, Cynthia. I don't want you to be our competition. We'll rep you as a 'special booking.' So when clients inquire about you, we'll tell them you only do seated or prone jobs for now. How 'bout that?"

I reached over and held her hand. I'm sure my look said it all.

I drove home with an excitement that's hard to describe. I'd landed an honest-to-goodness agent and had myself a great acting coach to boot. *Just watch me fly.* With things looking up, I felt more love and strength. Several days later, I spied a black kitten in a cardboard box in front of the local K-Mart. She looked like the runt and sickest of the litter, and I adored every inch of her. I named her Sadie, for the married lady in *Funny Girl*. She was my baby, so full of life. She instinctively knew when I was in pain and curled up on my chest to comfort me with her kneading and purring. We became inseparable. She always came to my call, even when she was out patrolling the wilds of our backyard creek. John loved her too. We weren't alone anymore. We were a family.

Meanwhile, Kate called often to tell me about piqued clients, and despite our talk, to ask if I could just stand for a particular job. *She's not getting it.* When she sent me on go-sees and auditions, I became even more frustrated. Clients who wanted me to sell exotic drinks, sports cars and perfume just couldn't wrap their heads around me being a special booking. After learning my lines and getting psyched, having to alert them to my limitations left me feeling awkward and disappointed.

Sometimes she sent me to meet photographers to get seen and drum up business. This didn't lead to anything, but these guys were always blown away by my back-story. And they couldn't believe I wasn't in L.A. or New York working all the time.

Kate finally started getting clearer about my limitations with the clients, and I quickly landed a print job. I'd be selling a slide-projector with a "husband" and "child." *I'll take it. Not glamorous, but it's a start.* The night before the shoot, Kate called to tell me that the client had backed out. I was devastated.

"They're freaked out," she told me. "They're just too afraid of you. It doesn't make sense to them that you look like you do, but can't stand up. They're not willing to take a chance, to gamble on you."

On the other side of town, Dr. Bailey had not given up. He told John and me that our only option was surgery. He would try the right leg first and, if successful, do the left. I was strongly tempted.

Maybe this was the answer. But my intuition loudly told me to steer clear, that I could be even worse off.

I told Dr. Bailey I needed to think long and hard. "I haven't even had a child yet, and I need to be well to be an actress. I know the surgery could make me better. But it could also make me worse. Right now, I feel surgery's too big a risk." We left it there. I felt dead in the water.

Then John saw an article in our local newspaper, *The Contra Costa Times*, that profiled a pain management doctor. The headline read, "The Doc To Go To When All Others Have Given Up." What hooked us most was that this guy only treated pain. We'd never heard of that, but hell, pain lay at the root of our problems. John was stoked when he told me the clinic accepted our Medi-Cal coverage.

Dr. Daniel Day's pain management clinic felt different from the start. The lobby had a comforting look, with a peaceful waterfall, bonsais and Japanese screens. Better yet, these folks believed me just as Bailey's staff had. They treated me with respect and true care. A lovely calm enveloped me. *That's pretty awesome for this girl. Two good ones in a row.*

We started off with a thorough physical exam. Day's associate peppered me with questions about my pain. Oddly, when he asked me to describe it, I couldn't find the words. I felt like an idiot. All I came up with was "excruciating." He probed further, suggesting words.

"Aching?"

"No."

"Tingling?"

"No."

Then he said it. "Burning?"

I was awestruck. "It's like my legs are on fire!"

He escorted me into Day's office. I was, unknown to me then, about to begin a medical adventure that could almost be a book in itself. Dr. Day gave me the big news right off. He felt I had a disease called Sympathetic Dystrophy. "Your symptoms are classic. It's a chronic pain disease that starts with an injury and gives the sufferer unrelenting, unbearable burning pain. Also, it spreads and the affected areas can turn purple or red."

I took a deep breath. *This guy talks about my life better than I can.*

"We'll try a series of pain blocks to confirm this and give you some relief. Your leg will warm up and your pain will be gone if you have Sympathetic Dystrophy. There's a small chance you'll have temporary paralysis of the leg, but the bottom line is we can make you better." It felt too good to be true.

When I arrived at Day's clinic Monday morning, I was given a hospital gown and placed on a gurney. I was surprised, and oddly comforted, to see and hear patients in various levels of pain and distress. Just like me. These people were writhing, moaning, even screaming. It felt like I was entering a secret club I should have joined years before. I empathized with my fellow pain warriors and felt happy for them—and for me—that we had found Dr. Day.

I got my first pain block that afternoon, though today I can't tell you what kind it was. I *can* tell you it frightened me, especially when I saw the 10-inch needle that was about to puncture my lower back.

Several minutes after the shot, I lay on my back with my head turned to Mom, who had come back from Manhattan temporarily to spell John who was now doing 40-hour weeks at AT&T as a temp. More mind-numbing work to pay the bills and save for our future. I was catching up on her happenings in New York when Day said my name. I turned and freaked out. He was holding my right leg straight up in the air, but I couldn't feel it. I was paralyzed.

Even scarier, the motor block that triggered the paralysis was working, but the sensory block was not. My pain raged as strong as ever despite my leg's toasty hue. Day was puzzled.

Each morning that week brought a new block along with more frustration and disappointment. Although the blocks differed, some hurting more than others, none took my pain away. Dr. Day alternated between anger and frustration, sometimes kicking the trash can, other times muttering to himself about not being able to "fix her."

I felt like a failure. Two excellent doctors who believed my pain and wanted to make me well couldn't help. *Somehow this must be all my fault.* I knew the pain was real, but I was freakishly non-diagnosable. Contaminated by Kaiser's abuse, I laid the blame squarely on myself.

But Day wasn't finished. During week two, he dusted off his fat medical books and began digging for any clue that would solve my mystery. He tested me for MS, Lupus and syphilis. All came back negative. That's when I remembered that during my initial consult with Dr. Day, he had described one block that involved the lumbar spine and an impossibly long needle. At the time he labeled this the last—and worst—option, but one that could tell us one way or the other whether I had Sympathetic Dystrophy.

I had nothing to lose. I told him to bring it on. We argued in his office. He felt I'd been "tortured enough" and insisted we quit. I leaned in just inches from his face. "But, this block might be it. If you say *no* now, I'll have to wonder about that for the rest of my life. And so will you." He sighed long and deep before agreeing.

John and my favorite nurse, Judy, were by my side early the next morning. This wasn't going to be easy and it helped to have them cheer me on. We were ready to go for it. Day inserted the needle into my lower back, pushing further and further until the anesthetic ran out and blinding pain erupted in my body. It attacked my head, toes, vagina, seemingly anywhere. He was digging in a nerve-rich area that could refer pain to any point. Each time I screamed, he inserted more anesthetic. We continued for what seemed like hours, with a pain level that would have made the Inquisition look like child's play.

"Her blood pressure has dropped too far," Judy warned Day in a frightened voice. "She's white as a ghost."

He didn't pause. I swear he was a madman that day. Instead he ordered, "Get her prepped. We're doing it again."

I wasn't angry with Dr. Day. I'd begged him for this chance to get my life back. But I didn't believe I could tolerate another procedure. John was glassy-eyed from trauma. Judy, clearly upset about the repeat, gripped my hand tightly, telegraphing me to hang on for dear life.

Somehow I survived the second round, but again the block failed. Without hesitation, Day told me I had two choices. "We can do this a third time here. Or I can hospitalize you where I can do the block under X-ray. That'll give me a better chance at hitting the right spot."

With sweat dripping off me, this was a no-brainer. Somehow levity kicked in. "Let's call it a day, Dr. Death. See you at the hospital."

This time, no one could be with me due to the radiation exposure. Just me and the needle. That day no one heard my screams, but that was okay. In some twisted way, Day and I had made peace with the certainty of pain and the possibility of healing me. This block didn't take either, but I heard Day call excitedly to John outside the room, his voice sounding like he'd discovered the cure for cancer. When he returned, he shared the news. "I can't believe it," he said. "The blocks aren't taking because the needle's too small for you. It's long enough for obese men and you're just a tiny thing. But because you were a ballerina, the muscles in your back are so over-developed that this needle can't reach the spot. I'll use a bigger one."

Hope can come in the cruelest form. My salvation could be dependent on an even larger needle.

The pain didn't lessen on the fourth go-round, but the block finally took. As I lay on a gurney with John by my side, my right leg and foot heated up to a rosy red as the drugs at last successfully dilated my veins. But this pushed the pain so high that I shook uncontrollably. Soon the dreaded words spilled from my mouth.

"This means I don't have Sympathetic Dystrophy, doesn't it, Dr. Day?" He kicked the wall next to him so hard it left a dent.

"No, you don't. But you just saved another professional athlete a load of agony. Next time, I'll get it right with one shot." After what I'd been through, I held on tight to that small dose of comfort.

During our last appointment, I ran Bailey's surgery suggestion by Day. I knew this man understood my body better than anyone. "I guarantee you this," he said. "If you have that surgery, you will *never* walk on that leg again. You'll be in a wheelchair for the rest of your life." I knew he was right. Fear raced through my being. I'd come so very close to stepping into the abyss.

Then and there, I decided to stop my search for the answer I felt certain was not to be. Instead, I threw myself back into the acting/modeling world. Even though my agent still couldn't find anything, I began landing jobs on my own. I gave my headshot to everyone in the business and an acquaintance pitched me to a client for a sitting job *without* telling them that was all I could do. Boom! I was on the cover of Hewlett-Packard's consumer magazine, even though I'd never touched a computer in my life. The client loved the cover so much that I felt comfortable confiding my whole story.

That got me referred to other clients. But I quickly tired of the work. Modeling is *really* boring, and I've never enjoyed being a brainless prop. Worse, I was reduced to selling medical equipment and home health products. There wasn't anything further from my coveted Ziegfeld Follies. Still, the work allowed me to hope again.

John's Take

Oh man, it was heartbreaking.

It had really looked like we were onto something with Dr. Bailey and even more so with Dr. Day, who announced that Cynthia suffered from a pain disease. I mean, holy smokes. Duh, pain. Right! It's always been the pain, the pain that never fucking stops. You take away the pain and she'd be doing cartwheels down the block. No more wheelchair, no more moans in the night. No more imploding life.

Manage the pain. Put a knife in it and turn the blade. Send it to one of those nuclear waste dumps 10 miles underneath some looks-like-Mars desert. Seal it with a cement cap and say adios forever. Day and his assortment of blocks and torture devices allowed me to think it was possible. At our fingertips. But just like everything else, the hope evaporates. It's just devils and dust. Back to square one. Back to the great search that leads to nowhere.

But this snarling bastard pain hasn't turned me to rubble yet. There are still a few pieces of my heart dangling. I have the strength to get up tomorrow, throw my shorts on. Get busy living or get busy dying. Damn straight. The answer is out there. It may be playing a game of hide and seek. And I may stumble around like some 7-year-old, a mix of drool and rocky road ice cream smeared across my shirt, dazed and desperate. But it can't run forever. I'm going to find it. And when I do, I'm going to free my girl from pain's shackles. I'm going to beat my chest. I'm going to thank God for delivering us from this evil. Then I'm going to lay my head down and sleep for a thousand years.

Where's our deliverance? Is it at the tip of a needle? Is it a pill hot off the presses from R&D? Is it some magic elixir brewed by a sub-Sa-

haran juju medicine man? Baby, I know it's out there. I feel it in my bones. Just hang on. When you're out of rope, tie a knot at the end and tighten your grip. Don't let go. Please.

NINE

REINVENTING CYNTHIA

My situation was simple. All I needed was something that would make a huge splash. *And* prove I could work in the business. *And* make me famous overnight. Easy stuff like that.

And then it hit me. Pose for *Playboy*!

Faster than you could say Marilyn Monroe, I had John pick up the magazine to see what was happening in Hefner's world. I dug out all the sexy lingerie I had. We cleared Mom's studio so John could take semi-nude pictures of me imitating poses from the magazine. What a kick. I even got creative and added Sadie to the mix. Something about black fur on white skin made the pictures sizzle, but that made keeping John on track even more challenging. My serious work of posing provocatively was foreplay for him.

"Why don't you bend this way, Cynth? Pucker your mouth. Point your finger there. Yeah. Move your knee here. Show me a little more of this."

The photos turned out better than we'd expected. I spoke with Verna about my submission. She gave me sound advice. "Cynthia, you'll stand out from the millions of other beautiful women with your killer story. Almost unbelievable. Use it with the pictures. They'll love you."

My brother David, an aspiring journalist, wrote my profile. I quickly submitted the package, sealing it with a kiss for good luck. I was shocked when I got a standard rejection letter a couple weeks later. I thought I'd be a slam-dunk and felt certain that no one had even glanced at my submission. Brushing off this setback, I got on the horn to *Playboy's* West Coast office in Los Angeles. I confidently held on until I got a photographer, Kim Mazuno, on the line.

Boldly, I asked for a test. Swayed by my story, he asked me to send my submission directly to him.

Kim called a week later. "Cynthia, you're *exactly* what *Playboy's* looking for. You don't need a test from me. These photos and your story are going to get you in. I'll submit them directly to the top." With that, a door opened and I felt the rush of recapturing my life.

In short order, David called *Playboy* headquarters and spoke with Gary Cole, the guy just underneath Hefner. David couldn't wait to get me on the phone.

"Cynthia, you're all they're talking about at Chicago headquarters. They want you to be a Playmate."

I was so excited I started pacing around Mom's dining room. *This is it!* I couldn't calm myself. Hell, I didn't want to. Needing a task to divert my frenetic energy, I started scraping paint from an antique pillar Mom had found for the house. As I pushed the scraper back and forth, fantasies of limos, guest appearances—and mostly the film career this gig would spark—raced through my head.

Before I knew it, my pain shot through the roof and an old familiar panic set in. After months of improvement, it didn't make sense that this good news would bring back the full-blown pain. But there it was. The dragon had spat its fire once again. That pain ripped me out of my partial recovery. Then, to make matters much worse, the brass at *Playboy* said I was a no-go. They'd already done a pictorial about a disabled woman, Ellen Stohl, a few years prior, and, "We never do a story twice."

I was devastated but didn't let myself fall into a depression. I *knew* I was perfect for this magazine. I barraged them with new photos every month. Finally, my "you're-making-a-huge-mistake" tactics paid off in spades. In July 1988, a *Playboy* press agent called.

They were searching the country for their 25th anniversary Playmate and would be in San Francisco tomorow. "You're the girl we want to see first. Bright and early. And don't forget to pack your bikini." Bingo! Fortunately, my pain had eased enough for me to do limited work and I was hell-bent on pulling this off.

The next morning, dressed in a denim mini-skirt, blue-fringed blouse and white cowboy boots, Mom delivered me to the St. Francis hotel on Union Square. Upon arriving at the penthouse, I was warmly introduced to the *Playboy* crew, including photographer Kerry Morris.

Despite early jitters, I soon found myself in my element. As local media milled around setting up their cameras and lights, I slipped into my peach and silver bikini to shoot with Kerry, who proved to be a doll. I told him I had a ballet injury, so he didn't have me stand for long. As I posed from mostly seated or prone positions, he cracked jokes and got me laughing and relaxed as he snapped away.

Meanwhile, Don Sanchez, an anchor from KGO TV, along with a reporter from the *San Francisco Examiner*, clamored for intimate details. I loved every moment. I coyly shared that yes, I had a boyfriend, and no, he wasn't upset. And that *Playboy* was the only magazine I'd ever pose nude for. I beamed white-toothed smiles. The cameras, the lights, the questions—everything was perfect.

I was a natural. My news spot ran that evening. I appeared bikini-clad in the *Examiner* the following morning. Suddenly, I was the talk of the neighborhood. Everyone wanted to see and talk to me. It felt like old times. Mrs. Jackson, the neighborhood gossip, moseyed to our front door to mimic one of my TV quotes. Vince phoned to say I'd turned Powell Avenue into "Po-Wow-WOW Avenue!"

I would have jumped for joy if I could have when *Playboy* sent me a letter a week later. They hadn't selected me as their 25th Anniversary Playmate. Instead, and perhaps better, they wanted me to sign a release so they could keep my pictures as they were seriously considering me for a future "special" pictorial. Again, my heart and head spun with possibilities. I was back on track. A different track, but a track nonetheless.

The months rolled by, however, with no progress. So I continued to bang on *Playboy*'s door. I'd gotten to know Stephanie, the photo coordinator at their Los Angeles headquarters. Because John and I were considering a move to L.A. to be in the center of the entertainment biz, I phoned Stephanie to let her know I'd be in town for a few days apartment hunting. My aim was to bait her into setting up a meeting. Stephanie took the hook.

Our meeting was great. She told me that in many ways I was a perfect catch for *Playboy*. Along with testing for a special pictorial, she asked me to consider singing and dancing in *Playboy*'s Vegas review. *Sign me up, but I can barely walk.* When I explained my limitations, she became frustrated because she could see my potential. It was the same old story. The way I looked and the big, positive energy I exuded didn't match up with my pain and disability.

At one point, Stephanie sat up exclaiming, "Wow, Cynthia, you're a perfect spokesperson." Her words exploded like fireworks in my head. *That's the one thing I can still do that really turns me on. I can be a face and voice for something I'm passionate about.* Truth is, I scarcely knew how accurate that assessment would one day be.

Stephanie said they didn't want to waste me as a Playmate. "With special pictorials, your smarts and personality are just as important as your looks. I'm going to give you a Playmate questionnaire to fill out, and we'll fly you back for a test."

That sounded great, but I was concerned. "Stephanie, I know there's been a special pictorial done with Ellen Stohl, and I've been told by Chicago they won't do my story because it's too similar."

She paused, then shook her head, "No, you're not getting it. This test is a formality. Just to prove that you photograph well and get along with the family here. You're in, Cynthia. Ellen Stohl's not in your way anymore." Relieved, I floated—well, with a bad limp—

out of Stephanie's office into the reception area. One of the Playmates breezed through, fabulous disproportions and all, trying with futility to answer a simple question posed by a *Playboy* executive from across the room. After stumbling through the first few words, silence fell. I took pity and finished her sentence for her.

Back at Mom's, I carefully crafted the questionnaire. Yes, they really do ask what your hobbies are. I titled my pictorial, "Cynthia's Sitting Pretty and Proves She Has Nothing To Hide." They loved it, and Stephanie booked me on a flight for L.A. The excitement mounted when she called to tell me about the first day of my shoot. *Playboy* was building a set for me and had assigned their top photographer, Arny Freytag. Stephanie invited me to stay at the mansion, but because John would be there as my caregiver, *Playboy* nixed it due to their no-boys-allowed policy.

Once in L.A., I was shuttled around town in a limo and put up in a suite at the swanky Le Parc hotel. The thrill of this visit more than made up for my pain, which spiked fiercely.

The next morning, I entered *Playboy*'s inner world. Giant Playmate centerfolds covered the walls, with mirrors seemingly everywhere reflecting the fantasy. I was amazed that my set, a pink-inspired bedroom and boudoir, only took up a tiny portion of the expansive shooting studio filled with cables, lights and equipment.

In my dressing room, which evoked my Vegas days, I was surrounded by a gaggle of creative consultants from "upstairs." Intrigued by every inch of me, they pulled at my arms, touched my face, pressed color swatches against my skin. Inspired discussions erupted over the texture of my hair. Straight or curly, down or up? Someone barked out orders to change the bed sheets from pink to peach as in "let's enhance her skin and hair color." No detail was too small. "Who's the girl?" I heard all day long from the shadows. Only a very few, as it turns out, are privileged to sit under these lights with the *Playboy* machine humming behind them. For me, this shoot was another performance, a part to be played. The nudity quickly became a non-issue.

But even with the glitter, posing was hard work. As Freytag shot off roll after roll and the phone rang with queries from the overlords asking about every detail, I did my best to follow the abundant rules. I had to drink with a straw. I couldn't touch my wardrobe or my body, especially down there since every pubic hair had been brushed just so. Sherry, my wardrobe gal, had to get permission for me to put on and remove my right shoe since it was too painful when she did it. I may have been the only girl in *Playboy* history allowed to adjust her pumps.

Arny blared a '70s soundtrack whenever we were shooting. I started laughing when I heard Fleetwood Mac's "You Make Loving Fun" as it brought back memories of my first boyfriend. *Boy, if Mitch could see me now.* I was on my back, lingerie strategically displaced, most of my body hanging off the bed.

"So what's funny, Cynthia?" Arny asked.

I laughed and played sexier than ever. We worked well together as I quickly responded to his precise instructions. He chirped, "I can't believe it, Cynthia. You're one of the few girls I've photographed who knows her right from her left."

"Maybe *Playboy* should work with more dancers," I quipped.

At six o'clock, this version of *Cinderella in the Nude* ended. I was exhausted, physically and emotionally. When I emerged fully clothed, John was waiting in the building's entrance, sharing a laugh with Arny, who had reported a great day. I was happy and proud as John wrapped me in a bear hug. I might have doubted my reality, but Sherry had stolen some Polaroids for me as a keepsake. She and my make-up artist, Alexis, ogled the pictures, gleefully asking, "Did you know you photographed *this* well?" Conversation turned to what national media I'd choose to promote my pictorial.

I naively asked if I'd get Phil Donahue. They giggled. "You can get anything you want. King, *People*, Letterman. The world is yours."

That night, back at our suite and sore from the shoot, I pulled out the Polaroids. John shook his head in disbelief. "These are even better than Kim Basinger's." I realized my life was about to change completely. I was going to get back much of what I'd lost. My fight for redemption was over. I cried as I wrote a letter to my brother David, my soul mate as he coined himself, telling him about the day and how excited I was to ride this rocket.

Back in Pleasant Hill, I prepped for the rest of my shoot and our move to L.A., barely able to harness my excitement. I was in suburbia only in body now. My head was already in the glitz and the lights. Stephanie phoned to say the photos were gorgeous and everyone was happy.

"Now, it's just a matter of paperwork by the guys in Chicago. The sign-off is a formality before we shoot the rest of your pictorial. We're all excited."

I was surprised when she didn't call the next week. Or the next. Whenever I touched base, she reassured me things were steaming full speed ahead. But my stomach was telling me something else. I stopped sleeping. My period stopped as well, my personal indicator of big stress.

Six weeks ticked off. Then I got the worst phone call ever. "Chicago is passing due to Stohl's story," Stephanie told me. "They don't do stories twice." Apparently they did do turndowns twice.

Stunned, I asked her, "Then why did they take the pictures?"

She stumbled over her words. "Well, ah, they always want to see the girl."

I'll never know why the decision changed. But I now know that in showbiz, careers are often made or torn to shreds arbitrarily. From my bed of despair, the curtains drawn tight to shut out the light, I wondered how I was going to survive this blow. How could I resurrect my spirit and my career? What new rabbit could I possibly pull out of my pain-filled hat?

The *Playboy* verdict followed a decision about John and me that was equally devastating. I had slowly accepted what I knew from the start, that John was the man I wanted to spend my life with. Being a wife had never appealed to me before, as that designation seemed conformist and submissive. But I now had a strong desire to marry this man. Our wedding would be a testament to our love and what we'd endured together. I wanted to shout to the world that we were forever.

Not so coincidentally, John had been experiencing similar feelings. He was now working nights at an entry-level job at Bank of America, saving his days and energies for my caregiving. Eyes red and blurry, he came home one morning and dropped to his knees before me as I sat in front of the bathroom vanity. Swiveling me around, he took my hands in his.

"Baby, all I could think about all night long was that I love you. And I want us to get married," John said in tears before placing his head on my lap.

Stroking his brown hair, I began to cry with him. "I've been thinking that too. I can't believe you'd come home today and say this."

I flashed back to the first time I'd seen John. "Who is that fox?" I asked during the opening-night cast party Mom had thrown after getting the lead in *You Can't Take It With You* at the local community theater. John arrived late and immediately captured every drop of my attention. He was wearing a gray vest with jeans and tennis shoes. The uniquely bold look in his blue-green eyes proclaimed that he owned the world and would forever be kicking up its dust. I'd never in my life been so knocked out by a guy.

Someone from the crew overheard me and said, "That's Ed."

"Well, I'm going to marry him!" Unfortunately, whenever "Ed" got within earshot, my heart pounded, my palms began to sweat and I completely clammed up. I thought I'd die when he approached me as I sat in one of Mom's blue velvet, antique chairs.

"Wow, everyone in your family's an artist," he coolly commented. "All the paintings and photos in this house are incredible. Are you an artist too?"

I could have said a million things to make him fall in love with me forever. Problem was, my throat wouldn't open and my brain went to mush. I finally burbled an awkward "No." He tilted his head, and said, "Oh!" After a long, excruciating pause, he made his excuses and walked over to the potato salad. Babette Bilger seized on the opportunity and soon monopolized him. My chance had passed and I hated Babette, that non-burbling hussy.

Later, Mom came over to introduce me to her fellow cast member, John, and "Ed" was forever gone. Laughing at mistaking him for his character's name, my nervousness melted as we connected with a sensual energy beyond anything I'd ever felt. When I discovered that we both attended Diablo Valley College and then planned to head to UC Irvine, renowned for its acting and dance departments, I knew our fate was sealed. Deep inside, I celebrated that feeling.

But I was celebrating all by myself. John had not yet seen our wonderful fate. True to form, he made his cool late entrance when the next cast party rolled around. I would later learn this wasn't an expression of style. No, John was always late because he was blind as a bat without his eyeglasses, which he refused to wear out of vanity. So he had to stop at every other road sign, and get out of his car to read them.

I was beyond excited to finally see him and then crushed—leveled to smithereens—when he barely spoke to me. I wept silently all the way home.

"David, I'm in love with John Garrett," I finally confided to my brother when John wound up as the understudy in a play where

David was handling props. "This is my last chance. Just tell John I want to date him. Tell him to call me." I'd never been so forward, but for me these were desperate times.

My brother did my bidding, but the phone never rang. Every night I blistered David for details about John—what he had worn, what he had said, what body part he had scratched. I talked non-stop about him, driving my family and friends nutty in the process. I dragged Vince to John's matinee and sat in the front row. Each time he spoke, I got goosebumps. Still nothing. Finally, I convinced David to invite John to the big summer bash that Beth's then boyfriend was throwing. Despite a total absence of encouragement, I knew this was it, the magic night when I'd break through.

Everyone at the party had heard about this mystery John guy Cynthia had a huge thing for. I was sitting on a bench, waiting for my turn at ping-pong, when a rumbling began. "He's here. John's here!" Without thinking, I beelined my way through the crowd into the house.

And there he was. John Garrett. *All to myself.* He smiled at me. Taking his hand, I introduced him around, then sat him in the kitchen and got him a beer. For the next three hours, we talked about everything from music to the Carter administration. Hey, folks, I needed to make sure he leaned to the right—or should I say, left—side politically. We laughed nonstop, never moving an inch from our barstools. We drummed with kitchen utensils and made hand puppets with potholders. I professed my undying love for his favorite rock band, The Who, though I couldn't name a single one of their songs, and for Bruce Springsteen, who I hadn't heard of beyond the fact that John was a huge fan.

A few days later, John actually called me. Me! Mom only had one phone in the house, and it was fought over like a prime piece of real estate. The phone cord reached all the way to the bathroom, offering rare privacy in this house full of noise and mayhem. But after hanging up, I was embarrassed when David and Vince asked where John was taking me on our first date.

"He didn't ask me out," I replied softly. We were stumped.

After a couple of depressing weeks, there was still no word from my beau-to-be. My sophomore year at Diablo Valley College had just begun. Walking from acting class, a sea of students flowed into the main plaza. One caught my attention. Time stopped and everything moved in slow motion. John and I locked eyes from 50 feet away. We walked slowly toward each other, mesmerized. If this had been a movie, I wouldn't have believed it. *Way too hokey.*

We joined hands and started walking together. It didn't matter where. John mentioned, "They're screening a movie this afternoon. Jane Fonda in *The Doll's House.* Wanna join me?" How fast can a person say yes? We had a date.

When we said goodbye, I raced to the nearest phone booth and called home. Mom picked up and I quickly spilled the beans. "John asked me OUT!"

Following the movie, of which I have absolutely no memory, John drove me home where we joined Mom and Paul's birthday celebration. Yes, they are on the same day. Once there, he shook his head in disbelief at the dozens of bunny rabbits that ran loose in our backyard.

Much to my delight, the following week John and I met each morning at the Humanities Plaza. But this guy was moving so slowly, a turtle could have whizzed past him.

Our first kiss (God bless America!) *finally* happened at a condo he was house sitting. We'd watched what seemed like a dozen episodes of "The Newlywed Game" while he got his nerve up. There was instant electricity and I stayed until early morning as we intimately discovered each other. Being old-fashioned, I didn't let him get around third base. But I knew, right from the start, we were going to be serious. My feelings never changed. Not even when I learned that John had a reputation as a heartbreaker or the reason why he moved at glacier speed. He'd never had a serious relationship before. The idea of emotional commitment—to say nothing of his new feelings—terrified him. While I was starry-eyed, certain and in love, John was taking his first big leap. Even his closest friends were betting on the exact date he'd dump me. But silly old me didn't worry one tiny bit. *I knew.*

Now, after all these years, he was asking me to be his wife. He looked up with his tear-soaked face and said softly, "Will you?" The smile through my tears said it all.

John began saving money for a ring and together we launched a search for an extraordinary wedding and reception venue that would represent who we were. We found it at San Francisco's Swedenborgen church, an intimate, historic stone building with massive wood beams, lit by a huge fireplace and candle chandeliers. Madrone tree trunks with original bark arched overhead to convey the beauty of a forest and a distinct feeling of the Renaissance. The non-denominational church welcomed all to be married, even gay couples, which at that time was rare. We loved the openness and tolerance of this breathtaking Pacific Heights landmark. For the reception, we chose the Palace of Fine Arts, a San Francisco jewel inspired by Roman and Greek architecture and framed by a swan-filled lagoon.

The plan was perfect. Now we needed to figure out how to get me down the aisle. I wasn't about to add an ugly chrome wheelchair to the beauty of the day. Mom, John and I had fun brainstorming some creative ideas, which included having me come down the aisle à la Scheherazade on a "flying carpet" powered by six brawny men. You could hear my squeal across the bay when they told me that one.

In the midst of the fun we were having with these plans, John and Mom visited the local Social Security office to make sure all of our T's were crossed. They shared the devastating news with me in the car. Marrying John would cancel my Supplemental Security Insurance (SSI)—and most importantly, my medical benefits. We couldn't afford that. Later, I learned this was often called Social Security's "marriage penalty law." Many people with severe illness either don't get married or divorce in order to keep their healthcare. So much for family values in this country.

With heavy hearts and a bitter feeling that we were being punished for my disability, John and I surrendered. Our wedding would not be.

I felt I was back at square one. Two major scenarios that seemed primed to succeed—my work with Dr. Day and the *Playboy* saga—had crashed and burned. Now our wedding had suffered the same fate.

Even then, beat up as I was, I knew I'd take another crack at something soon. I was going to find me another launching pad.

John's Take

I've failed again. We can't marry because we're trapped in this entitlement program nightmare. But we're only in it because we don't have any other means to pay for healthcare. It's hard to find a well-paying career—even one you hate—if you're caregiving 24 hours a day. I'm not making any excuses, but who's going to hire a guy who might need to be home at a moment's notice? Men my age need to be working 80-hour weeks to get ahead. They need to drop everything to cater to the boss. That's not me. But I can't stop thinking that I'm a gigantic loser for not being able to marry the woman I love.

What else can they take from us? They've already grabbed our health, our peace of mind, our ambition. Now let's just strip away the last bit of dignity. We're not even afforded the right of every man and woman of consenting age. This is just too much. People snap when backed into a corner.

We're boyfriend and girlfriend. So what, are we dating? People say, "You're married, even if not legally." I see their point—the relationship has stood up to more muck than most can tolerate—but we don't have that piece of paper. I'll forever check off the "single" box on forms that ask for marital status. If she gets sick and needs to go to the hospital, I may not be able to see her because I'm not family. Not family? This is bullshit.

I hate what's being dumped on us. We're caught in this trap, and it's pulling us down further and further. Hold on, I say over and over to myself.

But hold on to what?

TEN

LIFELINES

I couldn't marry. I couldn't dance. I couldn't land an acting job. I couldn't even secure the *Playboy* spread that had been assured me. But I could still sing and pursue a recording career. From *Backstage*, I located a vocal coach in San Francisco, who said she'd never worked with someone who had my potential. By the beginning of 1989, however, just talking created hot pain that stretched all the way to my throat. Singing became impossible. Soon my ability to talk vanished as well.

That was the worst. I am an addicted talker. I yak, I yammer. John and I joke that he'll never process even half of what I say. My mind breaks all speed limits. It pours out of my mouth, highly amped and often passionate, a verbal flood that I don't edit much. Amongst the Toussaint brood, I've always talked over everyone. I'm a communicator, pure and simple. And when I'm not talking, I imitate or sing. I'm almost always *on*.

John and I both feel the non-talking years were a special torture. Unfortunately, that scenario is not completely over yet. Pain regularly flares in my vocal cords, forcing me to be mute again.

When my voice first left, I went to a couple of Ear, Nose and Throat specialists outside of Kaiser. They scoped my throat, but all they saw was a tiny contact ulcer that had no business causing this level of misery. An endoscopy revealed a hiatal hernia that provoked more head scratching. Yet another unsolved mystery about a body that kept going haywire.

Unable to speak for a year straight (and on and off for another five), I wrote notes on Etch-A-Sketch-like boards that John bought at Toys R Us. They wore out after a few months, mostly because when inspired or enraged, I pounded the stylus over and over for emphasis. Like always, I had a lot to say.

Somehow, John and I shared long conversations even though I had to scrawl every letter. I often whistled to get his attention when he was out of sight. To this day, his head jerks when he hears a high-pitched sound. We even developed our own sign language, complemented by clicking sounds. And sometimes, in the dark of night, I fingered letters on his palm. I'd share things as diverse as my love for him and my growing despair about losing not only my speech, but also my singing voice. The voice that had been my last creative outlet and joy.

I now dreamed each night that I was dancing ballet. As John sprang from bed to go to work, I'd share every detail. What I had danced, where and with whom. These were the most vivid dreams I'd ever had. Some nights, I'd get to do an intense barre. I could feel every muscle in my body working again. Other nights, I'd be dancing a classical ballet, feeling the stiff, short tutu bouncing with my jumps. It was sublime.

Over the years, these dreams became haunting. The pain would seep in, and I knew that no matter how hard I tried, I couldn't work through the movement. Other times, I'd lace my toe-shoes only to find myself on ice. Sometimes, just before a performance, I'd make a last costume check only to discover I was wearing pajamas. Often, my partner couldn't dance, and I'd start falling.

Back in the real world, John and I cleaned anything and everything in Mom's house to fill the hours of sadness and isolation. John sat me on the floor and we emptied the fridge. Out came all the aging, moldy leftovers Mom had refused to pitch before she went to Manhattan.

Then we attacked the backyard shed. What a mess! Mom's endless piles of stuff were, yes, endless. This decluttering gave me a sense of control. *(Oops, Mom. So sorry for accidentally tossing your handmade wedding dress.)* We gathered trinkets to sell at massive flea markets, pulling in $200 on a good Sunday. As the sun pounded down, I strained to whisper prices loudly enough, frustrated that the buyers couldn't understand my pointing and gestures.

I read the classics, five to six hours a day. That ended when I got severe eyestrain reading *War and Peace,* 100 pages short of completing it. *Psst, don't tell me how it ends.* So much for that avenue of escape.

We also tried the movies. But it was almost impossible to get to the theater seat using crutches, and dangling my right leg while sitting up proved torturous. I remember seeing *Colors*, starring my favorite actor Sean Penn. From the first to last frame, it was all I could do to not moan out in pain. After John carried me home, he brought me two bags of frozen peas. Per Kaiser's earlier PT advice, I used them to ice both hamstrings. I did this religiously three times a day, especially since it initially numbed the pain. Hell, I'd do anything for a few minutes of relief. Later, after my diagnosis, I learned that ice spreads my disease. Yet another gift from that HMO.

I was mostly bedridden. Crawling had become so painful that at night I couldn't get myself to the bathroom. Time and again, John brought that dented stainless steel bowl for me to pee in.

And still I couldn't talk.

Each week, I'd physically save up for our one big event—the Garretts' Saturday night barbecue in Martinez. I loved Jack and Betty and their mouth-watering top sirloin with all the trimmings. But trying to engage them with silent communication at their dining room table humiliated me. Still, I went just to combat the devastating loneliness.

My kitty, little Sadie, handled my silence with unconditional love. Since I could no longer call her, she now came to my clap.

Swimming, which had been recommended by Penny, the dance physical therapist I'd found years earlier, provided the only light during those dark times. Gliding through the water had always felt perfect to me, and as Penny had predicted, seemed to improve my physical and emotional health. I loved it. John would lift me into the Olympic-size pool at Heather Farms in Walnut Creek and I swam a mile each day. Using a Styrofoam Pull-Buoy to keep my legs afloat, my stroke barely creating a wake. Outside the water I was badly disabled. But in this blue heaven, I was an athlete again. Free at last!

Finally my voice returned, albeit part time. Desperate to find a niche in the entertainment business, I decided that John and I would still move to Los Angeles. We used our savings from the illusion act for a down payment on a beautiful new condo in North Hollywood located a virtual stone's throw from the major studios.

We quickly settled in with Sadie. I immediately plunged into trying to find work, confident I could land a job as a spokesperson. I mean, I never saw Mary Hart or Elvira walk. The correspondents and hosts on E! Entertainment sat through entire segments. *That could be me.* I sent my headshot, resume and a demo to everyone I could think of. No one responded. When I finally talked to a producer from E!, he was put off, even enraged, that a disabled person had the nerve to waste his time. Clearly the prejudice against disabled TV hosts was much the same as it was for actors. Each door that slammed shut frightened me that much more.

I needed to meet someone with power in Hollywood, a person who could think outside the box. I sent a letter and headshot to Beau Bridges, who'd been my favorite actor growing up. His projects suggested a kind, open heart, so I wasn't surprised when he phoned me. By coincidence, he was filming the James Brady story. "How long have you been in the chair?" he asked pointedly. Put off, I made it clear that, "I'm not confined to the wheelchair. I just use it for long distances." I hadn't yet come to terms with the chair, a vibe he probably felt. In his kind, raspy voice, he asked me to send him a demo, promising to keep me in mind for upcoming disabled roles.

I also contacted Michael Landon, who I adored. He was well known for hiring disabled talent for his *Highway to Heaven* series. His publicist phoned to say that Michael loved my headshot, was certain he'd seen me before and was eager to meet up. We set a date. A few days later, I got the news that Landon had gone public about his advanced colon cancer. He died a few months later.

Still, these two connections inspired me to take the plunge. Bridges and Landon didn't think there was anything wrong with me using a wheelchair—and they were two of my heroes. So I finally did it. I rented a cool, jet-black wheelchair full time. That one-time enemy changed my life. I was no longer stuck at home or in the car. I immediately went into a mall for the first time in years. I'll never forget seeing its futuristic glass elevators. The world had progressed without me and I felt very ready to play some serious catch up.

It wasn't to be. The pain that had crippled my legs began to ravage both my arms. *Oh God, not my arms.* One day in early 1991, nine years into my illness, I woke and tried to unfold them. I felt the familiar burning, stabbing pain, and despite my frantic straightening efforts, my right arm stayed stuck. With one arm in a severe contracture and both in unrelenting pain, I could no longer swim or play the piano. I couldn't even do simple things like writing, washing dishes or petting a cat. With gut-wrenching tears, we sent Sadie to live with Mom. I felt more useless than ever.

I talked a lot to John about my despair. Afterwards I often felt guilty for having added to his load. With my condition worsening, a mortgage to pay and no family or friends to lean on, John crumpled. For the first time, he experienced anxiety attacks and night terrors. His face drained of all color. The fear in my poor Superman's eyes grew daily. He tried to drink himself to sleep and moved into the second bedroom. But the pressure of being the sole breadwinner and caregiver did not abate. He was, in a word, overwhelmed.

John could now barely make it through his workday. Shaking like a whipped dog, he wept as he left the house. "I'll give it my best shot," he'd say. But I never knew if he'd make it through his shift. Hell, I wasn't certain he could make it through a meal. Once in a fast food restaurant, he suddenly lay down, afraid he was having a heart attack. The fact that he didn't have health insurance and we were one hospital stay away from financial ruin compounded his fear.

Determined not to let John's nervous breakdown destroy us, I became *his* caregiver. I knew what faced us if he got fired or institutionalized. Our L.A. days would be over, and most likely our lives as well. I steeled myself to support him through his panic attacks. When he came to me hyperventilating, saying he couldn't go to work, I made deals with him.

"John, just go for three hours." I'd hold his hand or touch his face. "Then call me and we'll talk about whether you should come home or not."

Sometimes he'd make it for an hour without needing a pep talk. Other times I was certain he wouldn't make it for a minute. I was terrified, but worked hard not to show it. I wanted my strength to carry him through.

My Superman bent, but he didn't break. Eventually, John spent a Saturday at the county hospital where an MD took a brief history, assessed his life and assured him his heart was healthy. That immediately eased John's fear. This wonderful doctor referred him to a good psychologist at a low-cost mental health clinic in Van Nuys who told him his symptoms were a normal reaction to stress and chaos.

This time our medical system worked. John began a slow recovery. Every week, he returned home with a smile after his appointments with the psychologist. He also brought giant muffins, which they gave away at the clinic. I finally recognized my love again.

John's illness gave me a new outlook. I needed to carry more of my own weight and bring in some money. But what did I still have to sell?

My old college roommate, Melissa, helped me find that answer. She was living in Los Angeles and working in publicity at Paramount*. When she came to our condo, we both screamed like schoolgirls gone wild. She'd had a nose job, and I was surprised to see her long mane of crimped blonde hair. But otherwise she was the same spunky, go-get-'em gal. After catching up, Melissa said quite matter-of-factly, "Cynthia, your story's way too good for *Playboy*. It's a movie."

This wasn't a new notion. For years people had compared me and my story to Jill Kinmont and *The Other Side of the Mountain*. A movie maker and close high school friend of John's, Victor Salva, was the first to make that connection. John and I bumped into him at our favorite Pleasant Hill Mexican restaurant seven years after my hamstring injury.

"What do you mean *The Other Side of the Mountain* is your favorite movie, Cynthia?" Victor said over chimichangas. "Hell, it's *your* life story!"

His remark offended and frightened me. Jill's life as an Olympic level skier who reinvented herself following an accident that left her a quadriplegic had stirred me deeply. I'd seen her movie a gazillion times. She was my biggest hero growing up. Not only did she have endless courage, she helped many people with her example. But at that point, I hadn't come to terms with my disability. Not even close. Being compared to a quad, no matter how courageous, was no compliment. Even though I knew I'd never dance again, I still saw myself as a ballerina.

But once I accepted my new reality, I was fascinated and profoundly flattered by the comparison. And now here was Melissa, someone in the business, telling me that my story could be as powerful as Jill's.

We initially planned to contact actresses with the star power to launch a film. Since I couldn't use my arms, Melissa typed a letter to dancer turned actress Paula Abdul. She'd recently worked with Paula and felt she'd be ideal for the lead. "She'll understand the loss," Melissa said. Fifteen years later, in 2006, Abdul would announce she had the same disease as I, which would have made her perfect for the role. Too bad she never responded. But maybe my story hit too close.

Eventually, at Melissa's suggestion, I got my hands on a *Hollywood Creative Directory* that gave me contact info for every producer and agent in Hollywood. The mailing label for my fictional "Sadie Productions" ensured that my letters wouldn't get tossed unseen. I studied the directory like I was cramming for a final. We submitted to anyone who'd done stories like mine. John must have typed out 200 letters to producers, actors, managers and agents. In hindsight, I wonder how we survived before personal computers.

The response encouraged me. We got well over 50 calls and letters. I quickly learned I had to catch their interest in a matter of seconds with a story they couldn't walk away from. I became adept at selling my story, a skill that has helped me since, quickly figuring out how to improvise and change directions since every prospect had different questions and needs.

Most companies I pitched to wanted an outline. I wrote a three-page treatment, which Melissa edited. Unfortunately, the studios, networks and production companies weren't doing "soft" true-life stories. True crime and violence ruled the day. Plus, I didn't have the convenient Hollywood happy ending. But I kept at it.

Before long I'd made some good friends in the business. Dick Freed, producer of Lifetime's most popular movies, and Tom Kageff, who'd recently produced a couple of Robert Altman films, became big fans. Peter Stelzer, second in command at Ted Danson's production company, told me, "People in Hollywood will *always* do things for you they won't do for anyone else, Cynthia. You're just that persuasive." He would later hand my story to Christopher Reeve at the 1997 Emmys, during which Peter's company won best television movie for *Miss Evers' Boys*. Another producer, Ken Scherer, took my story to *The Other Side of the Mountain* producer. The latter passed saying, "I can't compete with Jill's story. It's just too similar." This Gang of Four became my show biz support system.

A couple years later, my story picked up traction when Rachel Harris*, a successful TV producer, jumped on board. Her company joined forces with two others, including Dick Freed's, with the aim of producing a premium cable movie that would highlight an indictment of Kaiser. We were moving fast and talking casting when I was told that Kaiser stepped in and threatened to sue everyone involved for slander. At that point Harris caved, I suspect due to the pressure, and everything came to a dead stop. Another crusher, but hell, I was used to that by this stage.

I've always enjoyed being a person who never gives up. I refocused on finding an actress to champion the movie. I knew we had a powerful role that would almost certainly elicit an Emmy or Oscar nomination. Phone calls from agents—most notably for Madonna, Brooke Shields and Drew Barrymore—rolled in and brought new hope. I wasn't dead yet, and neither was my project. I'd do whatever it took to make this fly. I felt driven, both for John and myself. We needed a big break from the disappointment that had shadowed us for nearly a decade.

John's Take

Yeah, things are a little better, but dark stretches of isolation still dog us.

Picture yourself in one of those sensory deprivation tanks. Not for an hour. Not for a day. Think weeks. Think months. Yeah, years. Days stretch on forever. Your body's incarcerated, but your mind is free to wander. But wander where? What else can we do? Stillness is your new friend. You shake hands with the infinite that is housed by walls and pain. Housebound. Limited by movement that brings the worst kind of emptiness. Your voice echoes in the chamber, but if there's no one there to hear it, do you exist?

I count the hours. How can I fill up this day? How can I keep Cynthia occupied enough not to drop into depression? I dance around like a clown, trying to redirect her. Let's go to the new Costner flick. Let's play backgammon. Let's clean out the fridge. Dance, clown, dance. Keep the poor broken pretty girl from feeling the truth. Tick, tick, tick. Night can't come fast enough. Then sleep will be our escape. If I'm really lucky, I can rest for a few precious hours.

But then there's another tomorrow that stretches on forever. I throw on the make-up, slap on the red spongy nose. I'm doing card tricks, but she catches on. She sees through the smoke and mirrors. Pain is the ultimate truth teller. It's only four in the afternoon and I'm out of tricks. Tell me how I am going to fill these hours.

Please. Tell me. I'm tired of playing this game.

ELEVEN

AND THEN IT GOT VIOLENT

My efforts with the movie world yielded connections, both social and professional, but no results. Even the strong initial response from the agents for Madonna, Barrymore and Shields faded, again in large measure because of the softness of my story. Hell, nobody was shooting at me and no one was chasing me in a car. As John's mental state improved, mine worsened. I felt we were the only soldiers on the losing side of a war with an unidentified enemy.

Soon after our move to L.A., I signed my Medi-Cal over to Kaiser to save money. That change, along with my preexisting conditions, prevented me from moving to a different insurance company. Despite my years of hell with Kaiser, I had hoped a new town might bring in doctors who cared. I chose a woman, Dr. Laura Mazarro*, as my internist. Maybe the fairer sex would be less abusive. Besides, I now had proof with my arm contracture that something was physically wrong. They couldn't say that I was nuts anymore.

But Kaiser held the line, basically ignoring my arm dysfunction. From the get-go, it felt to me that the Southern California doctors were more abusive than the ones up north. One physiatrist said I had "tendonitis from Mars" and pressured me to take a truth serum so he could prove I was making up the pain. Another said I was just a woman, suggesting that I shoot myself in the head. Yes, he really said that.

A neurologist, Dr. Shadid*, who would only speak to John with me listening in, dismissively said my problems were strictly psychological. Because he never looked at me, I had to wave my hands to get his attention. I challenged him to explain how he hadn't been able to straighten my arm despite his strength. He shot back, "You're folding up your arm with your mind just the way one levitates oneself." I wondered who was the crazy one here. He continued cryptically, "I don't understand why you don't accept our psychological-induced diagnosis. Chances are in 10 years or so, they'll tell you what it really is." Yeah, he really said that, too.

The most respect I got was from Mazarro, my only female doctor at Kaiser, who suggested that I was an enigma. But during one visit, my mother later shared that the doctor whispered to her, "She's never going to get care here because she's expensive. If Cynthia was my daughter, I'd get her out of the system." But I was trapped.

In the meantime, the pain was spreading like a grass fire. It was now torture to open my scorching jaw. The rest of my body kept my jaw company and I had the constant sensation of a hatchet splaying my back while hot oil cooked my innards. It felt as though the skin on my arms and legs had been peeled away. The agony ran my life, alternately turning me into a monster or a lamb praying for relief.

Depression set in again. I didn't eat and became dangerously thin. My descent into hell with John deepened as we struggled to survive. I wanted desperately to live, but this wasn't a life. Except for John, everyone close to me was gone. Even Melissa, after realizing this thing was permanent, disappeared from my life.

While John was still at my side, depression and sleep deprivation had caused him to gain 40 pounds. His heaviness reflected our unhappiness and amped my guilt. I found it unbearable to look at him. He was now invisible John, a painful extension of my misery.

I didn't hate this ghost of a man, even though we bickered often, but I hated the horror that was destroying us. Once again, my sorrow turned into anger that transcended anything I'd ever known. I felt warehoused in our condo, staring at the white walls while the months and years peeled away. The isolation, the unspeakable loneliness, often dwarfed the physical pain. I was plagued with the reoccurring thought that if John and I died, no one would notice. No one expected us. No one stayed in touch with us. Only the stench would alert the outside world to our demise.

I gained a sliver of comfort watching *Little House on the Prairie* each night and fantasizing about the family the Toussaints used to be. Otherwise, I was a loaded pistol with a hair-trigger. The tiniest thing would set me off. Sour milk curdling in my oatmeal. John shrinking my favorite Gap T-shirt in the dryer. Anything. I spewed my hate and anger at the world by throwing things in the condo, much like I had in the early years at Mom's house but with greater frequency and violence. The kitchen tile floor was often covered with fragments of porcelain and glass.

I usually targeted my fury at John as I screamed at the top of my lungs, not caring who heard me. I had so much hate in me, I needed John to hate everything too and share the load. I ravaged him with a degree of cruelty that's hard to admit and even harder to accept. "You're the loser I got stuck with," I ranted. "You're not successful at anything. Why don't you do me a favor and leave so I can kill myself? That's the best thing I'm ever going to get. If you hadn't stayed, I'd have been dead a long time ago. Fuck you, John Garrett!"

Somehow I felt my struggles gave me a pass to abuse the only person who wouldn't leave me. It felt good to dump my bile on him. He just took it silently. I hated him for not walking out during those rages. I hated him for his loyalty.

As I look back on those dreadful times, I can see—and learn from—what triggered my abuse. It was mostly a product of my judgments. Of John, of the people who deserted me, of the health-care system and everything else. What's most significant is that those judgments and that anger felt so God-almighty appropriate at the time. In truth, these feelings were destroying me.

When my violence finally drained, John would sit on the floor, his head slumped. He held his hands prayer-like, stretched out in front of him, pleading, "Please, no more." His tears spotted our light pink carpet.

Poor John. The only person who didn't bolt and this is his reward. This is what the hero gets. Then it would hit me. I never hated John in any of this. But in those moments, he represented all the loved ones who had left me. Only then could I look up, exhausted and filled with unspeakable sadness, to see the damage I'd done to the house and to John. And to us. I'd lie in his arms weeping in concert with his sobs. But a new cycle of hate would rise with the morning sun.

Years later, John told me he fantasized during this period in order to find a nugget of sanity. In one fantasy, I became someone else, a peaceful, calm person leading a satisfying life despite the pain and disability. In another, he lived alone, in full control, doing what he pleased, having the time and freedom to pursue his passions. His fantasies always involved leading a serene life.

Instead, he worked an eight-hour, overnight job dealing with irate bank customers. He'd then straggle in at 7 a.m., lusting for sleep, to an irate partner whose pain was making her crazy. Nowhere could he find any peace. He was constantly on guard, nerves rattled, like a soldier on a battlefield. Which bullet had his name on it?

The one thing we'd always held onto was the strength of "us," a force we were now losing. John grappled daily with the desire to put an end to our suffering. He purchased a self-deliverance book, *Final Exit,* which gave instructions on how one could—with assistance—take his or her own life. He bought it in anticipation of the day that seemed inevitable for me and perhaps for him as well. We did not have any other escape hatch.

To make matters worse, a new neighbor who constantly stomped around and ran his water faucets day and night, had moved in above us. I called narcotic officers who said the man was probably operating a meth lab. We were desperate to relocate, but the mid-'90s recession had leveled us economically. Once again we were stuck, with nowhere to turn. I reacted poorly, as I did to nearly everything during that time.

My ever-increasing anger terrified me. I had the energy for a hundred marathons, but no way to vent. Even when I knew I was about to explode, I couldn't go for a walk, let alone a jog, to ease the tension. When *Little House* was over and John was asleep, I worked every internal process to numb myself and hold the hate inside. Sitting there all alone, silently, I prepared as best I could for another night of emotional and physical trauma. Would I rage? Would I take my bitterness out on John?

Unable to sleep, I watched him slumber and once again felt the spite and rage I fought so hard to control begin to surge. Soon the emotional vomit became a runaway train and the violence erupted. I lashed out in fury. I screamed profanities, broke what I could, abused John verbally, spat and struck him again and again. I wouldn't let up. I wanted him to feel the same pain that was destroying me.

Finally, the ghost snapped from his sleep-deprived stupor. Temporary insanity transformed him into a lunatic. He threw me about, then put his hands around my throat. I felt his grip tighten. John's face was alive with rage and contempt as he demanded that I stop the madness. After these episodes, he begged me to call the police and turn him in. Anything to get out.

John had struck back the first time a few years earlier. We were in bed when I screamed in the pitch black and he backhanded me. But instead of striking my cheek, he hit my nose so hard, I thought it was broken. He took me to an emergency clinic where I was X-rayed. My nose wasn't broken, but I'd obviously been assaulted. The social worker encouraged me to turn John in to the authorities. I didn't because I wanted to protect him. I knew I always started the violence. He was a good guy in an ungodly situation who'd been pushed too far.

Now the violence was escalating. I thought more than once that John would kill me. One time, he threw me to the carpet where I'd dumped a large potted plant. He shoved my face into the dirt. "You're going to clean it up this time!" he screamed, rubbing my face back and forth, holding me down with his knee. I couldn't breathe. I tried to beg him to stop, but I couldn't get the words out. He was too far gone to have heard them anyway. I don't know what finally gripped him, but he let go. I hobbled into my bedroom, my face and breasts covered with dirt and blood from the abrasions.

Even so, I never assessed the inevitable consequence of my rages. I could only consider my pain and hate. They were bigger than everything. I knew John could very well end my life when he became violent. Almost twice my size, it wouldn't have taken much for him to stop my breath. But I was afraid to hold the rage inside—that could only lead to suicide. So I chose to take my chances with John, trusting that he'd maintain enough sanity not to kill me. The fact that we have both survived makes that one of my wisest choices ever.

That said, our lives became more hopeless. Even though we knew our anger was directed at the circumstances rather than at each other, our descent into this physical and emotional abuse became frighteningly routine. "It's all going to be over soon," John said just as he'd said for the last 12 years. This time, however, I knew he wasn't talking about the pain.

John's Take

I just want to rip out the pain. Shut it up. I want to take an axe and chop it into little pieces. I want to pour kerosene on it, light it up like a big bonfire, and dance around as it turns to embers and ash. It sucks the life out of anything. It mocks and makes the world around it dim and dark. It pokes me in the eye and smiles like a demon, daring me to do something about it. It laughs as it brings me to my knees and I beg for mercy.

The problem is it's inside of her. And it turns her into something unrecognizable. Then it infects me like a fatal virus. But it doesn't kill me. I'm not that lucky. It lets me stay alive as my life descends into chaos. It burrows into my brain, sucking out the last bit of reason. Then, as I turn into the beast it is, it fades away because it has won. Now I am it and it is me. The barbaric pain that lies within her has found a new host. As my fingers curl around her throat, my eyes turn black. I want this to stop. And the only way to stop it is to end the one I love.

There are no words for this horror. This nightmare has no measure. God have mercy on me.

TWELVE

THE CLOUDS PART

We lived with the rage for almost 10 years, as insane as that was. We could have a gorgeous mock wedding one day and be pounding on each other the next. But handling the tough stuff is a key part of who John and I are. We just don't quit. It never mattered how difficult our relationship became or how degrading and castrating it was. I remember someone saying, "Lovers don't finally meet somewhere. They're in each other all along." That pretty much says it for us. Just to see him smile at me and feel his essence. It's how we both knew intuitively, from deep down, that our partner wouldn't leave. Wouldn't kill us. Wouldn't give up the love that, on our good days, consumes us.

When the ugliness rose up, of course, neither of us fully understood this. But that truth is what saved us and saved our love. Eventually, John and I would move past fighting each other to fight as a team.

Communicating deeply helped us heal, at first temporarily and later permanently. During our darkest hours, John lay next to me and through his tears shared his feelings of failure.

"I'm so sorry, baby. If you'd found a guy with money or power, he could have put you in the right clinic or bought the right medicine. Maybe you should find somebody else, a man who can fix this."

Shaking my head in disbelief, I held him close. "I don't feel any of that. No one in the world could have loved me more than you. How can you be responsible for what's happened to me? When are you gonna take on natural disasters and stop all those lousy earthquakes?" I smiled, gently kissing away his tears. Then looking deep into his beautiful eyes, I said, "You stayed, John. That's my miracle.

You've given me the greatest gift there is. Just you being here. For me and for us. I'm *alive* because of you."

I'd finally found a silver lining to all the suffering. I discovered the real John, along with his strength and his passions. I also felt his love for me at a deeper level than ever, a love and support that propels me forward to this day. His essence showed me that there is great goodness in the world. And with all that, I began to find the steps to a higher place.

In May 1995, we decided to celebrate the relationship we had begun to reclaim, and to fulfill our courtship dream in Paris. We couldn't marry, but no one could keep us from taking a honeymoon. I'd fantasized about going to Paris since I was a child. In grade school, I listened wistfully to my French teacher, Madame Rose, tell us you could actually feel the Eiffel Tower sway on a windy day when you were at the very top. That took my breath away.

Things fell into place quickly. Mom gifted the money. I began studying French, my favorite language, with tapes and books, cramming up to five hours a day. I was busy, John was busy, and we both felt more joy than almost ever before.

I knew the trip was a huge risk pain-wise, but I didn't care. There were higher stakes involved. Much higher. Even though I didn't articulate this to myself, I needed to make this choice. I needed to stop letting "them" and the pain run me. I feel now it was about creative freedom at the soul level. Once again, I felt strong and in charge.

This trip to Paris was a game changer for both of us. We were the team with a huge halftime deficit and would go on to win the game. After Paris, our lives were still besieged by the same strains, but we were different. We started then to move forward and upward to places and events we never anticipated. I now see this journey as the springboard for that growth.

I knew the trip was risky beyond the chance it could greatly increase my pain. "I have to go, even though I know it might kill me," I told Mom. She accepted that quietly.

Upon our return, Mom would tell me I had a completely different expression. But my pain had become much worse. It stayed that way for several years and was eventually the reason Kaiser finally, finally produced a diagnosis for my messed up limbs and body. This discovery led to my first real treatment—another benefit from the Paris trip. I did hurt like hell and was virtually bedridden for three more years. But I had no regrets.

Being in Paris opened up my entire boxed-in world. I was in love, and now not just with John. The day after our arrival, we set our sights on the Eiffel Tower, which I had spied through the clouds as our plane made its descent. I couldn't wait to be there, to touch it, to get to the top.

The ticket salesman took one look at my wheelchair and said it couldn't be done. He would only sell us tickets to the third level. I purchased them and smiled with steely determination. I'd find a way.

Once inside the Tower, dizzy with happiness, I reached the third level as quickly as possible. Then I spotted the steps that had prompted the vendor to deny us tickets to the top. Undaunted, John and I scrambled about and found a wheelchair lift, outfitted with cobwebs and dust, that looked a thousand years old. We cornered an attendant who, after much pleading in my limited French, agreed to fire it up. The gods were smiling on me because that lift, slow and creaky, took us to the elevator that would carry us to the top. It was the ride of my life.

I couldn't believe I was going to realize a dream I'd held since childhood. Tummy butterflies fluttered as John wheeled me out. Then like a punch to the gut, I saw it. A steep flight of steps leading to the exterior observation deck, the ultimate top. I immediately looked around for another sympathetic attendant. And there he was, the young, idealistic gentleman I sought. Bless his heart, he was, indeed, a take-charge guy. After a few words, he shouted orders to the other tourists to clear the way, and they courteously complied. With John at the back of my chair and the young man bracing the front, we began our climb one hard step after another. One slip would end my dream and me. But eventually, each of the 16 steps had been counted off.

Cheers and applause from the crowd greeted us. *What do you know, we got us a rooting section.* We had made it. And as Madame Rose had promised, we were swaying in the wind. There was nothing but sky before us. From the top of the tower—the tallest structure in Paris—nothing obstructed our view. Holding hands, we saw the Seine, Notre Dame, the Left Bank and beyond. We were above it all. Above the pain. Above the hurt. Above the loss. We were so much closer to liberation because we hadn't given up.

By wonderful coincidence, while writing this chapter, John surprised me with a May 13, 2009, feature in the *Los Angeles Times* titled, "10 Things You didn't Know About the Eiffel Tower." Number 6 stated, "wheelchair users aren't allowed at the top." This "fact," coming exactly 14 years after our trip, tickled me and sparked my Cheshire cat grin.

After the honeymoon, we wanted— no, needed—to exchange rings to symbolize our commitment. But, alas, for me there was no ring. We'd searched far and wide for the perfect expression of our love, but nothing was quite right. One day it hit me. I already owned the perfect ring, a precious diamond heirloom that my grandmother had worn, and that I now wear every day.

And what a story behind it. Grandma Haering, on my mom's side, forever told the tale of how a field hand on her Minnesota farm had stolen "the diamond." Just before Grandpa died, he revealed to Mom that there was something special for her at the bottom of his World War I duffle bag. There she discovered the ring. My grandfather had taken it from Grandma Haering, a testament to their bitter divorce. Mom gave me the ring along with the story in a Christmas stocking, knowing how dearly I loved Grandpa, who raised and then cared for my Aunt Grace until her death. I think of them each time I look at this delicate diamond and white gold ring, which remains my most cherished possession.

To accent the beauty of the ring, we chose a slender Tiffany's eternity band that I wear with it. We decided to exchange rings and privately pledge our love in a snow-bound, Sierra cabin on New Year's Eve, my 35th birthday.

Scott Harris from the *Los Angeles Times* used our love story and upcoming ring exchange in his front-page Valley edition column titled "Illness Only Strengthens Couple's Love" in November. I couldn't be a bride, but how many couples who aren't Elizabeth Taylor and Richard Burton get a front-page spread?

Our plans changed when John and I went to Mom's house for a two-day visit right before our trip to the mountains. The spirited bustle captured us and we quickly realized we didn't want to leave the hoopla. Just like the old days, the Toussaints were having a blast, and I was once again truly happy. We knew this was the perfect time and place for a wedding. Okay, not a real wedding. I was, after all, fated to be single in the eyes of the government. But our commitment ceremony, complete with an exotic sushi and crab dinner reception, would be held right there.

"Hey everyone, we're going to have a wedding!" Mom announced in her megaphone voice. Excitement rolled through the house like thunder.

With only three days to make it happen, Mom, a.k.a. Hurricane Leona, sprang into action. With her artistic touch, she transformed the house into a sacred chapel adorned with white lights, bells and garlands. Lace and gold ribbon framed each doorway.

An origami-sprinkled Christmas tree crowned the living room. The Douglas fir, decorated by Maki, one of Mom's new Japanese boarders, was our grandest tree ever, almost hitting the highest beam. Every ornament from Japan was a jewel, every piece of tinsel placed just so.

Mom hustled up the perfect cake, frosted thick with yummy white and light pink (my favorite color) roses, along with fresh flowers of the same color and the mandatory garter. Then my childhood bedroom was transformed into a bridal suite complete with white lace curtains, scented candles, orange ribbons and roses. She accented our love nest with bed sheets and pillowslips with a delicate hand-crocheted trim, a wedding gift she and Dad had received but never opened. All this fuss and ruckus had me feeling like a very beloved, honest-to-goodness bride. Wow!

The day of the wedding, Maki and Junko, another of Mom's boarders, took a break from their frenzied sushi making to help me. It was time to pick a wedding gown from the vast array Mom had collected at the local shops. Because it was so difficult for me to sit up, this had to be done at home. The bright-eyed gals giggled as we tugged and pulled up the dresses from around my ankles. I modeled them in front of Mom's exaggerated expressions and the heavy oak mirror she could barely manage to hold up. We raspberried the duds, then oohed and aahed over the hot ones. Between changes, Maki surprised me with a gift of 500 origami cranes she'd made over two nights to bring good fortune to the bride and groom.

Then Mom surprised me with DeeDee, my hairdresser, who arrived loaded down with rollers, a blow dryer and her two-inch, hot pink fingernails. As Paul's wife, Tracy, clamored for makeup tips, this doll of a stylist morphed me into a curly headed bride-to-be, baby's breath flowing from my locks. My 9-year-old niece, Lauren, stared in awe at my transformation.

The ceremony would be in the living room, just as Mom had dreamed when we built the addition years before. It was perfect, down to the pink and white embossed napkins and confetti. Well, almost. My bridal bouquet pooped out in the fridge overnight.

Then it was New Year's Eve. Family members, friends and Mom's roommates sat in a circle. A quiet reverence filled the room. I lay on Mom's pure white couch in a strapless sequined gown and matching gauntlets, listening to the fire crackle. I took in the love, my smile now a permanent fixture, while John nestled himself next to me on a footstool.

Mom, tears welling, lit an antique kerosene lamp from the farm where she was born in 1932. Softly, she shared its history. As a child, her big sister, Grace, had lit her path with this little hand-blown lamp during the dark nights on the farm.

Each of us, as we spoke that night, held the lamp and basked in its warmth. John talked about our determination to marry legally one day. "But tonight, we're exchanging rings to confirm our love and commitment," he said with a wide smile. "Now and forever."

I then took the lamp from John. I thanked Mom for making this dream wedding happen so joyfully—and for raising me with the wisdom to choose John. Turning to John's parents, Betty and Jack, I choked back my tears and thanked them for creating the most extraordinary man on the planet. I saw the love and appreciation in their eyes as I struggled to speak. Jack, whose goodness is reflected in his son, stood and toasted the bride and groom. He thanked us, along with everyone in the room, for "adding to the magic of this most special night."

My big brothers' words especially moved me. From the fireplace, Jon read a loving tribute about how we had preserved our love during the years of struggle. Switching gears, we shared a great, rolling laugh with Paul. He confessed to a huge mistake. "I gotta tell you folks, it's beginning to look like I goofed big-time

15 years ago. That's when I told Cynthia not to date John because you can never trust an actor." He raised his glass, giving John his blessing with a wink.

Though our wedding was not recognized by the state, it was honored and held sacred by everyone in that room. John and I chose not to exchange traditional vows, having blown by those a lifetime before. Instead, we gifted each other with our own words. Mine were in French. "I love you more than words could ever say. You're my best friend, my hero and, just for tonight, you are my husband." I asked him if he could understand me. When he quickly responded, "Oui," I was tickled.

John, in turn, thrilled me by reading a poem he'd written that afternoon. Hearing his words proved to be one of the most beautiful moments of my life.

> *Windmills*
>
> *The Dancer and the Actor*
> *Under the trying canopy of life*
> *Swing and sway to the sweet rhythm*
> *Of wistful, mysterious fate*
>
> *He plays the grand role*
> *Of the strong, silent knight*
> *She, the impeded angel, nimbly jetés*
> *Across a pond of sorrow and hope*
>
> *Together; heart and heart, they tilt*
> *Forward against a steady headwind*
> *Toward that which is placid and kind*
> *Toward an oasis where dreams thrive*

My little niece, Lauren, adorned in a red, checkered dress, skipped over holding a satin and lace pillow that Betty had made.

Tied to it were our rings. We slipped them on each other's fingers, then tenderly held each other and kissed.

John's Take

Holding Cynthia's hand on top of the Tower, still breathing hard from carrying her, was one of the proudest moments of my life. We had the guts and courage and determination to risk all we had left—to take this dream trip. We turned our backs on what was holding us down. And we won. In France, we recaptured the spirit that has always been the best part of our relationship. It's what drew us to each other like a magnet—that zest for life.

Passion. Vigor. Boldness. Risk.

These are the goods we saw in each other. And they are the things we keep alive through the darkest of nights. We never gave up on each other. If there was a ray of light, we clung to it and reached back to grab the other's hand. We pulled each other up. And up. And out.

I look at Cynthia during our commitment ceremony, lying on her mom's couch, glistening in sequins and elegant in long soft gauntlets. She is perfect. Perfect in her beauty and perfect in her soul. Perfect in her courage to sprawl out before family and friends, not allowing her pain to make the rules. I realize I really love this kind of perfect. A perfect that steps outside the normal perfect of others. A perfect that redefines the word perfect. In all its glorious imperfection—the pain, the sorrow, the having to pass on a legal marriage, the lying down to exchange simple vows of love—we find our perfect, suspended above the earth, untouched and pure.

God, I love this woman. And no one and nothing will ever change that. In the soft light of that antique lantern, I exchange vows of love and commitment that I will never say to another.

I feel whole. I feel loved. I feel perfect.

Aunt Grace's 1943 graduation picture at Chaska High School in Minnesota
(Professional photograph by Werner Studios, MN)

Mom and Dad's wedding day in Minneapolis, 1954; I think they look like movie stars! (Professional photograph by Werner Studios, MN)

The Toussaint brood, 1965: from left to right: me, Beth, Daddy, Jon, Paul, David and Mom (Professional photograph by Unknown)

I was 12 when I snagged my first ballet solo, 1972.
(Personal photograph by Beth Toussaint)

When I was a 19-year-old ballerina, I had it all. (Personal photographs by Beth Toussaint)

Posing before a ballet performance; I'm 4th from the left.
(Personal photograph by Victoria Turner)

John and my first Christmas and picture together, 1980
(Personal photograph by Leona Toussaint)

Backstage with Bombay at the Reno Hilton, 1983
(Personal photograph by John Garrett)

John and I posing just before jumping onstage
(Personal photograph by Mark Kalin)

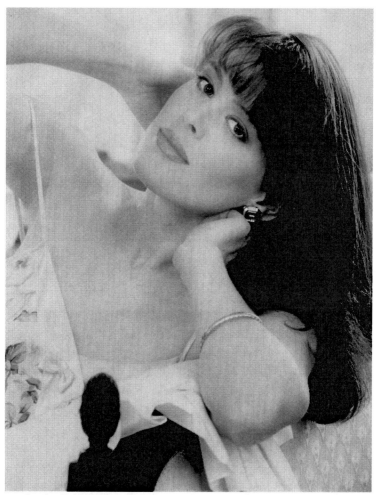

Yes, they do take headshots at Playboy!
(Professional photograph by Arny Freytag)

After making it to the top!
(Personal photograph by Unknown)

John and I are all smiles before our commitment ceremony on my New Year's Eve birthday, 1995. (Personal photograph by Leona Toussaint)

On my gurney beside John before the anti-HMO protest at Kaiser in Los Angeles; if you look closely, I'm holding my ballet slippers. (Personal photograph by Leona Toussaint)

Speaking to the media at the 1999 press conference before Governor Gray Davis signed sweeping HMO reform. (Professional photograph by David Crane for the *Los Angeles Daily News*)

Testifying at my 2004 Women In Pain Senate hearing. (Personal photograph by John Garrett)

For Grace logo created by Tricia Rauen.

With Los Angeles City Councilwoman Wendy Greuel, Councilwoman Janice Hahn and California State Senator Liz Figueroa after receiving an RSD Awareness proclamation at City Hall. (Professional photograph by Unknown)

Mom's gorgeous drawing, Metamorphosis; we use this as one of For Grace's thank you cards.

Finally in my cap and gown at my 2005 graduation ceremony at University of California Irvine
(Personal photograph by John Garrett)

*Campaigning during my 2006 run
for State Assembly*
(Professional photograph by J. Emilio
Flores for *The New York Times*)

*A loving afternoon in the park with
6-year-old Tessie*
(Personal photograph by John Garrett)

*John and I are decked out '50s style for my broth-
er-in-law Jack Coleman's birthday party, 2008.*
(Personal photograph by Leona Toussaint)

Celebrating my partial CRPS remission and 50th birthday by visiting Tanzania
(Personal photograph by John Garrett)

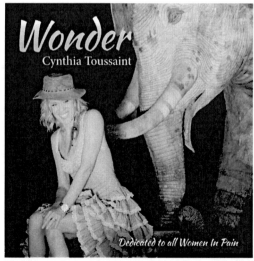

The cover art for my debut CD, released in 2012, was inspired by Africa. I'm wearing my safari hat and the elephant symbolizes the strength I now feel behind me
(Professional photograph by Dana Patrick; Designed by Michael P. McHugh)

THIRTEEN

BIRTH OF AN ACTIVIST

Before the exchange of vows, we had finally been given a name for what had dogged our lives for so many years. The diagnosis had been delivered, most off-handedly, on September 25, 1995. And the diagnosis had not been delivered to me, but to John, who was now seeing the same internist. He returned from Kaiser, his face a sickly white, and spilled the words. "Dr. Mazarro knows what you have. A disease called Reflex Sympathetic Dystrophy."

I was stunned, almost breathless. "She's right. That's got to be the 'Sympathetic Dystrophy' Dr. Day talked about all those years ago. That's the *only* thing that ever made sense." Although Dr. Day had said that I didn't have the disease when the block didn't work, that had been years ago when little was known about RSD. Since then, so much had been discovered. An immediate wave of relief rushed through me. After more than 13 years, my pain actually had a name. I'd given up on a diagnosis long before, despite John's certainly that we'd eventually know what had caused my suffering. And here it was. No one could ever again tell me it was all in my head. I was free from the disbelief and ridicule.

While this was an important breakthrough, the diagnosis couldn't have been worse. According to the National Institute of Neurological Disorders and Stroke, Reflex Sympathetic Dystrophy (RSD), now known as Complex Regional Pain Syndrome (CRPS), is "a chronic pain disease believed to be the result of dysfunction in the central or peripheral nervous systems." Too often called "The Suicide Disease," RSD is triggered by a trauma to the body that can be as major as a heart attack or as minor as a pinprick. In reaction to that trauma, the body's nervous system sends a message to the brain that says, "Pain!" This is a normal, healthy response, the one that tells us to pull our hand away from a flame. But with RSD, for reasons unknown, this signal to the brain can't shut itself off. Instead, it perpetuates and then amplifies—pain, Pain, PAIN! RSD, when diagnosed and treated early (usually within six months of its onset), often gets fixed. When untreated or inappropriately treated, however, the neurons sending the pain message to the brain begin sharing it with other neurons, and the disease spreads to the rest of the body. The intensity of RSD pain was later confirmed when the *New York Times* reported that it outranked cancer as the most painful disease on the McGill Pain Index.

John and I consumed every scrap of information we could find about RSD. Clearly, my disease was no longer reversible. But there were treatments available. Years later, one treatment would match the disturbing extremes of the disease itself. RSD sufferers are actually going to Germany to be put into weeklong, ketamine-induced comas. The notion is to reboot the brain, much like a computer, so the central nervous system stops sending pain signals. But all too often this procedure, which can be psychologically traumatizing, doesn't wind up working. Luckily, that one wasn't available for my consideration.

Fearful that she'd pull the diagnosis, I phoned Mazarro. "John told me you've diagnosed me with RSD. Is that true?" My heart was pounding hard when she replied, "Yes, Cynthia, that's what you have."

"I don't get it, Dr. Mazarro. Why now? Why didn't you think of RSD way back when my arm folded up?"

"I did, Cynthia," she said talking nervously. "I told you that you had RSD back then. I've known all along, ever since you've been my patient."

Her revelation stunned me. I chose in the moment not to challenge her, but as I tossed and turned that night, Mazarro's apparent deceit raced through my head. Five years. Five years of hell, pain and isolation. Would knowing what ailed me in 1990 have helped me physically? I'll never know. But it would have meant everything psychologically and emotionally. A lot of abuse and suffering would have been averted. And some of the many family and friends who fell by the wayside might have found a way to hang in with me if my pain had been named.

I had thought my diagnosis would bring loved ones back, but 13 years of chaos and doubt proved too much. My endless illness had scared the hell out of people. Now most everyone continued to stay clear of me, in all likelihood because there was no cure for RSD.

All of this said much to me about the social "crime" of chronic pain. We hurt lots, but don't follow the rules of illness. We don't die, and we don't get better.

Despite my RSD diagnosis, Mazarro and Kaiser continued to refuse medical treatment. No, that's not accurate. Mazarro did suggest I take two Tylenol twice a day to quell my pain. That would have been like telling a third-degree burn victim to take two aspirin in order to feel better. John was so desperate, he actually purchased the Tylenol. He keeps these bottles in his bedroom drawer as a testament to his folly.

This last indignity did it. The truth was abundantly clear. Kaiser's choices were based on saving money, not lives. Stronger in spirit because of my diagnosis, I resolved to wage war against them. Further, I would tell the world what these bastards had done to me so someone else could be saved. Eventually, my battleground would extend from the courtroom where I sued Kaiser despite the odds stacked in their favor to the pressroom where I nailed them. A few years later, this attack would move successfully into the halls of legislature.

For openers, Mom and John sent another volley of letters to Mazarro and Kaiser demanding treatment or an outside referral. True to form, we heard next to nothing. But I had an ace in the hole. I was damn good at telling my story. I just needed a soapbox.

The timing couldn't have been better. Miraculously, the dirty practices of the HMO industry were coming to light. A California attorney, Mark Hiepler, got a ton of press with his lawsuit against Health Net, in which he had asserted they killed his sister due to delay and denial of care. With awe, I listened to Hiepler's heart-breaking story on talk radio. *My God, this is my story—but I'm still alive.* He laid out step by step how HMOs (this was the first time I'd heard this acronym for Health Maintenance Organizations) used gag rules and physician bonuses for non-treatment to limit care—especially for the expensive chronically ill.

There it was. That was me. I was ready to shout my story from the mountaintops. Everything fell into place when Mom spotted an ad in the *Los Angeles Times* asking for HMO victims to call if they wanted to speak out. With tears in my eyes, I dialed the number and reached the Los Angeles-based Ralph Nader group, Consumers for Quality Care. CQC's mission was to expose HMO misdeeds, specifically care-rationing schemes. With passion to burn, I convinced their director, Jamie Court, that I was their ideal spokesperson. To prove my ability, I sent him the *Los Angeles Times* article Scott Harris had just written about me, which detailed my nightmare with RSD and Kaiser.

Jamie wasted no time putting me to work. Soon media was beating a trail to our condo for interviews, and I was frequently showing up on the local news from my bed. After being mostly sidelined and silenced for a decade, I had microphones and cameras capturing every detail of my struggle. I'd spent my life trying to find a spotlight. Now, I had a red-hot cause and the role of a lifetime. My story could save other people.

Saul Gonzales, producer for KCET's highly regarded *Life & Times* program, was floored by my plight and green-lighted an in-depth segment. His crew turned our condo into a mini sound stage to capture a day-in-the-life of John and Cynthia. After an intense interview, Saul went to Kaiser to get their side. He shared with me that not only was Kaiser stalling, they had also commented, "After you hear our side of the story, you'll realize there is no story."

I was concerned Saul would back out when Kaiser continued to stonewall. As the months ticked by, I put in regular calls to get a status report and keep the fires burning. At last, Kaiser offered up their assistant medical director, Dr. Joel Hyatt, along with two doctors, including a psychiatrist.

Although I had never met any of these men, Saul reported that they laid it on thick. On camera, they retracted my RSD diagnosis, saying that my problems might be psychologically rooted. They even questioned the very existence of RSD. Off camera, they added a new level of slander. Hyatt suggested to Saul that I was inventing everything because of deep psychological problems forged by my father's suicide.

"Are you comfortable with me sharing that statement in the segment?" Saul asked.

Without a blink, I urged him, "Please, use it, Saul. Let Kaiser bury themselves."

That they did. KCET poured extra dollars into the segment and it ran an impressive nine minutes. Just after it aired, I got a phone call from Beth. She'd caught the piece and was angry about what they'd said about our father. I told her I had no control over Kaiser's lies. To comfort her, I added, "People see the truth, Beth. Most everyone who watched knows that Kaiser is evil and that they're lying."

My producer friend, Dick Freed, called later, mirroring that public sentiment. "It was brilliant, Cynthia. Your guy flat out nailed them."

I was landing blow after blow on the chins of Kaiser and the HMO industry. But they weren't taking it lying down, especially when national media came knocking. One day, Jeff Simon, a segment producer with ABC's *Good Morning America*, phoned. After a short interview, he put me on a conference call with the network powers in New York who were planning a segment about HMO disasters with three real-life stories. "Cut the other two," Jeff quickly ordered. "We're running with Cynthia."

I was beyond excited to share the news with John. "We're going coast to coast. Kaiser's never going to shut me up now."

This was going to be a barnburner. After a lengthy shoot at our condo, I told Jeff exactly what Kaiser would say and the strategies they'd use to kill the piece. With a wave of a hand, he assured me, "They can't stall, Cynthia, because we're running this next week. I told them that if they don't talk right away, they'll be shut out. And that's the last thing they want."

Sure enough, a few days later, Jeff shared that Kaiser had said all of the things I had predicted. But they added a new wrinkle. They demanded that I be seen and diagnosed by an RSD expert before the piece ran. With only a few days left, however, there wasn't time to secure an appointment.

I was surprised when Jeff scampered to get my medical records to Dr. Franklin Kozin at Scripps Institute in San Diego for an evaluation. It appeared to me that Kaiser was leading ABC around by the nose. "This is a more difficult segment to pull off now, Cynthia, but it will definitely run next week," he assured me as he left the condo with a copy of my records. But I was itchy with uncertainty.

The phone stayed silent too long. Even in the early months of my media work, I had an intuitive sense of timing when things soured. I phoned Jeff, who was audibly upset. "Cynthia, I have really bad news. I just couldn't muster up the courage to call you."

"Oh, God. What happened?"

"Dr. Kozin said that without seeing you, he couldn't unequivocally diagnose you with RSD. We ran out of time. I feel horrible. Please let me do something. The interview's *so* good on tape. Can I send the raw footage?"

Heartbroken, I said, "No, Jeff. *Good Morning America* caved. I don't ever want to see what would have helped so many people if it hadn't been snuffed out."

The truth, John and I discovered, wasn't always enough. Corporate America owns the media and controls much of the flow of information. With a few well-placed calls from corporate lawyers, editors and producers will kneel to unreasonable demands or simply pull a story that the moguls don't want told. The realization was frightening, but it didn't for a moment stop my crusade to tell the truth about HMOs.

Fortunately, HMOs had become the biggest black hat in the country and the media continued to tap me as their story *du jour*. I was now the "Ballerina to Bedridden HMO victim." When John went into stores, he'd overhear people angrily talking about HMOs, often referencing me. I was getting known and people were squarely in my corner. More importantly, I was educating the public and changing perceptions. Soon, constituents began telling their California legislators that they wanted something done now to rein in these profit-over-healthcare machines.

An interview with KNBC confirmed this changing public sentiment. The station's producer called. She'd seen a number of my TV appearances and her nightly news show wanted to do an in-depth segment with anchor Paul Moyer. I was delighted. During a pre-interview with the producer, she told me that she wanted to hang Kaiser by getting Hyatt to parrot what he'd said in the KCET piece. I winked. "No worries; he'll stick to script."

Moyer cruised up in his shiny new Porsche Boxer that paid homage to his multi-million dollar contract as L.A.'s top paid broadcaster. John rolled his eyes, assuming this would be a career-enhancing, superficial dog and pony show. That attitude quickly evaporated when Moyer began talking. This guy was authentically pissed at Kaiser. He shared that his wife had caught one of my recent interviews and was deeply moved by my story.

In my opinion, Kaiser came off worse than ever in the piece, with Hyatt bumbling through his interview as he talked in circles and offered feeble illustrations to support that the HMO had provided me with extensive care and that "she's been treated for her chronic pain." KNBC's producer and I had a healthy laugh over his chair-squirming. Kaiser's game plan was apparently failing. I loved seeing the truth kicking their ass for all to see.

Soon I learned about another unethical aspect of the Kaiser empire from Consumers for Quality Care. It's called Mandatory Binding Arbitration. With MBA, cases cannot be adjudicated by a jury of the patient's peers. Instead, we get what many national organizations characterize as a "kangaroo court," a panel of three retired judges who essentially work for Kaiser. According to CQC, MBA mandates that all judge's fees are paid by Kaiser, a clear conflict of interest. CQC further argues that if the judges don't rule often enough in Kaiser's favor, they're not asked back. Lastly, they state that the pay is lucrative, and many judges rely on it as a cushy retirement. In short, this system is rigged from top to bottom.

My father had unknowingly signed away my right to a jury when I was 3 years old. Like most, he probably hadn't read the small print. Outraged, I talked to the media about why MBA was unethical. That's when a reporter quite appropriately asked me, "Have you actually been through mandatory binding arbitration?"

I must have looked like a deer in the headlights. *Oh shit!* I knew then that to be an effective spokesperson, I had to submit myself to this sham legal process.

I quickly retained an attorney and sued Kaiser for medical malpractice. I didn't know then that this would trigger five years of endless and emotionally draining interrogatories and depositions. For each hearing, I'd spend weeks reading reams of medical records, hundreds of letters, lengthy event chronologies, relevant media stories and more. I didn't want Kaiser to catch me stumbling over a single fact. Often, Kaiser's attorneys cancelled the day before. When the depositions finally did happen, they were nothing short of brutal. My attorney had advised them that I would need a room that wasn't air-conditioned, and a couch on which to recline if necessary. Despite this, hours and hours of grueling questions were directed at me in an ice-cold room that had no couch. The conditions shot my pain sky-high.

"Is your mother still alive?" the Kaiser attorney asked at one point. That felt like a threat. They even tried to intimidate me by videotaping my testimony, which was unheard of in medical malpractice depositions. In 2001, after five years of this, my case failed to proceed to the MBA stage due to a legal technicality.

Even the lead-up to MBA had been sheer hell. To this day, when people ask me if they should sue their HMO, I give them the same advice everyone gave me. Cut your losses and walk away. But in retrospect, suing was the right decision. It helped transform me into a much more effective spokesperson about HMO abuse.

On a brighter legal note, in early 1999 I caught wind of a class action lawsuit against Kaiser for false advertisement. *Hot damn!* I called one of the lead attorneys at New York's Millberg Weiss, the number one class action law firm in the U.S. and the one handling the case. I gave Joe Gugliomo a spirited monologue about why I would be *the* ideal key plaintiff. He was impressed by my passion and story. Despite a legal technicality that almost excluded me, I was brought on board. Things moved swiftly and efficiently, a polar opposite to my "kangaroo court" days.

I loved this lawsuit because Kaiser's commercials during the mid-'90s had driven John, Mom and me bonkers. A gentle, kind woman's voice, akin to how you'd expect Mother Teresa to sound, warmly assured the viewer, "Only our doctors make the medical decisions for our patients." This claim angered us to the point of insanity. So I was extremely excited to help fight Kaiser in a legitimate court case.

I was prepped for my deposition by attorney Gary O'Conner. He was sharp and I felt safe and comfortable with him. But the deposition was straight from *hell.* Kaiser had three icy attorneys staring me down as they tapped away on their laptops. They badgered me mercilessly hour after hour with questions they repeated again and again in various incarnations, all designed, I'm sure, to trip me up. I felt like my taut body was going to shoot through the ceiling as I strained to maintain control.

After six hours, we stopped for the day with plans to continue the deposition the following morning. As we left the building, Gary told me the other key plaintiffs' depositions had lasted only an hour or so. Apparently I was *the* threat. Then he added, "Cynthia, you hit a home run today!" Feelings of relief and pride rushed over me. But the result was even better than that.

Shortly thereafter, Kaiser settled the suit and agreed to change their ads along with other actions I can't divulge due to the restrictions of my legal gag order. A media ballyhoo followed that triumph. So did an increase in the harassing phone calls that had started a few years prior when I began to get serious media attention. Kaiser doesn't go quietly into the night. They fight tough and dirty.

Though we had no proof, we assumed Kaiser was behind the unnerving calls. Finally, I phoned Jamie and told him what was happening. I was somewhat relieved—and yes, emboldened—by his take on the situation. "That's a compliment, Cynthia. If Kaiser *wasn't* harassing you, you wouldn't be doing your job."

Soon after, I was invited by U.S. Senator Barbara Boxer to speak at what would be my first press conference. Together, we'd be introducing the Patient's Bill of Rights, a new piece of Congressional legislation championed by Ted Kennedy, to the Los Angeles media. I felt deeply honored, especially since I'd always been a big fan of both senators. But I still got a good case of the heebie-jeebies the weekend before, as I'd never spoken publicly. In jest, I told John I was too nervous to do it.

"Then don't," he needled back. His reverse psychology worked like a charm. We burst out laughing, which eased my tension. We both knew I wouldn't miss this opportunity for the world.

I could barely sit up at that point, but that wasn't going to stop me. We'd found a wheelchair that doubled as a gurney. By lowering the back of the chair and raising the peds, I could be lying flat, lickity-split, whenever my pain kicked in. The chair could even be positioned so I could lean back with my legs raised and bent, which quickly became my favorite position.

I entered the crowded conference room feet first. Upon seeing the crowd with rows and rows of cameras, my nerves kicked up and nature called. One of the nurses in attendance who supported the legislation kindly offered to assist me to the restroom. We were advised to be quick about it. Trouble was, I couldn't get into the disabled stall. It was occupied by someone taking her sweet time. I sensed the seconds ticking off. *Damn, I hate it when someone does this.* At last, Senator Boxer emerged, blushing pink. I eased the moment, chirping with a grin, "So even senators have to go to the can, eh?" We shared a laugh as Boxer's aide sped her off.

Though a tad tardy, I was immediately intoxicated by the energy in the conference room. After Boxer's poignant introduction, I delivered a passionate recap of my HMO experience. This was potent stuff. I felt empowered and knew my words would be heard by hundreds of thousands that evening.

Before leaving, Senator Boxer knelt next to me. "My God, you're still so young and you've been through such a nightmare." I was touched by her concern. She thanked me for speaking and added, "You'll get them in court." I think we both knew that the mandatory binding arbitration, which hadn't yet been decided at that point, wasn't going to go my way, but I appreciated the hope she projected.

Later that day, I was the teaser on most of the Los Angeles news channels. Besides getting the HMO word out, the press conference taught me something. Being a high-profile spokesperson was similar to being in the theatre. I prepare for the show. I overcome the stage fright. I love the thrill of the performance. Then I get the reviews on TV and in the newspapers.

My work as an advocate was feeling great. But my healthcare program was not. The care folks at Kaiser were out to lunch. I suspect Mazarro had caved in to her superiors, recanting my diagnosis with the media. Bizarrely, one day in January 1997, she forced me to come in by threatening to cut off my Klonopin prescription if I refused. A new law, she claimed, required physicians to see patients for whom they prescribed narcotics at least once a year. Two problems with her statement: First, Klonopin was not classified as a narcotic. Second, I spoke with three pharmacists, including one at Kaiser, who said no such law had been enacted, recently or otherwise. But I had no choice. The pharmacists also advised me that cutting off my Klonopin cold turkey could actually kill me.

I wasn't able to sit up long enough for the car ride and appointment, so Mom drove down from the Bay Area with her four-door

Honda Civic to transport me in the back seat. Though Kaiser had promised a gurney at their end, none was there. *Surprise, surprise.* Eventually, John hustled one up. Before long, I was glaring at the woman who had betrayed me.

I believed that Mazarro had forced me into her office in order to officially expunge my diagnosis. Instead she said, "Cynthia, you have RSD and I have another patient with it. It's a terrible disease and you're very unfortunate."

This insanity stunned me into silence. In the media, Kaiser said I was crazy. But in a private setting, I was a very ill patient with a legitimate disease my doctors refused to treat. I'd slipped into Kaiser's rabbit hole where the lunatics were running the asylum. And I was still trapped with no chance for care.

I soon fell into yet another deep depression. I'd waited over 13 years to finally get my diagnosis. But I felt more hopeless than ever. I stopped eating again and slept the days away as my body folded up from disuse. The reality of suicide danced ever closer.

Mom became terribly frightened, but she knew there might be one last card to play. Since my media exposure, a number of RSD folks had advised me of a way to bust out of Kaiser. I had to qualify for Medicare. That would make me a "Medi-Medi" beneficiary as I was already on Medicaid, which would allow me to use most any doctor or facility. Each time I checked this out with Social Security, however, I was told that I didn't qualify.

That didn't stop Mom. She set up an appointment, fully intending to beg for my life. When she got to the Studio City office, my caseworker had piles and piles of papers stacked on his desk. Hair disheveled, he looked up at Mom and quickly told her, "I think we've made a colossal mistake. Your daughter has been qualified for Medicare since 1988."

It turned out he was right. Federal law dictates that if you're disabled for 24 consecutive months, you automatically qualify for

Medicare. We still can't figure out why no one at Social Security ever told us this. If I'd known, I would have been spared a ton of hell at Kaiser's hands.

John and I thought we'd be elated if I ever escaped Kaiser. But it was a long, quiet day—one reserved for silent contemplation and stony relief—when I finally terminated my membership on October 1, 1997. We were too deeply damaged, physically and psychologically, to celebrate. Yes, I was free, but the scars of this war would never dissipate. Fighting Kaiser had proved far worse than fighting RSD. The disease was innocent, but my HMO was a vicious enemy that had dehumanized me. To this day, I wonder how all those involved in my case and so many others sleep at night.

But I was now on the path to better care. I called every pain management specialist I'd heard of in L.A., finally choosing Dr. Geoffrey Foley*, the only doctor who got on the phone with me. I heard true empathy and dismay in his voice when I told him I'd had RSD for almost 14 years with virtually no treatment.

I arrived at Foley's office on a gurney, folded up in a fetal position. After a thorough review of my history and a physical exam, this handsome, fiery English gent confirmed my RSD diagnosis. I was one of the most advanced cases he'd ever encountered, complete with severe muscle atrophy and contracted, discolored limbs. As I described my excruciating pain, he nodded with the tired familiarity of someone who'd seen too much of this.

First, he tried sympathetic nerve blocks, knowing there was little chance they would help because my RSD had almost certainly spread to my central nervous system. Unlike Dr. Day a decade before, Foley knew that RSD typically remains sympathetically-maintained (controlled by the sympathetic nervous system) for the first few years. It later becomes sympathetically-independent (regulated by the central nervous system). This is why Day's blocks hadn't worked and why Foley's didn't take either.

We moved on to medications for neuropathic pain, the pain category for RSD. During the consultation, Mom protested, "No, Dr. Foley, my daughter's not taking any drugs." Glaring, Foley told her, "Your daughter is very ill. I won't allow you to be in the room if you get in the way of her care." Then he turned to me, holding his hands up to his face as if to block out Mom and John. He said very softly, "Cynthia, you and I are going to work as a team to make you better." I wanted to hug him for taking control. We had a doctor who truly cared about me.

We tried many medications—opioids, anti-depressants, muscle relaxants. Finally an anti-seizure medication, Neurontin, worked like magic. With my pain at last eased, I worked intensely with a physical therapist, Victoria Lange*, who was an expert with a movement therapy called Feldenkrais. Since I couldn't bear to be touched, she used guided imagery. She told me to imagine myself in a relaxing place, suggesting the mountains or a beach. I surprised her by conjuring up a ballet class where the intensity would calm and focus me. While imagining elaborate dance combinations and describing them to Victoria, she was able to slowly touch and manipulate my body.

After just three weeks of this new treatment, I began to unfold. I could sit up again in my wheelchair, although limited, and walk short distances in our condo. It felt like a miracle. Soon I was going into restaurants and movie theaters for the first time in years. I'll never forget sharing the epic *Titanic* with a room full of people, even though I had to elevate my legs using the seat next to me.

Perhaps my biggest accomplishment was my new Reebok tennis shoes. I'd worn the same pair for a decade as every other shoe shot fire into my legs. Even though John had painted them time and again, they were ratty and humiliating. But now my shoe wardrobe tripled as I had spanking new white, black and beige Reeboks. For me, that feat was tantamount to climbing Mt. Everest.

On the emotional front, psychologist Dr. Debra Greenberg helped me untangle my pain trauma. In my sessions, I felt validated. She said my anxiety and depression, even my anger, were normal given the depths of my losses. Keen to HMO abuse, Debra encouraged me to share all the tragic, crappy feelings I harbored about my pain and my treatment. This was a major step because it launched a journey during which I developed a relationship with my pain that continues to this day and that has fostered increasing acceptance of my pain year after year.

For the first time in 14 years, I wasn't battling abusive doctors in an abusive system. With the help of these earnest healthcare professionals, I slowly began to heal. Like a battered puppy, it took months to believe that their care was authentic. But they were for real. Now that I had a nurturing place in which to become stronger, I could more effectively continue my battle against the system that had stolen so much of my life.

Often when you're ready for action, things happen. My opportunity came in a call from Elaine Burn at Consumers for Quality Care. She said there was an MBA-oriented California ballot initiative, Proposition 216, that desperately needed media support. If passed, this initiative would abolish mandatory binding arbitration. I can't remember being more stoked. Jamie and Elaine organized a major protest against Kaiser at their Sunset facility with me as the centerpiece. It was kind of like starring in my own movie, except in this one, I was fighting to right a wrong. Their press release shouted it in big, bold letters:

Bedridden Ballerina Crippled by HMO Abuse Delivers Empty Ballet Shoes to Kaiser in Protest of Care Denial

On that crisp October morning, I arrived on a gurney along with dozens of loud, chanting picketers from the California Nurses Association. I made my statement to the press. Then the show really heated up. John pushed me down the sidewalk, surrounded by the protesters. Signs waved as the crowd shouted, "With HMO, it's always NO!" Soon traffic was snarled on Sunset Boulevard as we headed for the main entrance. Kaiser's security goons arrived to intimidate us. We just kept walking. When we reached the administrators building, the security personnel locked arms, barring our entrance. Elaine, tussling with the guards, told me to show them my Kaiser membership card. They had no choice but to step aside.

Once inside, still on my gurney, I presented a harried Kaiser executive with my ballet slippers. "These are for you now," I shouted at the top of my lungs, silencing everyone in that crowded room. "I can no longer use them because Kaiser has crippled me for life."

As John and Elaine wheeled me out and the sun kissed my face, I knew I was no longer a victim. I was now a survivor. A survivor who was quickly becoming one of the major catalysts for changing public opinion about HMOs, changes that would soon lead to historic legislation. I felt renewed and empowered.

My years of dogged advocacy coalesced in September 1999, 17 years after I'd torn my hamstring in the ballet studio. Jamie invited me to speak at the mother of all HMO press conferences. California Governor Gray Davis was signing sweeping HMO reform legislation that would, among other things, make it easier to sue an HMO and give parity to mental health sufferers. It would also create a state agency to assist HMO patients. These laws were the first of their kind in the United States. And, very conveniently, it was all happening four blocks from our condo in North Hollywood.

When John and I arrived, excitement pumped through the crowd of prominent state leaders, their staffers and the public. Amidst enormous signs trumpeting "Patients First!" media from every news source swarmed the area, asking questions and taking pictures to commemorate the historic significance of this legislation and the fact that the HMO bad guys were finally getting their comeuppance. I was proud to have been one of the leading spokes-people who had helped make this day a reality.

When the media engulfed me with their mics and cameras, I emphasized the need to fight to the end to ban mandatory binding arbitration. As I scanned the press, I recognized many reporters I had worked with over the years. From the look in their eyes, I could feel their connection.

Afterward, I interviewed with reporters and greeted the legislators John brought to meet me. While I networked with all, I set my sights on California Senator Liz Figueroa. She'd been one of the leading champions for healthcare reform, authoring the bill to abolish "drive through" mastectomies. I knew I was meant to team up with this feisty woman.

"Well, when you're a woman, everything's all in your head," she said in response to my story of dismissal and abuse. We bonded immediately. I felt sure I could enlist her to chair a California Senate Informational Hearing about RSD. I just needed to get her passion wrapped around this disease.

I was charged with emotion throughout the entire six-hour event. I loved the fast pace of the young staffers on their cell phones—back then, these devices were something wonderfully new—and the excitement of seeing politics and media mixing it up. I knew this was where I belonged. I made a silent vow right then that I'd find a way to be in this world. *But how?*

That evening, my image and voice hit most Southern California radio and TV news stations. And the next morning I discovered I'd landed in virtually every regional newspaper. I even scored the much-revered front page of *The New York Times*. I was certain that this day would prove a significant stepping-stone in moving my story and cause up the chain to an even bigger stage. There were, I knew, so very many others suffering silently and needlessly.

My bold "dream of never again" had been born.

John's Take

It feels good to punch back. I don't know if I'd have the guts to confront a major industry—but I sure as hell love to back someone who does. I help Cynthia with some of the wording, suggest a sound bite or two. I keep her on point about who's in the room and whom she needs to tell her story to. I'm the guy in the wings, keeping an eye on the lead, making sure she's got her lines. It's an easy job. She always says the right thing at the right time. I'm just happy to grease the rails any way I can. As I always say, "Behind every great woman is a guy dribbling coffee down his shirt." I've got the stains to prove it.

Once Cynthia opened her mouth to the media, she made us targets. We're now free game for the HMO industry and their parasitic public relations henchmen. They can screw with us any way they want. They have billions of dollars at their disposal. I say bring it on. We're drawing the line in the sand. Their practices to a large extent are what have almost destroyed our lives. This is no time to bow to fear or intimidation.

It's time to rally with the Boxers and Kennedys in the great chain of power to drag this evil into the light. Let's bang this drum as loudly and for as long as we can. Let's challenge elected officials charged with protecting us to make new laws and levy ever-larger fines when those laws are broken. Public humiliation and actions that take money out of HMO pockets are the only weapons that our profit-driven healthcare system responds to.

I vow, here and now, to throw every inch of my being into making this come to pass.

Battle for Grace

FOURTEEN

THE BIG OOPS

Not all my decisions around that time were good ones.

During the onset of my advocacy work, which was spotty at best, pain and isolation continued to dominate my life. I measured my tenuous connection to the world with a visitor book that kept me company on my coffee table. When someone came to the condo—reporters, plumbers, carpet cleaners, anyone—I insisted they sign the book with the day's date and a comment. If I sometimes pushed too much, I didn't care. I *had* to have proof I existed. Even a few names a year meant I was still among the living. With so much of my life lost forever, my hopes for the future had focused on having a baby with John. We had always dreamed of the little girl we'd call Grace after my beloved aunt. And for a short time, it seemed possible that we'd have this joy in our home.

But the Kaiser horror show slammed the door on our baby. Their biggest gaffe had cropped up five years earlier. My gynecologist, Dr. Grubb*, reported a Pap smear that showed abnormal cells suggesting cancer on the surface of my cervix. He performed a loop electrosurgical excision procedure (LEEP) that caused me to hemorrhage. The subsequent cauterization without local anesthesia spread the RSD to my cervix and vagina. The pain from that felt like knitting needles shooting up and down my pelvic region. I could no longer sit on my stationary bike for physical therapy. Nor could I wear panties or tight clothing. Worse yet, intercourse became excruciatingly painful. As impossible, in fact, as our chance of now having a baby.

Before this Kaiser invasion, John and I had enjoyed a delightfully healthy sex life despite my mental and emotional pain. I experienced multiple orgasms—20 to 30 bursting off like fireworks. I didn't know why I'd been blessed with this sensual windfall, but I wasn't complaining. Being bedridden didn't offer many joyful diversions, so our lovemaking was an oasis in the desert.

Now Kaiser had stripped that away. Grubb referred to the fire in my pelvic area as "phantom pains." Again, they were calling me the crazy lady. Years later, my physical therapist Victoria gave me intensive pelvic therapy that restored our sex life. She also explained that my multiple orgasms were contractions caused by the RSD. "Think of this as the *good* part of your disease," she said with her booming laugh.

By 1996, our desire to have a baby outweighed all barriers. John and I were fighters. We knew that with help, I could get pregnant and carry our baby to term. But doctor after doctor at Kaiser didn't share our enthusiasm. They wouldn't guarantee artificial insemination, home healthcare and a C-section as services. Without these aids, a pregnancy was not possible. This was the cruelest blow of all. Having baby Grace was out.

John was virtually my only human contact as Mom had moved back to New York. And like before, he presented a mirror to my physical and emotional pain. It hurt to look at him and see his misery because I wanted so much for John to escape our hell. My rages ramped up again, along with the violence between us.

Adding acid to our wounds, the maniac upstairs escalated his bizarre behavior. Besides marching around the condo day and night and continually running the faucets, he had begun dropping what sounded like bowling balls on the floor above our master bedroom. We tried earplugs and ambient noise machines, but nothing worked. The noise burrowed under our psychic skin. Not even the short, sporadic reprieves helped. Instead, with increasing dread, we waited for the sounds to start again.

"Couldn't this be Kaiser?" a friend and colleague, Morgan Grether, announced. My heart sank because Morgan was grounded and wise. No conspiracy freak here. John and I had briefly discussed that possibility, but dismissed it because the notion was too awful. How could we fight a multi-billion dollar corporation dead set on making our lives miserable?

John had written to David Olmos, a healthcare business writer at the *Los Angeles Times*, to stir his interest in my HMO story. David had recently been a Pulitzer finalist for his exposé about HMOs, which helped break open that industry's misdeeds. Stirred by my Kaiser protest, he came to the condo for an interview in October 1996, accompanied by CQC's Elaine Burn. "This is really one cold guy," she warned me. "He's the toughest journalist you're ever going to meet. He doesn't even believe you were a ballerina." *That could be a problem cuz I sure as hell wasn't going to dance for him.*

Despite the warnings, I found David to be quite the opposite. He had a friendly face with eyes that were kind and engaging. We immediately clicked. The words spilled from me for four hours. Impressed that I was the real deal, he pitched my story to film producers the next day. He confided, "I've got my pulse on more HMO horror stories than anyone else in the country, and yours is by far the most extreme."

He then went to Kaiser. After three months and the same old stalling shuffle, they produced doctors who told him I was nuts. They reiterated that my illness was purely psychological, a direct result of my father's suicide. Then they added a twist of intimidation. They reminded David that *his* reputation was on the line if he wrote my story. Startled by Kaiser's gall, David told me, "They were very convincing." I sensed he had been knocked off his game by their potent threat. In the end, however, he believed me and encouraged my fight against them.

While John and I began to religiously follow David's frequent front-page stories, other media kept rolling my way. My "Ballerina to Bedridden" story was getting bigger and better known. I mercilessly badgered David for a year and a half, pressing him to write my story for the *Times*. But he hit a brick wall with his business section editors, who reminded him he'd already covered HMOs and then some.

Then we got a break. The paper started a Health section. David pitched hard, and mine was the lead story in the March 9, 1998, edition. Headlined "The Mystery of RSD," the article highlighted my scrapes with Kaiser. The best part of the article was that David reported a Social Security evaluation by Dr. Mazarro that I'd recently unearthed, which included her working RSD diagnosis. With this irrefutable evidence, he nailed Kaiser in their attempts to present me as a fraud.

This article got an enormous response and was picked up nationally. David's phone rang endlessly with calls from RSD sufferers who thanked him for giving them a voice. David informed me that Kaiser was so angry, they pulled their ads from the *Times'* Health section for six months. I couldn't have been prouder. Far fewer people would be led to their facilities.

I'd won another battle against this giant HMO, and it certainly hadn't ended David's career. Soon afterward, he was promoted to Health editor.

But life was far from good. John was becoming ever more angry and despondent. We could no longer see a future, only endless days, months and years of nothingness. With no baby and no place for peace, my last pillar of hope had been destroyed. Once again, I reacted inappropriately. To all my unfortunate coping mechanisms—called maladaptive behaviors—I would add yet another. I would have an affair.

During the time I was waiting for David's article to be published, I continued to work with the media and organizations that dealt with healthcare issues.

All of which led me to Martin Shea*.

He was an investigative reporter who cared deeply about people and justice. Very soon he would be resonating with the angst of my journey and my pain as he was falling in love with me.

We met when I spoke at a press conference. He was there with his sister, Cynthia (there are several of us), who'd suffered for many years from fibromyalgia and wanted to meet me to better deal with her pain. The three of us talked after my speech. I learned that Martin worked in the San Francisco bureau of a major daily and had recently written an exposé of a mega millionaire who made his money through a network of human trafficking mainly involving women. The details Martin shared touched me deeply, especially because this trafficker had been indicted as a result of the article and would soon be facing trial.

Martin was now in Los Angeles to visit his sister. I was drawn to him like a magnet. He felt like a kindred soul whose work for the paper frequently dealt with abuse akin to my experience with Kaiser. He wrote many articles about the little guy being victimized by heartless giants. Now he was taking on the HMOs. All of the folk at CQC greatly admired Martin. I seconded that. Since becoming ill, he was the first person who made me feel validated. His broad shoulders, quick wit and crooked smile brought me a special sense of security—a hero in waiting.

From the get-go, I knew Martin was attracted to me, even though he was married. I ignored his subtle advances, but they still flattered me. I was also nurtured by our conversations, which I soon began to crave as if they were a drug. I found myself thinking more and more about him. He continued to call to find out how I was feeling. When I was down, he'd be at the door with a smile and flowers when in town for family or work.

We were developing a powerful connection. I could lean on him. He was loyal and I knew in my heart that he cared for me. We both confided almost everything about our lives. For the first time since becoming ill, I had a close friend.

Martin began to find more reasons to stop by the condo to talk when John was at his bank job. We also hooked up often by phone. He loved to hear about my HMO media events and hell-raising. I'd been cooped up for so many years with only "invisible" John for companionship, and now here was a flesh and blood person actually flying in to visit me, spellbound by what I had to say.

I was taken by the way Martin's mind worked—his journalistic savvy, political leanings and natural sensitivity. I was flattered that this man whose attention was coveted by so many would drop everything when I needed him. I was moved most by his willingness to use his position to help underdogs take on the big guys. Inspired by my story, Martin amped his onslaught of the HMO industry. I became a key source for his articles. He soon had the HMOs jumping and many of his subjects got life-preserving care. He'd often compliment me on my tenacity. "I've never known anyone like you who just says what she's thinking, never editing, never backing down, in order to get the truth out." My energy pushed him to be more strident, more courageous in his work. Like all good relationships, we brought out the best in each other and loved the good feelings that gave us.

As my emotional need and yearning for his safety net deepened, my trust in him became my bedrock. He, in turn, spoke of wanting to be my hero, wanting to save me. "I'm going to be the one who will *never* leave you, Cynthia, the one who will *never* disappoint you," he said again and again. He told me he thought about me every waking moment and, yes, that he loved me. I felt treasured for the first time in years.

We started a ritual where he'd call each Friday to quell the loneliness I'd feel during the weekends when he was in San Francisco with his wife. The closer we became, the more painfully empty those two days felt to me. Not surprisingly, that was the time when I was most prone to the rages that provoked John's violence.

Over the next couple of years, Martin and I flirted on the phone and in person, but it stopped there. When he visited, he'd stare at me longingly and give me a few pecking kisses on the lips when he left. I knew he wanted more, but I always pulled away. I wasn't attracted to him physically.

I talked to my mother, to my psychologist Debra and to John about why I felt such strong feelings for this man. John, who'd been showing signs of serious caregiver burnout for years, seemed almost relieved—at least at the time—that someone else was carrying part of the psychological load. But he didn't believe Martin was interested in me sexually. "Cynthia, the man's married," he'd say with a laugh. "You're just imagining this because you've been cooped up so long." But a woman knows when she's being courted.

My feelings became more conflicted. While I felt a deep affection and appreciation for Martin, this was never going to be a sexual relationship. Although I was now feeling attracted to him beyond our emotional connection, I was with John. I needed to put the brakes on before Martin and I slipped across that line. Debra suggested I dull our mutual ardor by inviting Martin, his wife and newborn son to our condo for a visit when they were next in town. "Once you meet his wife and child, they'll be real to you and your feelings will change."

They came over, and we had a fabulous time. Martin's wife even promised to have us to their home soon when I visited Mom in the Bay Area. I was excited about the prospect of having a girlfriend. When she didn't follow through, I was deeply hurt. Years later I learned that Martin had called the shot on that choice. "Annie* brought you guys up a number of times, wanting to get together," he admitted. "But I always put her off because I didn't want to share you."

After that visit, in direct opposition to the plan's objective, Martin's pursuit grew stronger and my defenses weakened. He began to express his strong desire for an affair. He often confided his great unhappiness at home, the constant bickering with his wife and the "inevitable" divorce. I stayed strong until he mentioned his attraction for another woman at the bureau. I don't know if he wanted to make me jealous, but he did. I began fantasizing about being with Martin intimately. Besides, I feared he'd leave me if I didn't go further. I couldn't allow that to happen. If I couldn't find something to live for, I felt certain I'd kill myself.

John was a defeated man. He no longer woke with the fight to save me, to save us. Soon we had our worst bout of violence. As usual, I sparked the hate by screaming vicious verbal jabs and breaking things. John countered, strangling me by placing his foot on my throat and tugging my contracted arm in a blind, insane rage. From this darkness, my romantic feelings for Martin—a man unburdened by a lifetime of pain, loneliness and loss—crystallized. Through the desperate prism of my life, only he seemed to offer hope and a possible future.

Ironically, Martin had become the number one topic of conversation between John and me. For the first time in years, I had something meaningful to share, and John wanted to hear about the excitement. He'd lose himself in this new, transformed Cynthia. I became a happier, more energetic person when I spoke of Martin, just like the girl John had fallen in love with before the walls caved in.

With each encounter that inched toward intimacy, I shared my feelings of falling for Martin with John. Though he never wanted to share me, he saw how Martin put a glint in my eyes that hadn't been there for years. As I talked through tears mixed with guilt and utter elation, John calmed me, saying again and again, "It's okay, it's okay. He's making you happy. You deserve that."

Numbed by our emotional and physical pain, John sanctioned my intimate relationship with Martin before it began. In our countless talks, did John ever give me an actual green light? No. But neither did he ever tell me—or even hint—that I shouldn't go there. His feelings were revealed by his reaction to the gift Martin gave me for my 40th birthday—a vintage art deco porcelain ballerina lamp. When lit, a vanilla perfume would sweetly scent the surroundings. It was divinely, explicitly romantic. I promptly placed it on my nightstand so it would be the last thing I saw before turning off its light. The second to last thing I'd see was John's face. He was smiling, happy that I was happy. Pleased that my ballerina and Martin gave me joy.

The next time Martin came to see me, I fell into his arms and we kissed. He had courted me for four years, a strong confirmation of his devotion. Over the weeks that followed, his frequent reminders that he'd never leave gave me a safe haven. He became my second confidant. He told me to call him at work and leave messages during my rages to help stem the violence. He assured me he could take anything. His words and actions grounded me. He was like a protective big brother, perhaps even the father I'd never had. I was convinced that an intimate involvement with Martin would save my life.

The condo became a private sanctuary for long, passionate lovemaking. I drew the line at intercourse because it was sacred to me and was reserved solely for a lifelong commitment. Besides, John told me this act was off-limits, the single boundary he had drawn. He also said he was certain that intercourse with Martin would destroy me should things sour. Despite my trust and need for Martin, our relationship was far from sure, given the circumstances. I still loved and needed the man I'd exchanged rings with.

While Martin and I came together every month or so, John, who'd recently been laid off from the bank, got a respite from his 24/7 care-giving duties. While he recuperated at Starbucks, Martin and I spent hours sharing soulful talks, exchanging secret gifts, giggling and exploring each other while Natalie Merchant or Damien Rice sang softly in the background. My previous aversions melted away and in the quietness of the condo I fell in love with him. He spoke earnestly about his desire to start a new life, and I basked in the shine of being his "dream girl."

I even began to wonder whether what had started as a friendship for me might be inching toward marriage. He was my joy, my reason for living—the one thing that kept me from retreating into the darkness. I ached for him when I wasn't with him. He made me feel alive, desired.

As the relationship with Martin grew, so did my advocacy work. But my thoughts always turned back to Martin. I often broke up my hardworking, lonely days with an erotic email or phone sex with him. I loved enticing him away from his work with ever hotter, intimate promises. He was my audience of one as I verbally gyrated like a Sunset Boulevard stripper. His response told me he was as lustful for my affections as I now was for his.

Our lovemaking remained insatiable even though I never experienced an orgasm with him. He didn't know quite what button to push. Still, the emotional heat between us often left me breathless. I loved to wear sexy lingerie for Martin. At my request, he always wore black. Sometimes I'd surprise him by leaving the front door unlocked, allowing him to discover me naked in bed. We lit candles and spread chocolate on one another, feasting on our desire. He loved to cup my breasts from behind, whispering how he wanted to go deep inside me. We never tired of the endless kissing that chaffed our chins until they were red and raw.

After he left, the room would somehow change colors, taking on a warm, golden hue. For the next hour, I would taste him, dizzy with the knowledge that this would happen again and again.

"Cynth, I'm back," John called to me each time upon his return. Awash in my memories of Martin, I couldn't let myself consider what it must have been like for him to enter a condo still musky with perspiration, like a closed gym at wrestling practice. Beads of condensation still drenched the insides of the windows, and our bed sheets were rumpled and strewn. Dutiful as ever, John would wash and dry dishes he hadn't used. He knows I like things nice and neat, and he wanted to keep the woman he loved as happy as possible. "If she's happy, I'm happy" was the vibe I picked up as he nibbled on the cold leftover food I'd shared with Martin.

The affair was horribly unfair to John. Having him watch it unfold in his own home was worse. But at that time, I was lost in my addiction to Martin. He was what I got up for in the morning. He was my first and last thought each day. Just a quick exchange with him made it possible for me to tolerate another day.

Over the next few years, I remained balanced between the two saviors I needed equally. Martin was my promise of excitement and connection to the outside world, while John, despite a few fleeting thoughts of a more permanent relationship with Martin, remained my life partner and my foundation for stability. The feeling that I might not be long for this world partially explained my mindset. I'd recently discovered that RSD could evoke a heart attack. I could also develop cervical cancer that would progress unchecked as my pelvic pain now prevented any life-preserving procedures.

I was obsessed with the reality that precious few would care when I died. There would be no memorial service, no cards or flowers. *Now that everyone has gone, did I ever really exist?* I wondered. The love of these two men became the legacy to my existence. With it, I could die with some dignity.

The first cracks in this balancing act appeared when Martin occasionally forgot to call on Friday. I'd be up all night feeling forsaken and raging at John, making him pay for Martin's carelessness. Often Martin and I would connect the next morning. He'd apologize for forgetting, telling me he'd worried through the night. This would set me right. But over the years, Martin became less attentive, less responsive. He started breaking promises. Emails went unreturned and dates were canceled at the last minute.

At one point, in a major reversal, he confessed that my illness was too much for him to handle. "I'm not a hero like John," he admitted. Later, he added fearfully, "I'm afraid Kaiser's going to hurt me to get to you."

But I was hooked. I needed Martin too much to quit him. And despite his reservations, he expressed a deep desire to remain loyal. "I'm not going anywhere," he lovingly reassured me. We continued the affair, which kept me sane, but his changes were a constant threat to my security.

Eventually, Martin started running so hot and cold that he became my Dr. Jekyll and Mr. Hyde. Disappointment was the norm. In one phone call, I scrambled to bring back the "good" Martin, but he wasn't to be found. He spoke wearily of my lover's expectations, then casually mentioned that we would no longer be intimate. It was time, he felt, to just be friends. Desperate and betrayed, I screamed hysterically. The lynchpin of Martin's seduction had been that he'd never leave me. For the first time, I got a glimpse of a heartless stranger. After a lot more talk, Martin agreed to remain lovers and to never make another unilateral decision about us. The victory didn't help much, and I never again trusted him completely.

I became distraught and inconsolable as Martin's attentions eroded. I threatened to call his wife. Then one night when he wouldn't return my frantic calls, which he'd always agreed to do, feeling rejected and worthless, I made that call. Trembling with spite, I snarled at her, "Tell him an old friend called." Minutes later, Martin phoned screaming, "Damn it, did you call my house?" His wife now suspected an affair and he threatened to involve the police if I ever contacted her again. As usual, however, we talked it through, ending with "I love you."

After my call to his wife, Martin grew paranoid that my anger could eventually prompt me to contact his newspaper, which could possibly get him fired. Our tryst was clearly not okay in the world of journalism. It's frowned-upon for a reporter to become sexually involved with a news source because that would compromise objectivity, which is prized so much in the profession. Martin had violated that ethic with me years earlier. I was certain the shame of what could become a public scandal would blow up his world.

Still, flashes of devotion filtered through in our talks, residue of what had been. "I can't lose you, Cynthia. You make me feel like a man. Don't you see? If you're gone, I won't have anyone to talk to anymore. You're the only one who really knows me and cares. You're my best, my only friend." And after our lovemaking, we once again shared a calm, deep connection. For a moment, our relationship was beautiful again.

And then, suddenly, almost everything unraveled. Martin surprised me one day when he said, quite casually, he might have to leave the paper because of a row with his boss. He told me he'd probably move out of state since there were no jobs for him in California. *No job in California?* That was crazy. And it made me crazy.

Although Martin rarely wavered from his commitment to our Friday phone calls, he began to talk about his burnout and growing resentment toward me for being so ill and needy. He couldn't fix my monumental pain and loss. That devastated him. Helplessness so overwhelmed his reason, he urged me to commit suicide because "nobody in the world should have to live with this kind of pain forever." Though I'm certain he meant this with true compassion, his words devastated me. My only reason for living, this man who had given me a peace and joy, was now telling me I was better off dead.

The Shea family did relocate to Washington, D.C. The move punctuated several years of fighting, reconciling, making love and then fighting some more. When his wife discovered a series of intimate emails between us, Martin finally spewed his truth to me. "You've ruined my entire life," he howled over the phone. "I moved to get away from you. I hate my job here. And you, Cynthia, I hold you responsible for everything that's gone wrong." He went on to confess that he was plagued with guilt about our affair. He felt his soul had been "blackened" by his betrayal of his wife, his child, us, even John.

A couple of weeks later, John and I were in South Carolina visiting a colleague when I learned from Martin's voicemail that he was on a trip with his son. Not a radical event, but it marked another change on Martin's part. In the past, he'd *always* shared personal details like this with me. I was crushed. Coupled with the months of shouting me down in every conversation and the end of my cherished Friday calls, it all became too much. I exploded.

My eruption took place cocooned in our rental car during a pounding rain and thunderstorm. For two hours I purged myself, pouring my feelings of contempt and betrayal into his voicemail. Waves of sadness crashed over me as I sobbed into my cell phone until I could sob no more. After, I felt oddly refreshed and lightened. The relationship was finally, really over.

My breakup with Martin was the hardest thing I have ever survived. Worse than the malice of Kaiser. Worse than the ravages of

RSD. The toll on my body and spirit was immeasurable. During the strain and stress of our battles and especially during the aftermath, I suffered the worst depression of my life, anxiously obsessing on every nuance of our failed relationship. I feared I was destined for the psych ward if I didn't leave L.A. and the memories it held for me. I talked incessantly to John and my mother. I needed so desperately to figure out why Martin had transformed before my eyes from a loving, supportive companion into a monster.

During that time, I developed an overlapping condition to RSD known as Irritable Bowel Syndrome (IBS), a debilitating intestinal condition that can trigger an inability to control one's bowels. This became so severe I often was afraid to go out, as I might not make it to a toilet in time. Indeed, on more than a few occasions, I suffered the humiliation of losing it in my wheelchair.

I also developed body-wide eczema, an autoimmune disease caused by stress. For nearly a year, I was covered with a lizard-like rash that caused intense itching. Despite wearing mittens to bed, I bled from head to toe due to my excessive scratching. Even old demons sparked up. My right arm contracture went into such extreme spasms that I screamed in pain for days and nights, eventually becoming a regular at UCLA's emergency clinic.

Worst of all, my meltdown with Martin brought on a series of violent episodes between John and me. The last of these, which was the last one ever, left me unable to talk for months and cost me my singing voice, which I'd regained about 10 years before. Singing was the most authentic expression and greatest joy I had left, and hearing me sing was John's deepest pleasure. Losing that again at John's hands caused great sadness, which tainted us until quite recently.

It took considerable time for me to make sense of what had happened over my 11 years with Martin—four for the courtship, about three for the affair and the rest for our battles and his move to D.C. I chose not to have a final talk with him, since I feared it might further damage my body and mind. Martin, who appeared to be having a nervous breakdown, now frightened me too much.

Here's what I do know. The time I spent with him was born out of desperation. I now see it as a tragic means of coping with an impossibly sad, devastated life. And in the end, everyone got hurt.

I lost my way, along with my fundamental sense of right and wrong. My neediness blinded me to the fact that my actions damaged a marriage and a family. I live with this every day. I don't believe in regret because we make the best decisions we can each moment of our lives. But if I could go back and change one thing in my life, it wouldn't be that moment in the ballet studio. It would be the affair. And I've come to appreciate the extremes people, including myself, will go through to survive living nightmares. For me, this included the choice to violate my long-standing moral code. Understandable, but inexcusable.

The only possible saving grace was that Martin was there when John and I were literally destroying each other. Perhaps my connection with Martin, flawed as it was, kept me alive. I would have more peace if only I could be sure.

I still have bittersweet thoughts of Martin each Friday. Near the end, he shared that he would love me until his dying day. And once I love deeply, I'm not able to pull it completely away. Mostly, I miss my friend.

But I've come to realize that his inability to fully engage in the pain of my life was a gift. It tells me, loud and clear, how transforming John's love and strength truly are. John is my rock. He is the love of my life. Despite the intense feelings I had for Martin, I always knew in my heart that if I could ever get my life back, I wanted to live it with John. We just couldn't find a way during those years.

As for John and me, he asked me long ago to quit the memory of Martin, to find a path back to "just us." I resisted for reasons I can't fully comprehend. But over the last few years, I've found my way home. I hold John close every night. I find that I need him more each day, and I appreciate how extraordinary this man truly is. Most beautiful of all, I've come to "see" John again, perhaps more clearly than ever. We have survived the unimaginable and love each other more strongly for it. This binds us together now and forever.

John's Take

Why Martin happened is difficult to answer. Cynthia and I had shared trials far outside the scope of normal human endurance. There was the daily physical pain, isolation, regret, depression, dreadful anxiety about the future. And we had lost the normal rites of passage—careers, money-earning potential, children, marriage, building a social network of friends and business associates.

Every day we felt plagued as outcasts marginalized by illness, misunderstanding and ignorance. Sometimes I accepted this as our lot. Other times I'd get angry at the illness that was responsible. At still other times, I'd resent Cynthia, who was constantly angry at having her life stripped away. I'd blame her for the place of isolation we found ourselves in. I'd see the fear in people's faces when she'd speak about her loss, her pain. I wish she'd just shut her yap, but that's not who she is. She needs to tell the truth, to tell the whole experience in order to survive this madness.

I'd put myself on a treadmill to nowhere. Every time I thought we were moving in the right direction, it would fail. She would again be that bitter, angry soul talking every other day about suicide. This never-ending cycle reinforced the feeling that I was somehow to blame. She deserved so much more. She deserved someone who could right the natural order of things.

Maybe I allowed the affair out of self-pity, but by then I was a broken man. I was defeated and demoralized. I had done everything I knew to help her get her life back, but my burden was too heavy. I desperately wanted to be her knight in shining armor, slaying all her dragons. What a fool I was. I was driven by love and care, but I mixed that with unattainable goals that almost robbed us of our love.

Then Martin came into the picture, empowered with his prestige, the glamour of his work and the respect he had in the community. And she lit up like the Rockefeller Center Christmas tree. He represented the reward of the outside world. Not just any man could have gotten in between us. It had to be someone she respected and admired for his ability to make things happen. And who could be more of a savior to her than a man who had helped bring the HMO horror story to the world?

As his visits increased, it finally dawned on me. This guy was making a play. I was stunned, shocked and disgusted. But deep down, I saw Martin Shea as a possible escape hatch.

Now I want her back. I want us back. I can't erase that valley of hurt between us or pretend the Martin years didn't happen. But today is new. We can take the first steps to a different, better appreciation for each other. I regret what I allowed. Today, I wouldn't make the same choice. While Cynth and I don't disagree often, we do on this point. Now, if it were between losing her to suicide and having her in his arms, I wouldn't blink an eye. I would choose the former. At least we'd still have our self-respect and dignity. Those should be non-negotiable items—no matter how bad the storm.

It's not too late to heal. It's not too late to start over. Let's pick up the pieces and love anew. We've been seared from all sides. Now we've done it to ourselves. We've soiled our nest. Let's clean it up, slap on a new coat of paint, plant some flowers. Let's patch the foundation and clear away the brush that can catch fire. Let's rebuild our house of love.

FIFTEEN

I WANT TO LIVE

On a quiet, peaceful day, I asked myself *the* question that had been percolating deep down inside me. What is happening to all the people like me who have long-term RSD?

The first article about me in the *Los Angeles Times* had prompted many people with the disease to call asking for help, but not one had suffered RSD for more than two or three years. I was on year 14.

I put the question to John. He lowered his eyes before answering. "They're gone, Cynthia. They've taken their lives." *Oh, good God. The suicide disease is winning.* I felt like the survivor of a death camp.

But after so many years of being alone and clueless, I needed to connect with members of my tribe. I hooked up by phone with a local RSD woman, Alex Timberland*, through the Reflex Sympathetic Dystrophy Syndrome Association (RSDSA). Alex was warm and kind, seemingly untouched by the bitter aspects of the disease. Best of all, her medical treatment had resulted in a partial remission. I was eager to meet her because she offered tangible hope. But Alex shied away. I was devastated when I received her letter. "I can't be your friend," she wrote. "You're just too sick and it frightens me. You remind me of who I was."

Through the RSDSA I met other women with the disease by phone, but each broke promises of future ties. *Why are they all women?* It was heartbreaking to discover how dysfunctional the RSD community was. By and large, these unfortunate women were living lives turned upside down—just like mine—as they battled the demons of unrelenting pain, abandonment, depression and misunderstanding. Most spoke about suicide. Yet none wanted a relationship with me.

Finally, a single mom named Kimmie Lopez*, a fiery, knock-out Latina in her early 30s, befriended me. We spoke by phone once or twice a day, mostly sharing thoughts about RSD and my HMO reform efforts. Kimmie and I both had big energy and our talks nurtured us. Occasionally, when our pain allowed, we spent time together doing "normal" stuff like baking cookies or leafing through old yearbooks. I loved finally having a girlfriend. But what tied us together was our ambition to make RSD a household name.

One day, Kimmie mentioned that she wanted to start an RSD foundation with a fellow sufferer, JoJo, and me. "She's sharp, blonde and gorgeous, Cynthia. We'll be the Charlie's Angels of RSD." Her energy triggered a decision that had been cooking in me for several months. I would start a nonprofit organization to spread the word about RSD, a disease that was virtually unknown to anyone, including many of the people who had it. I knew widespread awareness of RSD was vital for sufferers to get good care and, ultimately, to escape from this killer of body and soul. We had a long way to go on that front.

During my HMO reform years when I was well enough to venture in my wheelchair to any nearby shops, people would recognize me from the local news. They remembered I had been a ballerina before Kaiser decimated my life, but not one could recall the name of my disease. Aside from what I had generated, there was absolutely no media focus on RSD. I felt strongly that I had the stuff to change that.

But I couldn't rely on Kimmie, who was becoming flaky. The last time I'd seen her, I was shocked by how over-medicated she was. She'd sat in the corner of a dark room like a zombie, barely slurring out my name, with a virtual drug store of pill bottles nearby. I knew Kimmie was giving up and feared being alone again. So

I was thrilled when she, seemingly inspired by the idea of the three Charlie's Angels trailblazing together, regained some of her spunk and invited me to her home on Christmas Eve to meet JoJo.

I was making small talk with Kimmie's adorable 14-year-old son, Sal*, and the family members who hadn't abandoned her when the phone rang. It was JoJo asking for me.

Excited, I answered and said how eager I was to meet her. A raspy, barely audible voice replied. "Cynthia, Kimmie's told me lots about you. You've done so much, and I'm really proud of you."

She told me she couldn't make it there that night; she was in too much pain. I could hear the depression and torture in her voice. "That's okay, JoJo," I said, masking my disappointment. "No worries. You've got to take care of yourself first. But I want a rain check."

After a beat of silence, she said, "We're all counting on you, Cynthia." Her words touched and troubled me. She was struggling with a level of pain that should be beyond human tolerance. I hoped she had the strength to hang on.

A few days later, Kimmie called and sobbed into the phone. JoJo had taken her life during the night. Soon, I got word that Kimmie was in UCLA's psych ward following her own suicide attempt with pills.

I never found out what happened to her. She stopped returning my calls and we never talked again. I miss Kimmie to this day. While I didn't get to know JoJo and don't even know her last name, her final words were a cry for help. Not for her. It was too late for that. She was begging me to help the millions of other women suffering in silence. To this day, whenever I give a speech, I tell my audience about JoJo, about her words, and about how we lost her far too soon.

"Today, I'm speaking on behalf of JoJo and the other women who've taken their lives," I say. "And for all those who *will* do so in the future—mostly because of the under-recognition and under-treatment of their pain."

Despite my ongoing flirtation with suicide, I realized I wasn't ready to leave. For starters, Beth and I had begun to reconcile. I was filled with joy—and more than a tad shocked—when she phoned me just after her daughter, Tess Olivia, was born. We'd barely spoken for more years than I cared to remember, but she wanted to bring the baby over. My pain went up to a 10 because I was so anxious about seeing them.

After a pleasantly familiar kiss, Beth shifted into her new mother, overwhelmed, what-the-hell-do-you-do-with-a-baby mode. And I shot into big sister mode, instinctively offering kindness and protective advice, soothing each fear that Beth confided. Those 16 years of babysitting and bringing up the neighborhood came in handy that afternoon. Despite the little one "hurling" (the word Tess and I assigned for spitting up) on my new teal couch—a joke between us to this day—our get-together began to melt the frost between my sister and me. It also helped me realize that people who leave can come back. Another damn good reason to stick around.

Several years later, the passing of John's dear brother, David, reinforced the value of life, however compromised. David had been diagnosed with stage IV prostate cancer in 2006. At age 52, he was a beautiful marathon runner who had just married the love of his life. He had missed his routine PSA tests due to lack of health insurance, his business having imploded with the dotcom crash. When finally discovered, the illness was too advanced to treat with any hope of success.

John and I were with David during his last few days. Despite hallucinating due to high doses of morphine, he died in his home surrounded by those who loved him. His death carried the dignity and elegance that had always marked the man.

David's passing showed me the finality of death and how much it hurt the family. That was his gift to me. As I kissed him one last time, I knew that death before my time wasn't what I wanted. I would never take my life.

Deciding to live meant I could no longer be a virtual shut-in. *Talk about life changing!* John and I realized that if I could get into the backseat of a car, I could see the world, meet the people, whatever. We tested this by renting a four-door sedan on weekends and it worked. We traded our two-door Toyota Celica for a cute little Dodge Neon that became my "get out of jail free" card. I'd lay my head against the window to ease the nonstop pain in my left leg. Then, as the world whizzed by, I yelped out my amazement to John. I felt like I had just emerged from a time capsule. I was especially enthralled by the L.A. women in their current fashions. I hadn't seen layered shirts or UGGs before. I also enjoyed their new tapered hairstyles with those trendy highlights. My strawberry blonde mop had turned mousy brown over the last few years, and I was squirming to get up to speed.

For darn sure, I wouldn't be doing that from the backseat of our car no matter how liberating those adventures initially seemed. That's when my new wheelchair-gurney took over and brought me back into the world. Sure, most people stared with looks ranging from confusion to downright pity. But I didn't care. You only live once, dammit, and I was going to live inside *and* out.

With my newfound freedom, John dusted off some interests that had percolated for years. He'd come across an alternative life-style movement called Voluntary Simplicity. A new local group was about to have its first monthly meeting. Their goal was to pursue authentic living by discovering their passions and by downsizing their material attachments. I wasn't interested. I'd always pursued my passions to whatever degree my life allowed. Besides, my last 15 years had basically been downsized beyond belief. I now wanted the opposite of simplicity—more people, more things to do, more busy-ness. If I simplified any more, I'd be in a freaking coma.

But John still wanted to pursue this and asked me to join him. He made it clear he was going with or without me. This was a major departure for John, whose every waking moment had been dedicated to my needs. In the past, he'd have felt too guilty to leave me alone.

These initial independent steps threatened me. *What if he finds something out there in the world that catches his fancy more than me?* I finally chose to tag along, despite feeling intimidated. How could I relate to normal people in a normal setting? And how could they relate to me? I'd been in my condo prison cell for what seemed like forever. The thought of interacting with people at a gathering that didn't revolve around illness or activism was inconceivable to me.

At the meeting, attendees introduced themselves, gave some life history and talked about why they were there. After reciting my elevator pitch of a life story, I bluntly said, "I'm here because my caregiver's here and not coming with him would mean three more hours a month of being alone. I don't want to downsize my life. I want to *upsize.*" I simply didn't fit, and I told the group I wouldn't be coming back. In some ways, I was lonelier there than at the condo.

After the meeting, a spunky, red headed woman approached me. Phyllis Gebauer, a writer with a warm, deep soul, had lived an unconventional life. Years prior, she and her recently deceased husband had followed their passion by moving to Europe to make movies. Now she was battling depression triggered by widowhood. Phyllis spoke her mind, just like me, commenting on the phenomenal love John and I clearly shared. "You two are extraordinary human beings for what you've survived together. What you have is rare. I hope you'll change your mind, Cynthia, and come to the next meeting." Her words touched me. I thought about her kindness for days after. No one had ever acknowledged the hardships John and I had endured, but Phyllis had noticed that first. So back I went.

I grew to appreciate everyone in the group. Our meetings became my favorite night of the month. Though I never embraced the Simplicity concept, as I needed no guidance on how to live an authentic life, this group gave me a wonderfully safe and nurturing portal back into the world. It was stimulating to be among the living again, with people who shared my core values.

My return to the world didn't stop there. I made a point of connecting with groups of disabled folks, a community with whom I deeply identified. For years, John had told me about Media Access, a well-respected talent agency in Los Angeles (hell, their headquarters were just a hop, skip and a roll from our condo) that represented "differently-abled" people for print, TV and film work.

When I finally went for an interview, old headshots and resumes in tow, I was inspired by this engaged, energized community of disabled talent. These people were bold enough to have their professional photos showing their wheelchairs. They weren't hiding their differentness. They put it front and center, confident and ready to show Hollywood they were as capable and professional as any working actor. In my opinion, they were much more so. I mean, look at the mountains they'd already climbed.

I adored the agents there, Gail Williamson and Gloria Castaneda. These phenomenally motivated women were hell-bent on getting disabled people depicted in mainstream media. Fortunately, due to all of my exposure and big energy, they had high expectations for me. The day after my interview, I got a print job selling Activans, retrofitted minivans for the disabled. We even got John into the act as my able-bodied husband. I felt just as beautiful and certainly more proud, than I did with *Playboy*. These vehicles gave the disabled access to the world, and that felt damn good.

I took free acting classes at Media Access. While I was already aware that disabled roles in Hollywood were virtually non-existent, I loved everything about this organization. The people, the classes, the parties—even the occasional auditions. I adored being surrounded by little people, amputees, paras, quads, the blind and the deaf who had all survived the "unsurvivable" as they boldly pursued their Hollywood dreams. It doesn't get gutsier than that. I'm proud to call these talented people my friends. We're beautiful misfits, banding together in a town that doesn't take easily to "different."

I soon learned from a disabled acquaintance about a magazine called *New Mobility*. This publication, with its tag line "Life on Wheels," became a very good friend. I read it cover to cover each month, learning much about the trials and challenges of being disabled. I related to the access problems, the legal issues and the deeply entrenched biases that confront the disabled. Through *New Mobility*, I became comfortable calling myself a crip, an empowering tag that helps undercut the putdowns of the able-bodied.

New Mobility and Media Access gave me a bridge to a deepening identity with the disabled community. These people who maintained their dignity in the face of pitying looks and stares provided a large dose of empowerment, pride and comfort in my differently-abled skin. In retrospect, these organizations also provided a strong foundation for the health advocacy work I'd soon embrace. In many ways, the disabled are a lost minority without a voice, a group that's still being dismissed and discounted in our society. Though not my life work, I'm always alert to do what I can to end this prejudice and the judgments that come with it.

I was on my way to forging a new identity and new purpose. But not until I was diagnosed with breast cancer did I fully realize how much I wanted to live.

In mid-2000, I noticed a lump in my right breast and alerted my internist, Dr. Edith Flores. She examined it and to my alarm told me to get a mammogram stat. After my mammo and ultrasound at a highly regarded university breast center, the technician told me that all was fine.

"You have healthy, young breast tissue, Cynthia."

"You're telling me," John cackled, relieved and grinning.

The petite young woman laughed and told me to get dressed. "The radiologist will just poke in and say hey before you take off." John and I embraced with happy tears. When it came to health issues, we weren't used to good news.

Dr. Swan* walked in and closed the door. Her brisk manner did not suggest good news this time either. She slapped my films on the backlit viewer. "Your lump was just a cyst," she said. "But here's the problem." She pointed to a small, circular cluster of white flecks on my left breast. "These are calcifications. They strongly suggest you have Ductal Carcinoma In Situ (DCIS) or early breast cancer. They're still in the milk duct so we've got time to get them out before they become invasive." After telling me I needed an immediate biopsy, she continued, "Cynthia, I know what your RDS (she misstated the acronym) has done to you, but this cancer will kill you."

My body slumped in the wheelchair. Just a few minutes prior, I'd been ready to skip this gin joint. My immediate shock quickly turned to anger. "I don't want to hear anymore. I can't deal with this. It's too much. And you don't have a clue what RSD has done to me because you don't even know the name of the disease. I don't know what I'm going to do or not do, but I need time to think. I *have* to get out of here."

Lying in the back seat of the car on the way home, I reviewed all my battles with the medical establishment and how their failings had made me sicker. I knew in my heart I couldn't survive breast cancer surgery. But perhaps this was just another one of their follies.

In that moment, a new feeling of empowerment entered my system. It was damn well time for me to jump off the medical merry-go-round. I would take control of my body and my care. I would no longer blindly follow their lead.

John was devastated by my new crisis. "I can't believe we've survived so much shit for *this*." We lay on our antique bed together for hours, quietly holding each other. That night I asked him to keep our bedroom lamp on because I believed I might be dying, and I didn't want to feel like I was already in my grave.

The next morning the phone woke me. After nearly two years of pitches, I had landed a feature in *Glamour* magazine. But for the first time, catching a big fish didn't make me spin with excitement. Heck, this was Moby Dick. But Ahab's boat had a hole in it.

I immediately told my contact that I'd been diagnosed with breast cancer. Though my stomach ached with dread, it was comforting to share the awful news. Oddly, she was excited by my diagnosis. *I suppose this makes the story even better. Doesn't the media have any shame?* I asked her to please not share the news. I didn't want this to turn into another breast cancer story. She assured me it would remain between us. A few hours later, I got my first call from Nanette, the editor assigned to my story. "It's so wonderful to meet you, Cynthia," she said just before exclaiming with excitement, "I hear you've got breast cancer!" I had learned not to trust media through the years, but this was a new low.

Nanette apprised me that my writer, Dina Stein, would be flying out from New York for the interview. Then we'd do a photo shoot. That perked me up. And it got even better. The article would get picked up by most everyone at ABC, where *Glamour* had a strong connection. This included *20/20* and *Good Morning America*. I was filled with excitement thinking about all the possibilities. Maybe this turn of events was enough for me to survive losing most of my left breast.

To avoid a biopsy that I knew might spread the RSD again (the disease can spread from anything that causes nerve trauma), I decided to show my film to several doctors hoping for a different read. But they all agreed I needed to move quickly because I definitely had cancer.

Then I checked in with my physical therapist, Victoria, to figure out how bad my RSD might get. She was kind and caring, but also straight with me. She confirmed that breast biopsies typically spread the illness. "If you opt for the surgery, I'll come to the hospital to treat you immediately," she added. "You'll need that because RSD, when amped by a lumpectomy or mastectomy, has brought on some of the worst cases I've ever seen." Not exactly encouraging.

Mom, John and I went to my oncologist appointment a few days later. Cold and indifferent, this attractive Eurasian woman told me I could skip the biopsy. However, if I wanted to live there was no way to avoid a lumpectomy followed by chemotherapy and radiation. To show us that the procedure wasn't so bad, she brazenly unbuttoned her blouse, exposing her lumpectomy scar like some badge of courage. I told her I'd think on this, but most likely would opt for no treatment.

My mother broke down, pleading with me to reconsider. "I just want them to take it out of you," she cried out, certain her daughter was choosing a death sentence.

"Mom, you know better than anyone that doctors don't know much. I'm going to learn about DCIS, and you have to trust me to make the right decision."

Before John and I began our planned vacation in Banff and Glacier National Park, we searched the Internet for information about DCIS. I was surprised and more than thrilled to learn that studies showed most DCIS cases never became invasive. I had a good chance of surviving without treatment.

In Glacier, John and I stopped at the summit of the famous "Road to the Sun." I sat alone, marveling at the snow-ringed, glacier-fed lake before me and its reflection of the crystal blue sky above. As the majestic mountains whispered their timeless wisdom, I decided to forego any treatment for my breast cancer. I couldn't risk starting the whole RSD cycle again. I'd monitor my DCIS with bi-annual mammograms. This was *my* decision. Informed and educated, I was in control. I wouldn't allow myself to be terrorized by doctors.

Not surprisingly, the doctors all freaked out. Mom did, too. But I stood my ground, and John was behind me 100 percent. He'd long ago learned to trust my gut.

The *Glamour* article got killed, and I had a sneaking suspicion Kaiser was behind that. It stung because I knew how much the world needed the information in that beautifully written story. But I was still kicking. I felt certain there'd be new opportunities just around the corner.

The DCIS never grew and never became a danger to my health. Nine years later, my radiologist proclaimed me at no risk. I learned a few things along the way. DCIS treatment has become controversial because the surgeries it supports nurture the bloated breast-cancer industry more than the patients. Women frequently approve unnecessary treatment because they've been brainwashed to believe they need this surgery to save their lives. Two articles in *The New York Times* written a decade after I made my choice reveal how inappropriate that counsel is. On July 17, 2009, *The New York Times* ran a feature titled "Forty Years' War; In Push for Cancer

Screening, Limited Benefits" that examined the overuse of early cancer screening and how it harms much more than helps, particularly among low-risk patients. Further, on July 20, 2010, *The New York Times* ran a feature titled "Prone to Error: Earliest Steps to Find Cancer." This article focused exclusively on DCIS and its over-treatment, prompting many women to sue their physicians for unnecessary disfiguring surgeries.

On a personal level, becoming my own healthcare advocate showed me how effective I can be at making medical decisions that are good for me. Not following my doctor's proposed treatment for my breast cancer is why I'm not fighting a new level of RSD pain and, quite likely, another reason why I'm still alive. I'm proud to be my own brand of breast cancer survivor.

Yes, I want to live. On my own terms.

John's Take

With the cancer scare behind us, we continue to take tentative steps back into the world. One step, one false move, one fall can send us back to the bed and a world dictated by pain. Most people, myself included, haven't experienced what it's like to know something in your body can betray you at any moment. If you're able-bodied, you take things for granted, like having legs strong enough to support you. Or that your nerves will send healthy messages to your body instead of sending constant waves of pain.

But Cynthia and I are stronger now. We have better doctors since we left Kaiser. So let's get out there any way we can and reclaim our piece of the world. I'm ready. I know Cynth is, too.

She has no inhibitions. She's shameless. Her eyes are wide open as we wheel into the store. She's practically flat on her back, her wheelchair-gurney extended out. As I try to cut a corner, I take out a display of Beanie Babies. The store clerk raises her brow. But we're having a blast. Cynthia just keeps saying, "Go over there. Go, go, go." She's hungry for everything—the sun, the shops, the people. She doesn't care if they point. Freedom inoculates you from the stares and petty comments.

I'll wheel her from one end of the country to the next if that's what she wants. I love being her legs, her locomotion. She's a lover of life and it's a sin to keep someone like her bottled up. As long as I can push that gurney, I'll stay behind her. I want to give her the chance to feel a sense of normalcy. We're not freaks. We're not going to stay caged up. We've got things to do and people to see. We've got dark empires to overturn.

Let's saddle up them ponies and ride into the blazing sun. Let's leave a mark that neither time nor tide can erase.

Battle for Grace

SIXTEEN

ADVOCACY AND THEN SOME

I had moved from victim to activist for myself and for all those damaged by malicious HMO healthcare. But that wasn't enough. Not by a long shot. Millions of people across the country—no, the world—were being leveled due to the ignorance surrounding RSD. I wanted to become a voice for everyone afflicted with this disease. I knew their suffering too well and wouldn't rest until our pain was recognized.

First on my list was to make that RSD Senate informational hearing happen. After hooking up with Senator Figueroa at the HMO press conference, I called her office on a regular basis to connect with her staffers. In the process, they got an earful about how RSD had changed my life. But I hadn't made my case in a way that everyone on her staff could hear. I had a bad flu when her top legislative consultant phoned me. Her call, at first, perked me up. Charlotte Kuiper* was sharp and talked with head-spinning rapidity. *God, I love the quick minds and fast pace of politics.* But apparently Charlotte didn't understand my passion and cause. She told me, "I'm going to strongly advise the Senator *not* to pursue this hearing. I feel it's a poor use of resources."

After clearing my sinuses with a hardy nose blow, I brushed off Charlotte's words, rolled up my jammie sleeves and went to work. I knew a couple of things that could make a difference. My story and I were persuasive enough to make this hearing happen. Plus, Senator Figueroa was firmly in my corner. I'd also picked up considerable points with her chief of staff, Liz Fenton. I put in yet another call to Fenton and emphasized the great need for an RSD hearing. There was no Plan B. One of my building blocks for accomplishing my goals is my strong belief that every *no* is a future *yes*. I was confident that if I kept knocking on this receptive door, Charlotte's advice would be acknowledged, but not followed.

Sure enough, I got word from staffer Kristen Treipke that the Senator had green-lighted the hearing, which she and I would organize together. This was a big deal, a sentiment that Kristen confirmed. "Legislatively, when California sneezes, the rest of the country catches a cold," she shared. The political truism made me even happier and prouder. My message about RSD would not just rock my home state; it would impact the nation because California was a trendsetter.

The planning moved quickly. Even in the early stages, I could feel the electricity of working with bright, capable people, most of them attorneys, intent on bringing RSD into the spotlight. In turn, I had the respect of these insiders. No decision was made without my approval and that was a thrill. I felt the responsibility and the urgency of suffering people counting on me for better days ahead. There was no cause closer to my heart.

With Kristin working the inside game, I handpicked the MDs, psychologists, physical therapists and researchers I wanted to testify and personally invited each one. After hearing Dr. Scott Fishman, director of pain management at UC Davis and author of *The War on Pain,* on the local NPR affiliate, I immediately inquired about his availability to testify. He was articulate and an impressive patient advocate, just the sort of person we needed. I got a return call from his assistant.

"Dr. Fishman is having a difficult time understanding exactly who's spearheading this hearing," she said.

"I am."

"No, no, you're not understanding his question," she stammered. "Dr. Fishman wants to know the name of the *group* you're representing, the group that's actually championing the hearing."

It took a call from the Senator to confirm that it was indeed "Cynthia, and only Cynthia" who had persuaded her to chair the event. Dr. Fishman agreed to testify, but ultimately was unable to do so because of a schedule conflict. Nonetheless, he did add his support to many of our future legislative activities.

After a half year of convincing government agencies to get involved and planning the agenda, advising presenters about testimony, generating media and coping with delays that nearly stopped my heart, the hearing was set for May 11, 2001. I decided to publicize the event by asking the Senator to pass a resolution proclaiming May as RSD Awareness Month in California. I did the same for Los Angeles through my City Councilwoman, Wendy Greuel, a move that generated both TV and newspaper coverage.

I was flying high in my new world and enjoying every speck of it. I met some of the key players in California politics at many of the speeches I gave, and began receiving proclamations in recognition of my efforts. I sure as hell wasn't staring at four walls anymore.

The hearing day arrived. As I drove downtown (yes, Los Angeles does have a downtown) past the pink and white blossoms bursting like popcorn from the trees, I could barely contain myself. Then I wheeled into the hearing room in the Ronald Reagan Federal building and felt like I was once again mounting the Eiffel Tower.

The room was packed. Senator Figueroa and her staff, along with state agency officials, filled the chairs of the panel. Dr. Foley and a number of other pain experts, along with members of the public, faced them. This was better than we had ever expected.

I was to give the key testimony, my first ever, and excitement danced the tango with my nerves. To steady myself, I used a trick that always helps me walk into the lion's den. "Grace under fire," I whispered to myself like a mantra. Then I thought of all those dark, voiceless years of lying in bed and to my old mantra I added a new refrain. "Today, I *have* a voice."

My testimony couldn't have gone better. I felt strong and articulate, as the unstoppable passion that surged through my body communicated itself in words that echoed off the marble columns. From my wheelchair, I told my story to an audience that sat so still they seemed to be holding their breath. I talked about the untold others suffering with this straight-from-hell disease. I also told them about my nonprofit in the making. And I gave them my bottom line: that together we could take the first steps to stop the torture.

Following the Q&A, Senator Figuroa thanked me for being a voice "for all those who don't have one." Her words touched me deeply because this had been my goal from the start.

The event gave me another insight. I could save lives by sticking my neck out and working my ass off in and out of my comfort zone. It often surprises me that people label me "fearless," because I get scared like everyone else. My hands sweat, my mouth parches dry, my heart beats like a bass drum. But I *never* let fear get in my way. Whatever hesitation or caution might creep in is quickly overwhelmed by the mighty needs of my co-sufferers. To this day, whenever I get butterflies before a live TV interview or a stage appearance where one misspoken word can make me look like an idiot, I say to John with a laugh, "Oh God, I *don't* want to do this. Oh please, I'd rather die." He always answers with a grin, "Better you than me, babe." And I start those interviews with a smile.

The success of the hearing gave me more confidence and what felt like a stronger base to work from. I was ready, truly ready, to establish my nonprofit. I had a clear vision. I wanted worldwide awareness that made RSD a household name like breast cancer or diabetes. I wanted to help the millions of people, mostly women, crying out in pain and not being believed. One sufferer might take her life today, another tomorrow. I had a moral imperative to do the work. Now.

Some months prior, I'd gone into my bedroom and cozied up with a comforter to decide what to name the nonprofit. I didn't want to use the disease's name since that could get us pigeon-holed. I also didn't want stuffy words like "national" or "association" that everyone and their grandmother used. I needed everything about my nonprofit to be creative, different and bold.

I rested my eyes on Aunt Grace's antique figurine, one of my dearest possessions. It sat quietly on the oak dresser my dad had refinished when I was a toddler in Michigan. *Grace will be part of the name*, I realized almost immediately. Because Aunt Grace had essentially raised my mother and I never got to meet her as she passed so early from leukemia, her memory was bigger than life to me and a big spark for my spirit. I thought of my dear aunt and the little girl John and I would have had. We'd have called her Grace. If this organization had been around when Aunt Grace was ill, perhaps she wouldn't have died in pain. And if it had been around when I first got RSD, John might be bouncing baby Grace off his knee right now.

I whispered to myself the name I'd come up with. *For Grace.* It felt awesomely good.

The look and essence of my nonprofit would be inspired by a pen and ink drawing my mom had done three years before I became ill. I had immediately fallen in love with *Metamorphosis* and the mysterious woman sketched amongst butterflies. I knew in a blink that this drawing would hold an important place in my life. Its shapes and lines, its lyrical etchings swirling like a ballerina's movement, spoke worlds to me. Now I knew the woman in the drawing was Grace and that a butterfly would be our logo. It was time to fly.

I quickly became a one-woman phone bank, calling anyone and everyone to tell them about For Grace. I asked for advice and for participation. I pursued Board Members and advisors. I even courted "supporting artists," since my vision included the use of performance to paint a metaphorical mural of the pain experience and to educate people about pain and healing.

Not all the new people in my life were encouraging. I was told that starting a nonprofit is the *hardest* thing in the world to do by Greg Stewart, my favorite minister at Pasadena Neighborhood, a progressive Unitarian Universalist church that John and I attended. Greg was one of my heroes because he had the guts to be openly gay and had endured a lot of nastiness as a consequence. He unabashedly had his commitment ceremony televised to protest a California proposition prohibiting gay marriage, and I was proud to be in the pews that day. If that weren't enough, he and his partner of 20 years, Stillman, had adopted five African-American crack babies. Talk about tough roads. His response to my nonprofit news chilled me, especially when he repeated his words looking intensely into my eyes. Greg knew I was serious and capable, but he was concerned I was biting off more than I could chew.

By this time, I'd repeatedly been told I should avoid reinventing the wheel and hook up with a nonprofit already doing good work in this arena. That, too, gave me pause. Perhaps I *could* get more done faster under someone else's sails. So I hesitantly approached Cliff Ashton*, Executive Director of Stop RSD*. I'd heard from one of their chapter leaders that Cliff was a manipulator out for his own gain and I should steer clear. But perhaps what I had to pitch would intrigue him.

When Ashton didn't return my calls, I apprised him by email of my desire to explore the possibility of working together before deciding whether or not to launch a separate nonprofit. I knew his organization wasn't generating any coverage about the disease and figured that my media track record might catch this attention.

It did. Ashton was keenly aware of my media savvy. He asked me to procure reprint rights to my *L.A. Times* article for his use. He also wanted permission to quote me as an endorser of Stop RSD. I did what he asked in good faith. Unfortunately, he offered nothing in return. Not even a thank you. After several more emails, it seemed clear that Ashton had no intention of partnering with me.

With time ticking and people suffering from lack of public awareness, I decided to incorporate. I was convinced my nonprofit would at long last bring RSD into the light.

I didn't know how to start a nonprofit, so I met with every well-placed individual I knew who had knowledge about the subject, including my old producer friend, Ken Scherer, the current Executive Director of the Motion Picture and Television Fund Foundation. MPTF had most every big name in Hollywood, including Steven Spielberg, on their Board.

Ken agreed to meet with me at their Burbank headquarters. I arrived early and was escorted into an enormous conference room. I felt like a bug sitting at their 24-seat table. Glass brick, Greek columns and pin lights added to the effect.

"I booked this room special for you, Cynthia, because I know you think *big*," Ken said as he entered with a grin.

We had a fabulous meeting and I came away with two great questions to answer before launching. "What's sexy about RSD? It's got to have sizzle to sell," Ken advised. "And who are you going to partner with who is as passionate as you about the issue? You can't pull this off alone."

Sexy came quickly. That was easy. While tragic, the reality is that "The Suicide Disease" tagline catches everyone's attention. As they say in the media business, "If it bleeds, it leads." Who wouldn't listen?

The second question, however, posed a challenge. Who would ever have the same level of commitment as I? This one stumped me until February 2001 when John came home with the news that his department at the bank was moving to North Carolina due to a merger. He'd been given a choice. He could relocate with the unit or be laid off with a severance package. John was clicking his heels over the idea of finally being freed from the misery of his bank job, even though he was already using a good chunk of his time there to work on a For Grace brochure, craft a business plan and research funding opportunities. The realization hit us at the same moment. John would be my co-pilot.

With this decision in stone, we moved full steam ahead. Between John's severance and unemployment, we had about a year before one of us had to pull a paycheck or craft a lifestyle around eating potatoes and cabbage. No one believed we could actually make our nonprofit organization a reality. Most people just talk about this sort of thing, but few follow through. "Impossible" was mentioned on a number of occasions. I think I've grown to like the word. Even though it's not in my personal dictionary, making the "impossible" happen is always sweet.

For Grace would focus like a laser beam on RSD awareness since that's what was most urgently needed. On the road to a cure, everything follows awareness, and both John and I knew this was my major strength. I would be the face of this effort with media, speaking engagements and legislation. John would handle the backroom responsibilities like paperwork, grant-writing, volunteer coordinating and the dreaded finances that made me glassy-eyed.

John and I set about learning the nonprofit biz from the ground up. I quickly caught wind that the founder of a nonprofit has to wear every hat, not just the gussied-up ones. All of this was new to me. So much for my just being the face of the operation.

We hooked up with a number of L.A.-based nonprofit support and legal assistance organizations to start the process of incorporating and securing For Grace's tax-exempt status. We worked full-time attending workshops, conferences and seminars. Whenever I had a spare moment, I networked by phone. I was a relentless bulldog. I'm certain more than one person gave me what I wanted just so I would unclench from his or her leg. Case in point, I wrangled the domain, forgrace.org, from Sara Lee. After speaking with a number of employees, I researched the CEO and discovered that we shared a love of ballet. During our chat about Joffrey's new season, I managed to convey that I wouldn't let up until I got the domain name. Before we hung up, Mr. Sara Lee signed over the rights.

It was thrilling, if intimidating, to learn the nuts and bolts of nonprofit management. It was also frequently as dry as the Sahara. Numbers and regulations and forms and policy. This square peg goes into this square hole. *Boring.* Performers typically don't adapt well to this right-angle kind of mindset. But with time, I demystified the gobbly-gook and enjoyed getting an education that I'd never expected.

On April 2, 2002, we incorporated For Grace. We didn't even celebrate. There was too much to do. I formed a Board of Directors, calling upon colleagues I respected who were well established in the business and civic communities. To get start-up funding, we approached family, friends and acquaintances and raised a few thousand dollars. John funded most of the early phase, which included filings, a phone line, post office box, gas, copies of educational materials and more, using his severance and unemployment benefits. Part of our learning experience involved attending conferences hosted by nonprofit pain organizations. I persuaded Southwest Airlines to give us free flights and sponsorship to cover hotels and attendance fees.

Even so, money got really tight. We worked out of our second bedroom with papers, binders and file cabinets encircling us. We were putting in mad, long days—12 hours wasn't uncommon—and we rarely took a Saturday or Sunday off. Most often, I didn't get out of my pajamas because I couldn't afford the time. I was scrambling to engage the Board, identify and cultivate potential funders, launch project work and hustle up media and speaking engagements. On the side I squeezed in conferences and workshops. That's when I wasn't dealing with the various problems that erupted. At times, I felt like I couldn't come up for air. I'd always been tough on myself, and I was just as tough on John.

RSD, however, didn't cut me any slack just because I was doing noble work. My physical pain, which had remained constant, could get worse at any time. Ironically, when things went well and I felt the most jubilation, my pain almost always shot up to a 10. Years later during a radio interview, Dr. David Bresler, founder of UCLA's Pain Control Unit, would say, "Winning the lottery would be the worst thing that could happen to Cynthia." He went on to explain that any emotional arousal, good or bad, activates the neurons that drive RSD pain. Though John and I had learned the truth of this over the years, I'd always been afraid to tell a doctor because I feared yet another cuckoo label.

I pushed on despite the pain, even when it peaked. I'd lie in my reclining wheelchair to work at the computer and talk on the phone, scribbling notes as I crafted ideas. I was always amazed at how this work helped me cope with the hell I'd grown to know so well. During my occasional breaks, awareness of the pain filled the vacuum and I'd lie in my chair moaning.

Despite the pain and frenetic pace, I was happier than I'd been in years. I had a purpose, a reason to get up. And I loved the feeling of being shot out of a cannon every morning. I was at last needed. For Grace couldn't flourish without me.

My heart skipped joyfully at our formal kick-off. By then our elegant logo had been finalized, along with our website that would win an international silver medal for design soon after it was launched. And we hadn't spent a penny, thanks to graphic and Web designers Tricia Rauen and Stan Evenson.

Then Beth's husband, Jack Coleman, of *Dynasty* and later *Heroes* fame, offered their beautiful Hollywood Hills home for our ribbon cutting. This gesture deeply moved me.

Mom flew in from the Bay Area to help host and map out the menu. The first guest to arrive was Senator Figueroa, dressed to the nines in a low-cut, peach number and elaborate hat. Putting her finger to her lips, she swore us to secrecy. "No one knows yet, but I'm going to run for Lt. Governor. Now what can I do to help out?" she asked, slapping on an apron.

Guests started to arrive, meet and mingle, all in support of For Grace. After Mom's homey barbecue dinner under the stars, the Senator and Dr. Foley spoke eloquently about the importance of RSD awareness. Then I spoke about what had moved me to this mission. I talked about my niece, Tess, and the next generation of children who, unlike her, might never face the confusion that "her aunt hurts and has to sit in a chair with wheels." After speaking, I blew Tessie a big kiss and she caught it, a smile spreading across her 3-year-old face.

From the day Beth had brought her to my house, Tess had taken center stage in my life. Over the years, she morphed into a mini-me, a bundle of energy that whirled like a dust devil.

"I don't understand Tess," Beth exclaimed one day with a puzzled look. "She's just like you. All she wants to do is sing, dance and speak French."

Tessie and I just "got" each other. She'd earned her nickname, The Tessinator, because of how fiercely protective she was of those she loved. Physically strong beyond her years, Tess insisted on pushing my wheelchair, even though she could barely peer over the back on tippy-toes.

Once after doing each other's hair and make-up identically, we asked John if he could tell which of us was who. "Cynthia's the one with the wrinkles," he said with a laugh. Taking exception to his tongue-in-cheek putdown, Tess, then age 7, bolted over to John and in one swift move, which she'd recently mastered in Judo class, dropkicked him to the carpet, laying him out flat. "I take it back," John said with a grunt.

Though Tessie was only a wee one the night of the kick-off, she reveled in my joy. Her connection to For Grace would strengthen as she got older. She always wanted to know what was shaking and whom we were helping. She asked about other women in pain and followed our media coverage. I tried to protect her from the "ugliness" of the pain experience, but this is one tough young lady with a big heart.

At age 10, Tessie surprised me when she asked if she could do her fifth grade written and oral history final about For Grace. Although she had interviewed me twice, I had no idea what was in store for me. On May 7, 2010, John and I went to her school's chapel where her class would give their oral reports. We heard presentations that ranged from Henry Ford and the fixed 1919 World Series to Walt Disney and For Grace.

Being me, naturally I was nervous for her at first. But Tess quickly put me at ease and then left me overwhelmed and speechless, a rarity for me, with her innocence and passion for the work of For Grace. She used a slide show to accompany her three-minute speech, which focused on the good and was devoid of all the heartache that comes with the work. Of all the generous awards and acknowledgements I've received, Tessie's words will always be closest to my heart.

Not only had my nonprofit been launched in 2002, it was already making a splash with a ton of local and national media in the newspapers, as well as on radio and TV. "Nobody gets this kind of media," exclaimed Laura Morgan, a former *L.A. Times* media relations director and Board Member. "Other nonprofits spend hundreds of thousands a year on PR professionals and never even touch this." Of course, those professionals lack the personal commitment that 20 years of a disease can plant in a person. If it took a hundred calls, that's how many I'd make. If I heard even the slightest hint of interest from a journalist, producer or civic leader, I locked on and didn't let go until I reeled them in.

I wasn't getting a paycheck and neither was John. Nonetheless, we were getting our reward. RSD was finally coming out of its very dark closet. It didn't matter if they focused on For Grace or not. I just wanted to get the stories and information about RSD out there. But we would soon be victimized, in a way, by our success.

Women with RSD—it was invariably women—were contacting us from around the country, grateful to at last have a voice. Many were inspired to help us raise awareness. We had no staff or resources to accommodate this flood of volunteers until John brainstormed a manageable project he called NAC, short for National Awareness Campaign. His concept was an online community that would support and encourage individuals to do RSD awareness work in their local areas.

With our multi-talented, in-kind Webmaster, Morgan Grether, we spent weeks developing the project. The site was chock full of great awareness ideas, downloadable tools and resources, along with printable posters, cards and brochures. Tricia added a great visual with a bright orange logo that trumpeted our tag, "Trailblazing a New RSD World."

Just before we launched NAC, Cliff Ashton sent us an email stating he was upset we hadn't asked for his input. "Frankly, I feel left out," he said. We were surprised because it seemed to us Ashton had never shown interest in our work. In fact, people had told us he was spreading the word that For Grace's efforts weren't legitimate. We told him his input would be more than welcome, but never heard back.

This proved to be just the first salvo as others in the pain advocacy world began dissing us. They must have felt threatened. For Grace was the only pain advocacy organization doing effective awareness outreach on a substantial level, and we were doing it on next to nothing. In fact, as a fledgling nonprofit, we'd raised so little money—a few small grants and scant individual support—that we were thinking about selling our condo. Our success was being accomplished purely through passion and hard work. Perhaps these other organizations didn't appreciate the mirror that our lean and mean operation was unintentionally holding up to their over-funded shortcomings.

Though many attempted to pick petty fights, we never engaged. We had quickly come to terms with the sad truth that the nonprofit world was not about locking arms and working together for a good cause. In actuality, nonprofit work is too often about turf wars and securing funding for directors' big paychecks. That wasn't our bag.

NAC went live in late 2003. Soon, women from across the nation were coming aboard, but a couple of initial problems reared up. NAC members were reluctant to chat online with anyone besides John, our volunteer coordinator, Deana, and me. They weren't becoming the self-sustaining community we'd hoped for, which we felt would be the cornerstone of a successful project. A second failing was as disappointing as it was puzzling. We'd expected that spreading the word would be a natural among those committed to RSD awareness. Instead, we wound up trying to cajole, persuade and empower this group that seemed too intimidated to do the work.

John and I devised a new plan. If I could generate local media stories for NAC members, we felt that seeing their names in print would inspire them to carry the awareness torch further. So I pitched the story of local NAC members to their town newspapers. Though working with all that media was like juggling 20 balls at once, we eventually landed newspaper and TV features for RSD individuals coast to coast, literally blanketing the nation. I even scored the first-ever RSD feature in *La Opinion*, the largest Spanish-language paper in the U.S. I was proud to give these women a spotlight. Many spoke on NAC's site about how their family members, friends and neighbors finally validated them after seeing their stories in print. But the project wore and tore at John and me, so we decided, in what was an emotional choice, to drop NAC and move in a different direction.

Meanwhile, I was continuing to land bigger and better media, including a *Newsweek* cover story and a feature in the *Orange County Register* that was picked up nationally. I was keeping my legislative doors open by continuing to earn proclamations, and always showing up to receive them before TV and live audiences. Speaking engagements were becoming increasingly easier to land. Sometimes they even called me. With each speech, the audience was floored to learn that more people in the U.S. had RSD than breast cancer, HIV/AIDS and Multiple Sclerosis combined. Each time, I wrapped up with the same thought: "It is awareness, along with early intervention, that is the difference between a life saved or a life ravaged by RSD."

In the midst of all this growing and stretching, we were thrilled to receive a donated office for a year, smack dab in the section of downtown L.A. dubbed South Park. Our spacious penthouse suite, accented with polished cement floors, exposed ceilings and top-to-floor windows, overlooked Staples Center (which was transforming into L.A. Live, the city's version of Times Square). It was the perfect space for us to build and strengthen For Grace.

As a follow up to NAC, For Grace launched a narrative-therapy project, Share Your RSD Story. We posted first-person accounts and photos on our website as a way of giving voice to people with the disease. One story chilled me to the marrow. Alaska Moore, from Arizona, had been in so much pain and dismissed so often by her physicians that she finally attempted to shoot her afflicted hand off with a .22 caliber gun. When that failed, she purchased an electric saw, and in an attempt to force her doctors to amputate, sliced through a significant portion of her wrist.

Harrowing and heartbreaking, each story provided yet another layer of understanding of this malicious disease—along with a depiction of the courage and bravery its victims used to maintain dignity and life force. These stories gave both the writer and reader the sense of a community whose collective experiences had much more in common than not.

I began to understand why this group of people, me included, was so damn dysfunctional. Virtually every woman I talked with discussed her suicidal thoughts. One swore that if I couldn't save her, she'd jump off a balcony. Another sent me a dozen phone messages and emails threatening to abort her fetus if I didn't talk to her. I realized we were all "adapting" as best we could to an upside-down, intolerable life.

To put this in perspective, think about how torturers attack their targets—primarily through intense, non-stop physical pain and sleep deprivation. Welcome to the world of RSD. I realized that our bad thoughts and actions, my own included, were desperate attempts to stay alive. As ill construed as they were, I came to the hard fought understanding that they were actually adaptive behaviors.

Shortly after we incorporated, our tiny, spitfire pro-bono attorney, DeAnne Ozaki, strongly suggested we hook up with Community Partners, a highly respected "fiscal sponsor" for start-up nonprofits. With their assistance, we could cut through much of the red tape and administrative hassles that derail good projects like For Grace's early on. There we attended classes and workshops with other founders, all truly inspirational people dedicated to civic good. I felt a special kinship with these people though I didn't yet understand why.

I got the first part of the answer while being interviewed on a live TV show hosted by L.A. broadcast legend Bill Rosendahl. "Thank you for being such a great leader," he said on the air. I was baffled. *Why did he say* leader? *I've never thought of myself that way.* But as John and I continued to attend Community Partners events, surrounded by people with similar energy and heart, people who didn't let fear stand in their way, it dawned on me. They were just like me. Leaders.

Although I've never been into labels, since becoming ill, I've always been defined by others. Activist, marketer, advocate, entrepreneur, leader. One creative journalist came up with "a wheelchair-bound star of a one-woman show." I enjoy the labels that bring such high praise, but I see myself more simply. I am, in fact and indeed, a devoted follower of my passion. Someone who wants to help a ton of people on a large scale. I do the work because I care that much. And because I can. If that makes me a what-cha-ma-call-it, I'm good with it.

John's Take

Yes, let's make For Grace happen together. It will be bold and unique, built only from our sheer will and good intentions. It will bring nothing sure, nothing guaranteed. We'll be the ones on the trapeze, twisting and spinning in midair, blindly grabbing for the next swinging bar. Will I fall? Will we fall?

We won't do it for the money. Who knows if we'll ever get paid? But after all those years working a job that made me sick with its sameness and conformity, we'll now be making something wonderful out of nothing. And we'll have the satisfaction of transforming 20 years of insult and suffering into hope for others.

No one should ever have to live through what we've experienced. This is our "dream of never again."

SEVENTEEN

GETTING POLITICAL

Sometimes truth does prevail. That happened in August of 2002. John dropped a pile of papers in my lap and his words exploded in the silence.

"They call it 'The Girl Who Cried Pain: A Bias Against Women in the Treatment of Pain,'" he practically shouted at me. "It's exactly what you've been saying for the last 15 years!"

My head spun as I read the report. Published in the *Journal of Law, Medicine and Ethics,* this remarkable game-changer authored by Diane Hoffmann and Anita Tarzian confirmed my belief that gender bias against women in pain was an epidemic. So did an article in *The New York Times* inspired by this groundbreaking report, entitled "Hurt More, Helped Less." The conclusion in both was identical: Even though women are likely to suffer *more* severe pain than men and tolerate it *less* well, their pain is more likely to be disregarded.

The medical establishment tells us that our pain is hormonal or psychosomatic. This abuse stains our psyches so profoundly that few of us ever truly recover. Men in pain are believed more readily and given pain killers instead of the sedatives and psychiatric referrals offered to women.

The *Times* article laid out word by word what John and I had been fighting against for the past two decades. Profiled as hysterical, histrionic and hormonal, I'd been a punching bag for the medical Old Boys Club and their condescending smirks and brushasides. It all added up to four little words: "all in her head." But now we had the groundbreaking "Girl Who Cried Pain" and *The New York Times* feature to put the lie to that dismissive diagnosis.

There couldn't have been a better opportunity to widen the scale of our work and introduce For Grace to a larger audience. Instead of helping the three to five million people in the U.S. with RSD, we would reach out to the 40 to 50 million women dealing with chronic pain, including migraines, pelvic pain, fibromyalgia and all the rest. It was time to put out this fire.

With the last piece of my pain puzzle falling into place, I wrote and posted a "Women In Pain" petition, complete with a bill of rights, demanding that doctors take a new look at women impacted by chronic pain. I also requested testimonials from women who were suffering and being abused by their healthcare providers. Over 4,000 poured in almost immediately, each more powerful and heartbreaking than the last. One woman, like JoJo, said she was going to kill herself that very night, then went on to beg that we take on the medical establishment and win.

The need to help alleviate people's suffering drove me in my work. I increased my media program, focusing on gender bias in addition to RSD. Journalists, especially female reporters, responded so strongly to the women in pain angle that I realized we could generate enough media to spark a full-blown movement. But where to start? The answer came swiftly: I would reprise my first Senate hearing, the one that introduced RSD, with one that would shine a huge national spotlight on gender bias, which for us was now Public Enemy No. 1.

During the summer of 2003, I made a list of my Sacramento contacts and began burning up the phones. Everyone I spoke with—committee assistants, staffers and legislators—said it would never happen because of the state's historic budget deficit. Sacramento was broke, but I remained focused and didn't flinch. I knew I could get key people to listen, and once I grabbed their attention, they would appreciate the urgency of this cause and I'd be able to close the deal. So I continued on the phones. When I reached the end of my list, I started over.

For each rejection, I had a basic message. "The under-treatment of women's pain is the most inhumane and unethical inaction I know of. It's also the most flagrant form of patient abandonment a physician can practice." I always backed this up with my story.

My rant was usually met with stunned silence followed by "there's really nothing I can do." Then, from somewhere deep inside, these hard-boiled politicos invariably shared a personal anecdote about what had happened to them or to their mother, daughter or niece. To my amazement, they *all* had women in pain stories. I was certain it was just a matter of time and pressure before this logjam would burst through.

Soon the Capitol was abuzz with women in pain conversations. *Bingo!* Legislative liaison Jackie Koenig, in Senator Nell Soto's office, offered me a carrot—an informal roundtable hearing with legislative staffers through the Women's Legislative Caucus. As thrilled as I was by this offer, I didn't accept it. I was convinced this gender bias needed a full-blown Senate informational hearing.

"If no one testifies, Jackie, none of this is important," I argued. "We need an official hearing and a ton of media. Television, radio, the papers. We've got to get enough coverage to rattle their cages and put this horror story on the map."

I took a breath. "Who do we need to make this happen?" She named the Senate Health Committee members. "Then let's get cracking on *them*," I told her. And we did.

Finally, the stars aligned. Not one but *three* female Senators— Liz Figueroa, Nell Soto and Deborah Ortiz—agreed to co-chair the event at the Capitol. Senator Soto even agreed to officially proclaim a Women In Pain Awareness Month to honor the event.

The hearing brought something new into our lives, namely Big Pharma. That's the nickname for the mega pharmaceutical companies that work vigorously behind the scenes to further line their already overstuffed pocketbooks. We were contacted by Purdue, which makes the painkiller, OxyContin. Unbeknownst to John and me, Purdue was apparently using grassroots nonprofits like For Grace to counter the bad press they were getting about their prized painkiller, a practice known as "astroturfing." The media had claimed there was an epidemic of "hillbilly heroin" addiction. This involved people who got the Purdue drug illegally and then crushed and snorted it or shot up for a heroin-like high. This diversion of OxyContin had caused a sensational up-tick of overdoses, providing sexy headlines much to the concern of Purdue.

We felt the reporting was dangerously unbalanced and were concerned that stories about misuse could limit access to this potentially effective painkiller. We believed OxyContin was preventing untold suicides.

At the time of the hearing, we were still essentially self-financing For Grace, so John and I were excited about hooking a major funder for our efforts. Since we were unaware of how desperate and sinister the marketing efforts at Purdue had become, when Purdue said they wanted to fly one of their advocacy personnel, Robyn Lane*, and regional lobbyist Dean Stanton* to Sacramento to attend the Senate hearing, we could barely wait. But all was not well in paradise. I began to suspect this when Robyn suggested a list of ideal women to testify along with me. My gut told me that was wrong, but the women seemed to know the pain game and came across as passionate, capable and eager to help. So I went along, at least at first.

The morning of the Senate hearing, John and I met with the Purdue folk, including Robyn, Dean and their public relations people. The first moment I saw Robyn, I suspected she was trouble. Something about the way she looked me over. Granted, I was still sick with a severe case of the flu I had refused to let sideline me. Working on the hearing from my sickbed, in addition to the usual For Grace madness, had exhausted me. But this was a hearing, fostered in part by "The Girl Who Cried Pain," that *I* had to make happen.

The Purdue team reviewed my testimony. To my amazement, they suggested some revisions, including not mentioning their name as a supporter. *So, what is it that you've got to hide, anyway?* I was furious; I felt they were trying to strong-arm me over what I was going to say—or not say—at my own hearing. In retrospect, I believe they were sizing me up, a test of sorts, to see if I would play ball for future collaborations.

John and I had a big-time argument in the men's room just before entering the Senate chamber.

"Just go along," John argued. "There aren't that many changes. Bottom line, this could ultimately benefit For Grace."

In the end I agreed, but I entered the hearing room filled with anger.

Despite the hassle with Purdue, the standing room only hearing was hugely successful. Nobody left when it ran two and half hours overtime. "This *never* happens, Cynthia," Kristin told me. The long hearing gave us even more exposure as it was televised live via the California Channel and covered by the Sacramento papers. Plus, I'd already landed an Op-Ed in the *Los Angeles Times* about the pain gender divide and the hearing.

But it was the texture of the hearing itself that amazed me. Several female legislators shared women in pain stories about family members and friends. In fact, two Senators were moved to tears. Phrases like "they could have killed her" and "I never saw anyone suffer so much emotional abuse" filled the room. To this day, the video of this hearing is the most requested in Capitol history.

After the hoopla, Robyn invited John and me, along with the women they'd asked me to invite to testify, to a celebration dinner at a restaurant frequented by Sacramento's movers and shakers. As sick as I was, I accepted in the spirit of good business relations. This was our first taste of being wined and dined by Big Pharma. As I sliced through my grilled salmon and sautéed asparagus tips, I couldn't say it felt bad.

Suddenly a woman came up behind me and covered my eyes with her hands. "Guess who?"

I didn't have a clue. "Who?"

To my joyful surprise, I saw one of my political heroes, Senator Sheila Kuehl, who I knew had attended the hearing. "Oh my God!"

Sheila twinkled, "You're an actor, aren't you?"

"Yes," I exclaimed, probably a bit too excitedly.

"I could tell. That was the best speech I've heard since Jane Fonda spoke out against the Vietnam War."

I was speechless, my brain frozen solid from the power of her compliment. The Senator excused herself as I stuttered a thank you.

Back home and still dancing (at least figuratively) over the hearing's impact, I figured we were home free. *Now Purdue will eagerly fund For Grace, step back and watch us do what we do best—be a leading voice to raise the profile of pain as a major health issue.* But I was still naïve about the pharmaceutical companies' ways.

In the weeks that followed, Purdue amped their involvement. I was invited to give the keynote for pain advocacy conferences they were underwriting in Denver and Philadelphia. The purpose of these events—or so I was told—was to train and inspire pain leaders to effectively interface with media and policy makers. I was surprised and insulted when Purdue insisted I take an on-camera media class. In a taped, mock interview with their crisis management consultant, I was asked, "What treatment do you advise when a person gets an RSD diagnosis?"

"Well, there's a whole range of options out there, including alternative ones," I answered, spreading my hands a yard wide. "Remember, what works for one person may not work for the next."

The consultant chided me, suggesting that "as the up-and-coming pain star," I should "rethink" my answer. *Rethink my answer?*

"The correct response is OxyContin," several individuals in the class suggested. I felt like I was trapped in a *Twilight Zone* episode. Then it got through to me loud and clear. Based on my observation, Purdue was seeking to buy my endorsement for an instructional symposium on the virtues of their cash cow. Apparently, I was the only schmuck in the room who didn't know this. As a queasy feeling came over me, I told my "coach" there was nothing for me to rethink.

Shortly after, we severed our relationship with Purdue and lost their funding. On a conference call with the women from the hearing and a Purdue media relations employee, I hammered the last nail in the coffin. "I won't be a whore for a pharmaceutical," I announced.

In 2007, I was relieved to read on the front page of *The New York Times* that Purdue had gotten caught for their bad deeds. *Big time!* Three of their current and former executives pleaded guilty to misleading the public about OxyContin's risk of addiction. Purdue wouldn't be the only company to feel the heat. In 2010, a Congressional Investigative Hearing, chaired by Iowa Senator James Grassley, investigated the inappropriate influence of pharmaceutical companies on patient advocacy organizations.

Despite the funding road bumps, we were able to keep our downtown office after our donated year was up, but only through substantial financial sacrifice. John would continue to pull his pittance of a paycheck ($18,000 a year) and I would continue to work for free, which I still do. This was the only way to avoid selling out while hanging onto the office. John and I agreed it was worth it.

The downtown space provided a great meeting venue for our now professional Board and associated committees, as well as a sanctuary from the trappings of our condo office. It also gave me a chance to work next to Gary Erickson, president of a successful nonprofit consulting firm and a legendary fundraiser who I wanted to attract to our Board. In all, it took five invites in five years before Gary jumped aboard. Time well spent!

Throughout 2004 and 2005, I delighted in the invitations I received to panel and keynote for legislators, healthcare professionals and pain advocacy groups. The honorariums helped fund For Grace, while the travel helped make up for all those years of lost adventure. There was another benefit from this activity. My growing connection with legislators and the healthcare industry prompted me to move in a powerful new direction. I would champion legislation to create a full-blown RSD education campaign coordinated through the state's Department of Human Services. This bill would take us light years beyond our wonderful RSD hearing a few years earlier because this would be a program for the masses.

My appearances at these events throughout the U.S. helped increase For Grace's visibility, but they made running our newborn nonprofit that much more difficult. In the Dark Ages before the BlackBerry, catching up on emails meant the public library. During one such library mission, a message that caught John's eye would become my digital calling card to landing worldwide RSD attention. Two RSD friends told me about a Cliff Ashton email—funny, it somehow missed our inbox—alerting people that Discovery Health was doing a segment about RSD for their popular *Mystery Diagnosis* series. They wanted to profile someone who had waited years for a diagnosis and had a "Hollywood ending." My hand trembled as I scribbled the producer's name and number using one of those stubby library pencils. *Oh my God, this is it.*

In less than a minute, there in that Augustine, Florida, public library, I tuned out the world and psyched myself into pitch mode. I knew this story was mine. Despite a lightning storm outside, my cell reception was excellent. From my wheelchair, with librarians shushing me, I caught True Entertainment producer Timothy Hedden on the third ring. As I introduced myself, I felt like a racehorse busting through the gates at the bell.

We connected right from the start. Over the next five minutes, I laid out everything about the power of RSD to destroy its victims and gave him the details of my experience with it, right down to the happy ending of running a nonprofit to save others from my fate.

"Okay, Cynthia, I've spoken with dozens of people with RSD. You're the first one who doesn't sound kooky," he said when he could get a word in.

Switching into advocacy mode, I explained maladaptive behavior to him. "They mean well, Timothy, but they're desperate. We're all swimming in hell."

He told me, "Everyone I've spoken with wants the show to help them win *their* court case or settle their worker's comp. That's not what we do here. Is there *anything* you're wanting for your personal gain?"

"Yes, there is." I replied firmly. "I want your program to bring RSD awareness into every home in the country. That will help sufferers get diagnosed and treated early. You and I, we can give them a chance to walk, and I mean literally walk, away from this nightmare of a disease."

I heard his sigh filter in from New York. Then, "I love it. I'm going to take this straight to the top. Where can I reach you in an hour?"

With national media, it's a long process to actually get your green light. I interviewed regularly and sent photos over the next nine weeks, and with each approval, I moved up the chain, oddly confident I was going to land this treasure.

"Media's nuts, babe," John reminded me. "You're making a big mistake. They love you one day, then leave you the next. You know that better than anyone."

That was absolutely true. But I just knew this would work.

I had to line up three other interviewees, including a doctor, in case the show was a go. The producers liked the story better with each interview. Timothy reported, "The senior producer had approved two others, but went nuts over yours. She tagged it 'The best story we've ever had here.'" Still, I waited.

Early one morning, I was doing physical therapy on the bedroom floor while John worked at the computer. Timothy called. "Well, I got the final word, Cynthia." Silence at my end. "They turned it down." More silence as my heart caved. Then he laughed like a hyena. "Oh, where's your sense of humor? I'm kidding. You're in. All the way in. Truth is, we wouldn't have done an RSD segment without you." The news couldn't have been better, though at least half of me wanted to wring Timothy's neck.

Then the real work kicked in. I did a new round of interviews with my segment producer, Gabriella Spierer, a recent graduate of NYU's film school. She also interviewed John, my mother and Dr. Foley. In May, True Entertainment sent a crew from New York. The shooting was like nothing I'd experienced before. Gabriela interviewed me in a pitch-black room, spotlights virtually blinding me. Think prison interrogation.

My interview took three grueling hours. I was shocked that I burst out crying a number of times while describing my years of pain. The challenge wasn't just psychological. Because of the shot setup, I had to sit in an unnatural position. That, combined with the heightened emotion, drove my pain higher and higher. Still, we continued to work.

Every second proved worth it. The segment reached 20 million viewers in the U.S. before getting picked up by The Learning Channel and ultimately by Home and Health Worldwide. As of this writing, this 18-minute RSD exposé continues to run regularly in the U.S. and across the globe.

The response at For Grace was awesome, far beyond anything our two-horse shop could handle. We once again found ourselves the victims of our own success. Everyone already thought we were a well-funded, fully staffed organization. And now, due to the quality and scope of this *Mystery Diagnosis* segment, people must have assumed we occupied three floors of the Chrysler Building in New York. We were hearing from RSD sufferers all over the world and in most every language. We scrambled to find volunteer translators to respond, even recruiting my brother Jon, who'd lived in Brazil, to handle the emails from Spanish-speaking countries.

Almost every caller wanted to talk to me. Out of self-preservation, I rarely answered the office phone. When I did pick up, I pretended to be a receptionist. Hearing callers refer to "Cynthia" as some sort of messiah, the one who found the Holy Grail of RSD relief, struck me as bizarre. No one could be that messiah because no one figures out "The Suicide Disease." I was dealing with the same frustrations, anger and loss as they. And being projected through the rose-tinted illusion of media didn't separate me from that reality.

All this exposure didn't remove the sting from the end result of our year-long, hard-fought legislative action for a California RSD education act, which had become Assembly Bill 1648. Our efforts, which included securing letters of support, signing up groups of physicians and nurses, writing press releases, testifying in Sacramento and getting the rest of the California RSD community involved, were successful. I'd gotten our RSD bill onto Governor Arnold Schwarzenegger's desk in its first year, something the Sacramento pros said almost never happens. But the Gov vetoed it due to "lack of allotted funding."

When I heard, I lowered my head and closed my eyes. I thought about the people who would suffer just as I had, plus all those who would take their lives because of the swoop of one man's pen. I had to take action to counter that. But what could I do? What could I do that might generate even more awareness than if he had signed? The answer popped into my head with a full-throttled excitement rarely equaled by anything in my lifetime.

At Community Partners' holiday party, held in the swanky VIP club at Dodger Stadium, I seized the mic. To a crowd who profoundly understood the angst of good work cut-short, I hollered my intention to right a wrong.

"I'm running for a seat in the California State Assembly!"

The applause was thunderous. If I'd been able to stand, I know my knees would have buckled.

John's Take

The woman's nuts. She's bonkers. Not all the dots are on her dice. An enchilada short of a combo plate. I can't believe she's actually going to run in this race. These are career politicians who will trade their firstborn for a paid seat in Sacramento, complete with perks, no-deductible healthcare and a cushy pension. They don't tolerate fools kindly and they don't like outsiders mucking up their highly financed dog-and-pony shows for the electorate.

I tell Cynthia to think it through, then laugh at myself as these measured, reasonable words sputter out of my mouth. I don't recall the woman ever taking a measured, reasonable action in her life. Why would this madness be any different? And she's got a band of enablers supporting her notion—beginning with nonprofit legend Gary Erickson, Web guru Morgan Grether and award-winning producer Dick Freed. No slackers there. They think this move is the best thing since sliced bread. They're nuts, too.

I'm out-numbered even as my first reading of campaign finance regulations and election disclosure filings sends shivers down my spine and make me want to poop in my shorts. We don't know the first thing about running a political campaign. We're supposed to have a respectable grasp of the issues. We're supposed to know the insiders in the party. We're supposed to know the number of our district. Okay, that one I can Google. As for the rest, heaven help me.

Oy. Same old, same old. Fling it up there and see what sticks. Cynthia's stuff usually sticks a lot because it's all about heart. So, fine. Sign me up. Let's work some magic. We're going to find out how dirty and oily this machine really is—from the inside. And by the time we're through, maybe Cynthia can sprinkle in that best part of her—her authentic compassion and care for people—and turn this whole campaign on its head. Just maybe the people will see what's truly good for them.

Heck, I wouldn't mind being the significant other of an Assembly-woman.

EIGHTEEN

RUNNING FOR THE CAUSE

"You shouldn't run," Assemblymember Paul Koretz, who I'd met when I spoke before his healthcare committee, told me over kosher pickles at Jerry's Famous Deli. It was early 2006 and he was terming out in November. The two leading candidates in the race to replace him—Mike Feuer and Abbe Land—were well-funded career politicians.

"Besides," he added, "this will be the nastiest primary race of 2006." A familiar whiff of "impossible" overtook the scent of my pastrami brisket and John's corned beef.

This was an important lunch, one where I needed to be my best, just like all my meetings those days. But I had a health issue that was affecting my focus and concentration. I'd finally been diagnosed with fibromyalgia (FM), a debilitating condition I'd had for about six years. I'd never before seen a doctor about it because I didn't want another ailment piled on me, another oppressive label to make me feel more like a sickie.

The muscle pain triggered by FM in no way rivals my RSD, but the condition has its own brand of torture. It provokes, especially under stress, long, debilitating periods without restorative sleep. I became so sleep deprived I literally bumped into walls, breaking a toe in the process. I now measured my life not by the scorching pain endured, but rather the devastating fatigue that swamped me. Dulled by fibro-fog, as it's known, and exhaustion, I struggled to maintain the appearance of a sharp, capable pain leader and spokesperson.

It would take me years to finally accept the reality that the stress of going non-stop was taking a major toll on my health. Ultimately, I would make a pact with my hard-driving demons to take time off each weekend to balance my life.

This choice was largely sparked by Dr. Marc Brodsky, a UCLA Center for East-West Medicine physician who introduced me to integrative medicine. He treated me with respect, and his advice to avoid invasive procedures resonated strongly. This contrasted sharply with my Western doctor who urged therapies that included an intra-thecal pump along with two spinal cord stimulators. Even before Dr. Brodsky, I knew these treatments were wrong for me.

My connection with Dr. Brodsky marked a gentler approach to wellness that allowed me to take responsibility for my pain care. At first, I felt threatened because I didn't know how to fix me. But with time, my partnership with Dr. Brodsky changed my mindset. I learned that, ultimately, I was the one who had the answers. Often after relating my symptoms to Dr. Brodsky, he'd ask what I thought we should do. Soon, I learned to fix problems using my inner wisdom. It felt logical to have a doctor trained in both Eastern and Western medicine give me the benefit of both worlds.

During my worst bout of FM's non-restorative sleep, I spoke desperately to Dr. Brodsky about my depression and suicidal thoughts. I still remember his words. "You're going to get a lot sicker before you get better, Cynthia. But ultimately, you're going to get well."

The timing for my improved wellness was perfect. I was on the scent of a political campaign that would spotlight my cause. I wasn't going to end this quest no matter what anyone, including Paul Koretz, said.

"I hear you, Paul. My campaign just doesn't compute in your world. But it's the Holy Grail and then some in mine!"

I looked at him for a moment. "I'm going to give the media and all the good folks out there a very personal view of 'The Suicide Disease.' And, yeah, of gender bias. And of our broken health-care system."

As the conversation deepened and I displayed my knowledge and passion, I felt an evolving respect from this life-long public servant. Even though we'd clearly bonded during our meeting, I was astonished when he said, "Okay, Cynthia, I've already decided not to endorse Feuer or Land. If you can raise some serious money, I'll consider endorsing you." I swallowed hard. He continued. "I want you to call a campaign consultant, Fred Heubcher. Use my name, and try to persuade him to back you. I won't be surprised if he does."

I phoned Fred as soon as John and I got to the car. After giving him the skinny on who I was and the reasons I was running, I got my first lesson in brass-knuckle politics. Fred raked me over the coals, telling me that Feuer and Land were the best-qualified politicians in the state.

"If you were Erin Brockovich, you couldn't win this race," he announced. I resisted asking him, "What if I were Julia Roberts?"

Still, to my surprise, Fred offered to meet with me, probably as a favor to Paul. Though he dropped that ball, he did offer some advice after suggesting that I watch the movie *The Candidate*, evidently as an exercise to quell my idealism.

"Hey, listen, Cynthia," he said in an almost fatherly tone. "I hear your passion. If you're running to gain attention for your cause, then I say go for it. That's savvy. But if you're in this race to win, forget it. Choose another one."

During the campaign, which lasted nearly six months, I didn't admit to Fred or anyone with the exception of my closest advisors, that I was running almost exclusively to raise awareness about pain and our state's despicable healthcare system. But I had another, albeit decidedly more minor, purpose. I'd always been politically strong-minded and loved working with legislators to evoke positive change. On several occasions, I'd realized I probably had the stuff to be a good politician. I wanted to explore the process from the inside. Perhaps one day I'd run to win.

Nonetheless, I'd decided up front that I'd give this campaign everything I had. Two days later, I met with L.A. County Democratic Party chair Eric Bauman, who gave me the same spiel that Paul and Fred had. Something must have registered, however, because he invited me to speak at their meeting the following night. Stoked by the anticipation of the heated election year ahead, I immediately plugged into the electricity of the packed room. Still, I was brand spankin' new to this kind of show biz. My nerves were tingling. John spotted Feuer and pulled him over.

"So I understand you've thrown your hat into the ring," he said with what I interpreted as cold reserve. I knew right off this guy wasn't my cup of tea. He shook my hand, and with an even less sincere, "Good luck," he went off to work the room.

All the candidates who wanted to speak to the club's membership of about 200 lined up. When my turn came, I couldn't reach the podium's mic from my wheelchair. No matter, I was in my element. I belted out an inspired appeal for my candidacy, expressing my anger at our state's busted healthcare system. The audience whooped with approval. Apparently, a woman in a wheelchair who was the real deal stirred these political cynics. I sponged up the energy, which evoked memories of my HMO reform days. Out of the corner of my eye, I thought I caught Feuer leaving in a huff. A couple days later, I got word that Paul had endorsed him, teaching me the golden rule of politics: Trust no one. Sad, but true. And while I adore and respect Paul to this day, this is the nature of the beast.

Then came one of my biggest media events ever—a live, in-studio segment about pain and the gender divide for ABC's *World News NOW*. Sitting in Peter Jenning's chair at ABC's Los Angeles bureau, I let my story rip. This was the first time we'd landed worldwide media attention for women in pain, and I savored it. The timing was perfect because we'd soon officially expand our mission at For Grace to ensure the ethical and equal treatment of *all* women in pain.

Back at HQ, John was immersed in the paperwork to make my candidacy official. Challenge No. 1 involved getting enough nomination signatures from registered voters to get my name on the ballot. Since we scarcely knew anyone, I attended farmers markets each weekend. This part of the campaign scared the hell out of us. We were deeply concerned we'd never get enough signatures. I'd been told that many of those who signed up would be disqualified, so we collected triple the number of names required.

In the process, I often got into candidate mode and was soon talking issues and listening to people's concerns. I loved every minute of it. It quickly became apparent that everyone was tired of the status quo. They liked me because I was *not* a politician. The fact that I was a passionate person who had experienced real hardship resonated with many voters.

Framing myself as something different, I began to court the media. My advisors told me to make sure to mention that I'd posed for *Playboy* as that would grab attention. How ironic! "Are you sure that you want to pose nude, Peach?" John had asked me at the time. "Could it ever come back to bite you in the ass?"

"Well, I'm never going to run for office," I'd answered. "So, yeah, I'm sure." *How's that for taking a wise look into the future?*

And, natch, there was one time I felt like a dim-witted Playmate. During my first interview, a journalist hamstrung me on a basic question about my district. I managed to fake my way through, but decided I needed a much more respectable grasp of the issues to have an authentic campaign experience.

So I began cramming with John, who proved merciless when it came to flashcards. I'd always been keen about political matters—

pro-choice, anti-capital punishment, pro-public schools, pro-universal healthcare. But now there was a wide range of state issues I hadn't previously considered important. Things like eminent domain, immigration, transportation, term limits, etc. I was getting yet another education and found myself surprisingly opinionated about these newfound civic concerns.

With Morgan's assistance, I set up a blog as my campaign website. Via regular postings, I gave people the opportunity to discover "Citizen Toussaint."

"Don't articulate your position in print," political insiders advised. "You may need to flip-flop in the future."

Wait, you mean I have to have flexible morals to be a viable candidate? That was the first red flag that I might not be cut out to be a politician.

I joined Land and Feuer at over a dozen political clubs. These groups meet regularly and during campaigns hold endorsement meetings that candidates can attend to seek that club's endorsement. The other two Democrats in the race never showed, apparently intimidated by the Q&A portion of these events. Although I initially felt as capable as a frog when grilled about the issues and my qualifications, I sensed that my honesty and passion elicited respect.

"My God, you're the first candidate in my 10 years of endorsement meetings who actually answered one of the questions with an *I don't know*," a gentleman from the Westwood Democrats told me. "The rest of your crowd absolutely knows it all."

A member from the Stonewall club commented, "I've been sitting here all day, Cynthia, and I have an entire note pad filled with lies. You're the first candidate who has actually told the truth. Thank you. You made my day." Then he added in a tired tone, "I only wish we could vote for you." That's when I realized that candidate endorsements were preordained. Red flag number two.

Number three would be raised when it took phoning ahead and much on-site maneuvering just to get me, chair and all, into the Hollywood hillside home where an endorsement meeting was being held. I was growing increasingly concerned that the disabled element wasn't considered politically significant, either as candidates or club members. And this from the party of inclusion. *Hmmm.*

I received confirmation of my progress with key party players at the next endorsement meeting. This one, at the San Fernando Valley Democratic Club, was the biggest and most prominent of the primary season. When my district was up, Land went first, stumbling through her speech with what appeared to be a bad case of the jitters. Then Feuer did the same. I went last and delivered the goods in a speech that remains one of the best of my career. "I am a living example of the terribly botched healthcare system we have in this state," I began. I must have hit a nerve. The club didn't endorse either Land or Feuer because I siphoned off some votes, something I would accomplish again during my run for office. These club endorsements were like gold to the candidates, as they trumpeted them on the zillions of mailers that clog mailboxes as the election ramped up. The SFV club's endorsement was one of the biggest, and this little guppy had influenced its outcome, which defied the odds.

Assemblymember Lloyd Levine came over just after with a smile. "I have one piece of advice for you, Cynthia. In the future, put a little *passion* into your speeches." Everyone within earshot laughed.

That evening, I attended a single-payer universal healthcare event hosted by Senator Sheila Kuehl. The crowd included an interesting assortment of heavyweight celebs such as Ed Asner, Cindy Williams, Lily Tomlin and Ed Begley, Jr. Everyone who was anyone in local politics was there. They all seemed to give me high points for the speech I'd nailed that afternoon.

At the event, Levine approached again. "Cynthia, are you serious about running for office?" he asked, squatting in front of me.

I paused for a moment. "Not if I have to sell my soul."

He said it wasn't exactly like that and handed me his card, asking that I make a lunch date. "If you're serious about winning a race, it's just a matter of when and where."

I soon noticed—for the first time, really—that the people there didn't demean me for using a wheelchair. Everyone wanted to meet me, shake my hand and wish me well. The traditional pitying looks had evaporated. I realized that as a "celebrity," being disabled wasn't an issue. By running for office, I'd gained instant admiration and respect. And while this attention was flattering in the short run, ultimately its hypocrisy left me with a bad taste.

Within weeks, my campaign was rolling with email bursts, media and, yes, the dreaded robo calls, those automated calls that rain into homes during election cycles. This activity was made possible by the $5,000 we received from friends, family and supporters of my work at For Grace, a budget that would probably cover the coffee and Danish for most campaigns. I made sure to show up for all the candidate nights, my favorite part of this incredible circus. I got to yelp about my pain and healthcare platforms and, just as good, to slam Feuer and Land for the obscenity of their money raising. I'd learned that leading candidates spend two to three years raising money for their race, consequently owing big favors once in office. I enjoyed pointing out this despicable practice. "I can't imagine these candidates doing much more than paying off these debts and making deals for their next gig during their time in office," I said night after night as audiences howled with approval and John shared that my opponents looked like they wanted to crawl into their respective holes.

Although Land had a legitimate reason to be pissed at me as I was threatening to peel off some of her girl-power vote, she remained polite, authentic and warm. I was certain she understood why I was in this race and even respected me for it.

My regard for Feuer continued to drop. He rarely spoke to me, apparently threatened by this truth-spewing woman in the wheelchair and her miniscule campaign war chest. By this time, campaign insiders shared that he'd raised nearly a million bucks and had been calling in favors for six years to win this race. Now, here I was jamming up his endorsements. (Since then, just like any self-respecting politician, I've taken the liberty of flip-flopping when it comes to Mike Feuer. As an Assemblymember, he co-authored the For Grace-sponsored bill, AB 1826, in 2010. This bill, which has since evolved into another, will reform Step Therapy, a drug prescription practice used by health insurance plans at the cost of pain patients in California. Thank you, Mike, for being a good guy after all.)

To get as deep into the fun and games as possible, in late April John and I attended the California Democratic Convention in Sacramento. I went to this event still asking myself if there was any way I could fit into this game without compromising my values.

The energy was high and exciting. Delegates were stumping for their candidates. Ridiculously young campaign volunteers were banging drums and chanting for the next governor and the din confirmed, hey, this is damn important stuff. So listen up!

I now knew many of these insiders. Senator Figueroa was there because of her controversial run for Lt. Governor. At the Disability Caucus meeting, she immediately introduced me to the crowd, making a motion for me to speak. I could have kissed her.

The convention redeemed my faith in the Democratic Party. I'd long been angry with the Democrats for falling into line with Bush after 9/11, thinking they'd been a bunch of spineless patsies to accept his New World Order. But in Sacramento I found a progressive group that wanted to impeach Bush and stop his never-ending wars. Every room buzzed with challenges to the status quo and talk of restoring social programs for the aging and needy.

Yes, I could see myself in this people-helping, compassion-embracing party. And if I won an election, I could also see myself encircled by layers of people sharing my energy and passion. I would not be alone as I served constituents, fought for legislation and supported fair and humane policy. And, almost unbelievably, I'd collect a paycheck for my work. Hell, I'd even have a paid staff. What a dream.

With my faith in the Democrats reaffirmed, I snagged a phone meeting with Senator Kuehl to further explore the reality of a future win. "Cynthia, living in Sacramento half the week and my district the other is physically difficult for *me*," she shared with her typical candor. "And I'm healthy. This is something you need to think about." And for about the billionth time, I did.

The campaign started heating up in May. As I'd been told early on by insiders, the two frontrunners got ugly. Despite the warnings, I was shocked and sickened by the daily negative mailers that chewed up the bulk of their campaign dollars. This was where the election was bought. "The only winnable campaign is one that goes negative," fellow disabled candidate Jim Alger had told me early on. "That's what the people want. And whoever draws first blood will win."

I didn't want him to be right, but that's exactly how this race played out. Feuer attacked Land first. She countered by asking me and all the other candidates to sign a pact that we wouldn't go negative, as if the rest of us now had political influence. When this failed, she retaliated. The ambushing and name-calling was as childish as it was degrading. I felt like I needed a shower after each candidate's night.

Near the end, Land confided to me with a weathered voice, "Oh God, I can't wait until this is *over*." Feuer had continued his negative ad assault and she'd spent the week defending her integrity. I could see the burnout in her eyes. I held her hand, realizing that she was a decent person in a wretched game.

I would have loved to go toe to toe with Land and Feuer, but they were the only two invited to the televised debates. I called the *Beverly Hills Courier*, which sponsored the last debate, demanding equal time, but got blown off. So I made my case to the editor, landing a feature titled "Candidate Does Something Impossible Again."

Not long after, the media actually called *me. New York Times* writer Kathleen McGrory was planning a story about RSD, now called Complex Regional Pain Syndrome (CRPS), because her mother had the disease. Like any good journalist, she'd done her research and wanted to feature me for a couple of reasons. First, her mother had been a dancer, too. And second because "no matter who I talk to, I'm told that all the CRPS awareness is coming out of California due to your work at For Grace. Now, your run for office is amping the spotlight."

I was stunned that people in the CRPS world were acknowledging For Grace's achievement, as we'd never heard a nice peep before. In fact, quite the opposite. It warmed my heart to know that our truth had bubbled to the top.

"Is this a good time to do the interview, Cynthia?" Kathleen asked.

I was naked, about to jump into the shower before heading downtown, so of course I replied, "Now's perfect." What followed was an engaging three-hour interview, due just as much to Kathleen's acute interest as to my answers that at times went on for five to 10 minutes. Her mother's progression had been similar to mine, evoking a special intimacy. We found ourselves laughing and talking over each other. Without a doubt, this was the best CRPS interview I've ever given. I got to discuss everything. The good, the bad and the damn ugly.

In short order, Kathleen knocked off a 24-page article chronicling my CRPS experience that was approved by *The New York Times Magazine*.

But the media gods weren't smiling upon me this go around. The magazine had closed another pain story that same week, knocking Kathleen's out. Still, the consolation prize was pretty awesome. Our feature landed on the front page of *The New York Times* Health section, complete with a photograph of me campaigning. This was *huge*. CRPS had never been mentioned, let alone featured, in "the paper of record." This article would single-handedly legitimize the disease. The whole pain world was buzzing. I was enormously proud that my political run had brought this baby home. No one could ever again doubt and diminish those of us who survived this killer disease.

All was eerily quiet when voting day finally arrived. After feeling like a hamster on a treadmill for months without letup, the lull felt anti-climactic and a bit surreal. No one, myself included, was surprised when Feuer won the primary and Land picked up most of the remaining votes. I still have no clue how I didn't come in last. Other than John and me, I could identify few of the 1,600 votes I received.

After the race, I was courted by the National Women's Political Caucus to attend a campaign-training seminar with a phenomenal coach, Cathy Allen. She'd been responsible for getting women all around the world into office. I now knew that, yes, I was electable.

I thought about that, all the pros and cons. But being a legislator doesn't feel right for me. I couldn't live with the compromises it requires. Like giving up your beliefs and ideals. And like the relationships lawmakers sometimes have with their financial supporters.

On the other hand, I have positive feelings about a different legislative role. Using my connections, friendships and the media, I could promote laws that help people in pain—and in many ways, all patients—find effective health and healing. From this perspective, I can look back on this spirited adventure and still feel the joy of it.

The nuts-and-bolts results of my campaign were even more than I'd hoped for. We spotlighted pain as a major health crisis, as well as California's tragically inadequate healthcare system. Plus there were the stories—*The New York Times,* CNN, *Woman's Day, The Washington Post* and all the rest. Thanks to my $5,000 campaign and everyone who helped make it happen, women in pain were center stage.

John's Take

What a hootenanny! Once I got past my initial reservations, I dug watching Cynthia pound her fists on the podium, pointing out the disgracefulness of our electoral machinery. I soon grasped that she's above this silliness. She's not made for a world of compromise and half-measures, of ethics reconsidered. Her stride is too long. I'm proud I stood in her corner all the way.

The happenings of this past year are just one of our many rides together. I've met people, gone to places, done things that would have been the stuff of fiction otherwise. Playboy, ballet, Vegas, the Eiffel Tower, Senate hearings, worldwide media, on and on. Even one of these would have been the story of a lifetime.

It's not uncommon for me to be standing in a place of power and influence, of spectacle and wonder, of comfort and aid. I look around in awe and pinch myself. How did I get here? What force of nature has guided me to this higher place? Why am I the guy who's assisting this woman in her destiny? Divine intervention. Law of attraction. Dumb luck. Who cares? I'm just pleased as punch to be in this game. Talk about a beautiful life.

I've always believed in the power of us. We compliment each other's strengths and pave over the other's weaknesses. Like any good partnership, the whole is greater than the sum of its parts. We found each other, and despite the cracks and the meteor hits, we triumph. We celebrate with a dance to a symphony only we can hear.

We've harmed each other. I've said things that are despicable, beyond cruel. She's lashed at me with fury so fierce, I've wanted to hide in a hole and disappear forever. Indescribable pain stirs this pot. We know that, but it still blindsides us sometimes.

In this storm, we hold each other. We kiss, we touch. I love this woman. Madly. Deeply. Nothing's going to change that, ever. Not a disease, not a man, not a flurry of slaps. She taught me how to love. She taught me self-respect. She taught me how to stand tall no matter what. She has shown me the things that make me a man.

She's taken me to the edge of heaven. I see the outer rings of the divine. As I lay my head on her chest, my ear pressed tight, I hear her heart beat. Steady and strong. Like the woman.

I'm hanging on to this comet for as long as I can.

NINETEEN

A NEW WAR

In the years since my injury, I have fought for my own health and the health of countless other women. The windmills I've tilted against have ranged from the HMOs and pharmaceutical companies to putting a catastrophic disease and pain gender bias on the map. Unlike Don Quixote, I've won significant battles. But one quest remained unfulfilled. I had not graduated from UC Irvine. I still didn't have my diploma.

This had become an urgent matter for me. I know it can be hard for some to understand, but the absence of this piece of paper hurt me deeply.

"You have to give up, Cynthia," one of Senator Figueroa's staffers urged when the University of California chancellor himself informed the Senator that I would never be allowed to earn my dance degree from UCI. His communication had been triggered by a few years of action—letters and calls from Senator Figueroa and myself—and by the UCI dance faculty's vote against my chance for the diploma.

But giving up wasn't an option. Higher education had always been emphasized in my family. My mom earned her degree from Hamline University in Minnesota. All my siblings went to college and, except for Beth who left school early to model, each earned at least a BA. And my Dad's PhD topped our list. With that background, I never doubted I'd earn my own diploma. Even before my injury when I was up for a lead role on the TV show *Fame*, I knew I'd graduate before cranking up my career in show business.

In the years after my hamstring injury, I wrangled with the top people at UCI, asking that I be allowed to complete my degree.

Even during my darkest years, I sent letters. "I'm just a few credits shy of graduating," I argued time and again. "Let's figure out a way for me to complete my coursework and earn my diploma."

I guess the idea of a disabled woman obtaining a dance degree from her wheelchair didn't excite the university brass. Once, they even said they couldn't give me an honorary diploma despite the fact that I hadn't asked for one. I wanted to earn mine. Another time they said if they accommodated me, it would open the floodgates to everyone wanting a degree. Over the years, I talked to dozens of people who made promises they didn't keep or passed me along to someone else who made more promises that were not kept. The only consistent response was the word "No!" Not even Senator Figueroa's influence could break this impasse. When her staffers, Kristin Triepke and Laura Metune, read the chancellor's denial over the phone, I broke into sobs.

"We know how driven you are, Cynthia," Laura said, "But you'll never win this one."

There was no way in hell I would accept the chancellor's decision. Like the turtle I love in John Steinbeck's *The Grapes of Wrath*, I had to keep going for it.

I called, wrote and told every influential person I knew about my struggle. In early 2005, Gary Erickson agreed to use his connections to convince the university to reconsider. That was great news because Gary is as well-connected as he is empathic. Not only did he know Barbara Bodine, one of the UC Regents and former Ambassador to Yemen, he was a major fundraiser for UC Santa Barbara. Over the years, I'd often seen how money makes every institution jump.

The next week, after meeting with Barbara, Gary delivered the good news to me in person. Standing before my office desk, hands on his hips and looking even taller than his imposing 6'3" frame, he said, "Barbara wants you to write a letter to Alan Terriciano, the Dance Dean."

"I know Alan. He's one of the dozens there who hasn't returned my phone calls."

"Well, Cynthia, things change. He just didn't know that Barbara's on your side. And as a UC fundraiser, I'm no slouch," he said with a smile. "Barbara has a message for him. She wants you to tell Alan she feels there's no rational reason why he can't get creative and find a way for you to earn that degree. Especially since you're so close to it credit-wise."

Gary put his arm around me. "She also has a message for you. That your work helping women avoid what happened to you is pretty damn special." He winked. "I'll bet that's worth more than a few college credits."

I sent off the letter that same afternoon. Like magic, Alan immediately wrote back. This Dance Dean was now my new best friend. He invited me to meet with him, after which I could speak to the dance department's Injury Prevention class, something I'd requested repeatedly. The audience would include that same faculty who had decided a few years before never to let me return. Overwhelmed, I shared the news with Gary and accepted Alan's invitation.

It seemed like UCI couldn't turn me away now, but I wanted to hedge my bet, so I pulled in another powerful friend, the media. Mayrav Saar, the *Orange County Register* journalist who'd already written a feature about my CRPS struggles, loved the tale of me returning to fulfill my dream. She promised a front-page story called "Second Chance." As additional insurance, I introduced myself to the editor of the UCI paper, who agreed to run a feature. That story, a heart-tugger titled "It's All For Grace," which included a full-page photo, ran the week before my appointment with Alan.

John and I drove the familiar roads back to the place where my life had shattered. The moment was spooky, haunting and exciting. The years I'd spent there felt a million miles away and, at the same time, like yesterday. As I set foot—okay, wheel—on the Fine Arts campus, every memory about who we used to be hit me. Bittersweet pictures flooded in. Waving to Olympic hero and drama major Greg Louganis in the hallway plaza. Choreographing a dance about my beautiful sister on the plaza lawn. John meeting me outside Studio Two so we could walk together to the Commons for dinner before one of our rehearsals.

With a mixture of trepidation and confidence, we met Alan in his office. His hand trembled as he gave me a parking placard. He mentioned nervously that the media had phoned and would be joining us during my injury prevention presentation. Trying hard not to grin, I talked about my speech and assured Alan I wouldn't frighten the audience. "My story is alarming and dancers are at higher risk, but I'll make sure the ballerinas understand that information is power when it comes to CRPS."

I then brought up the six-word phrase that had brought us together. "So what about my diploma, Alan?"

His expression told me he'd been waiting for the question.

"Well, yes, I've been thinking about that," he blurted, shifting in his seat. "I think, I think I have an idea. You'll need to sign up for two independent study classes, Cynthia. Projects that we agree on."

"Sounds good," I said, almost in disbelief that we were having this conversation.

He moved to his computer and tapped lightly on the mouse. An image of an older dancer popped up. "I was thinking you could write a research paper about choreographer Anna Halprin. I mean, if you want to. As you're likely aware, Anna is well noted in the dance world for how she uses movement for healing."

"A perfect match," I agreed.

Then I pitched my idea for the other project. "I want to choreograph my pain experience on a ballerina. I want her to tell my story, to make the pain beautiful." Alan's brows shot up, tipping his approval.

"Then we're in agreement, Cynthia. I suggest you begin looking at our dancers next fall."

"No, Alan. I've already waited much too long. Twenty-three years to be exact. I'll find my own dancer. I've got four months, and I'm going to graduate in June." Alan nodded.

There it was. All tucked, everything in place, so easy to do in that moment and so impossible for all those torturous years.

A few minutes later, back in the studio that held so many memories, I quickly connected with these young dancers. I felt eager to share all I knew about CRPS and injury prevention. They were in full ballet garb, sitting on the familiar wood-paneled floor in stretching positions, their bright eyes directed on me in my wheelchair. I wondered if any of this could make sense to them. Then I spied Kiera Lai*, who seemed to be hiding behind a pair of oversized sunglasses. She had been one of my dance professors all those years back and one of the faculty members who had made the decision not to allow my return.

Pushing my resentment aside, I introduced myself to the class and spoke about my experience with CRPS. Then I shared how dancers could protect themselves should they become afflicted. In the background, Mayrav, whose ordinary posture stood out in this crowd of contortionists, scribbled in her notebook as her photographer snapped pictures.

Then I saw it. The spot where Meg had asked the question. God, I hadn't thought about that for years. I was stunned. Somehow, my talk with these dancers was taking place in the same room where it had all started. I stopped speaking as I relived that moment. I chose to tell the ballerinas about my conclusion that I would kill myself.

"Right now, sitting here with you, I can look at that spot with joy because I've survived and can now make a difference for women in pain. And, in some way perhaps, for one of you.

"Each of us has great inner strength that is rarely called upon. None of us knows what we can survive until we're faced with it. When I look back on my pain experience, living in a wheelchair has been one of the easier aspects. Now, this chair represents my freedom. Today I saw the campus from my wheelchair rather than from my toes. And it still looks damn good to me."

I told them I'd be receiving my dance degree 23 years late from this chair right alongside them in June. They clapped, screamed and thumped their toe shoes on the floor. Afterward, they lined up to hug me, to thank me, to kiss me, a couple of them crying uncontrollably. I held one ballerina, repeating, "I'm okay. Look at me, sweetheart. I'm okay."

The girls invited me to class. Before I went, I thanked Kiera, reaching up to hug and kiss her. The woman who had been so strict, unsupportive and downright arrogant when I studied under her, and who then rigidly argued against my graduation, broke down.

"God, you're such a hero," she whispered. "Look what you've done with your life. And I'm just a big, fat loser."

I whispered back, "You're beautiful, Kiera." I sincerely wished her well, then rolled off to class.

I started choreographing my dance the very next day. I already knew where I'd find my ballerina. Some years prior, after speaking before the Burbank Rotary Club, a woman, Natasha Middleton, had dropped me a note. She wrote that she, too, was a survivor, a fellow ballerina who at 21 had broken her neck in a car accident. The doctors had said she'd never walk again. Soon, I was on the phone with Natasha, who was not only walking, but managing her own ballet company. She could no longer dance professionally, but she could teach.

I began attending Natasha's Media City Ballet performances and was seated at the back of the theater one night when I spotted Ellen Rosa, a dancer with my height and body type, plus similar high arches and extensions. I loved the expressive way she communicated through the dance. She would be me.

We started working together. Suddenly I was no longer just watching. I had returned to my greatest love and discovered a new role that I treasured. The ballet studio could now live not only in my dreams at night, but as a real part of my life in a way that was more important than ever. On this beautiful high, I dared to be bold and allowed my arm contracture and endless tears to come elegantly to life through Ellen. With Natasha's help, I choreographed to "Never Again," a ballad about my life-long struggle presented to me as a surprise at a For Grace fundraiser.

I wanted to bring John's character into the dance. Natasha quickly recruited her top male dancer. Strapping, gorgeous and imported from the Ukraine, Arsen Serobian brought both strength and emotional expression to the choreography. When he lifted Ellen from her darkest point as she lay on the floor having succumbed to the horror of CRPS, I felt John's strength and how he had picked me up and helped me to live once again.

I also brought in "Grace," a little 5-year-old dynamo of a ballerina, to represent the child John and I could never have.

Then I faced my biggest fear, incorporating the wheelchair into the dance. In my eyes, there's nothing more beautiful than ballet, and to bring in the "ugliness" of the wheelchair was scary. But I needed to tell the whole story. One of my deepest pleasures with ballet has always been its power to make the earth-bound heavenly. Sparked by my creative juices and the dancers' skill and adventurous spirits, I found the courage to make that wheelchair beautiful.

Deep into rehearsals, I started shooting with Discovery Health. Almost immediately, I got the idea to bring their camera crew into the studio to capture that dance. I figured worldwide media couldn't hurt if Irvine pulled a nasty trick at the 11th hour. The crew was mesmerized as they'd never been this close to ballet. They shot the dance and decided to include it in the program they were doing about my illness.

Even more importantly, this ballet was a significant gift for me. Until then, no one really understood how my injury had occurred, which weighed heavily on me and made me feel alone. Most people don't understand the nuances of ballet, so journalists and producers always incorrectly described the movements that led to my injury. In fact, the depictions were often physically impossible. Even John couldn't capture in his mind's eye the moment that had changed our lives. But now I'd been given the remarkable opportunity to reenact it with Ellen.

As I snapped my fingers for rhythm, this accomplished ballerina followed every instruction. "Left leg behind you on the barre. *Pas de bras*, Ellen. Now bring your upper body down to your right leg. Beautiful, perfect. Stretch your back out as you bring your body up."

"Should I stretch it out more?" Ellen questioned, her large, brown eyes focused intensely.

"Yes. Let's do it again." She repeated the movement to my snapping. As her body reached the point of the stretch where it all went wrong, I called out, "Now!"

Ellen jerked in pretend pain, simulating my collapse. And the camera caught it. A ton of bricks—no, a mountain of bricks—lifted from my shoulders. I was floating out of my wheelchair. Those hellish bricks could never again hold me down. Everyone who watched this sequence would now hold one of those bricks. I would no longer bear my burden alone. I was free.

I completed the requirements for my dance degree while working full time at For Grace, pulling more than a few all-nighters. Then that day was upon us, the one where the impossible would come true. John and I, at long last, attended my commencement on a beautiful, sunny June day in 2005. A wave of excitement rushed through me as our Saab hit the campus. We were immediately surrounded by laughing, celebrating students in their black caps and gowns. Good God, my graduation was *really* happening. The tingle went down to my toes.

This was a commencement and for us a very special reunion all wrapped into one. Amidst the exuberance of it all, with people pressed together everywhere, John never left my side. We were greeted by Keith Fowler, one of John's favorite drama professors who would be announcing my name, to discuss a bit of special choreography needed to get me and my wheelchair on to the stage. As John and I lined up, I was congratulated and hugged by students I'd spoken to before, along with a number of former teachers and others who knew my story. The great El Gabriel put on my cap and tassel as we laughed together. I was amazed by how his presence somehow warmed me. This was better than a perfect triple *pirouette en pointe*, better than mastering a Bach piano concerto, even better than the lights of Vegas.

"Walking" with the Fine Arts department, we entered the spanking new Bren Events Center where thousands of people applauded and cheered. I looked up at the gigantic, gold UCI emblem backed by a blue banner a football field wide. Still in a partial state of disbelief, I struggled to hold back a flood of tears. My joy turned to fierce pride. Without a doubt, this remains the proudest moment of my life, my high of highs.

Then I got the cherry on the top. Little Tessie. There she was in a blue cotton summer dress and pink sun hat running down from the bleachers to kiss me. She placed a purple lei around my neck and handed me freshly picked lavender, smelling as sweet as she. I held my precious 6-year-old niece tighter than ever. I didn't want to let go. I wanted this moment to last forever.

"You made it, Auntie," she squeaked.

Up in the balcony, I saw my family arriving late in classic Toussaint style. My heart jumped when I spotted my sleepy-eyed big brother Paul. The night before, we'd had a bit of a row when I heard he wasn't coming. Steamed and hurt, I got him on the phone lickity-split.

"Cynthia, I just can't swing it. I'm going to be up all night with Ryan's high school graduation party. I'm afraid I'll fall asleep in the car driving down from Santa Barbara."

I love my nephew, but I needed Paul there. "You're the closest thing I've ever had to a father, Paul. It took me over two decades to do this. It will mean the world if you come."

And he had. Beth was there too, stunning as ever, with her husband Jack who was manning the video camera to document the event for Discovery Health. What a prince. My mother, dressed all in white like the angel she is, wasn't having much luck holding back the tears. I waved up, and my smile must have told them all they needed to know about how I was feeling.

Having taken in my family, I looked around and noticed that all the graduates were kids. *Was I really that young when all of this started?* I thought I owned the world back then, something to play off my fingertips like a yo-yo. Life was going to be fast-paced, non-stop glamour and fun. These kids had the same look in their eyes. But they hadn't yet tasted very much of the world—the bumps and pitfalls, the disappointments, the slap-in-your-face realizations. I felt protective of this brood. I wanted to wrap my arms around each of them and say, "This is beautiful. Don't forget it." But I realized that no matter what anyone said, it wouldn't matter a damn. And that was pure truth. These dancers would find their own way.

When it was the dance department's turn to be recognized, John ramped me up to the rear of the stage, as instructed, where we were hidden by a row of palms. I felt a bit silly peering through the foliage like Arte Johnson in that old bit from *Laugh-In*.

John and I were to go first. Suddenly I realized that Professor Fowler was waiting for us. Yikes!

"Oh God, John," I yelped in a panic. "Go now!"

John blinked confidently. "No, sweetie. He's supposed to call out your name first. We can't blow this."

Fowler moved on, and I immediately knew I'd missed my turn. Funny how these monumental moments play out in our heads, all perfect and precious. Instead, I was now Lucy trying to find a way to break into the act. I had waited 23 years for this? I turned to John with a grin. "We're the only adults here and we can't figure this out?"

"Oh hell, Cynth, let's just go."

John shot me into the middle of the commencement parade, almost clipping one of the other graduates. Fowler did a double take, but pro that he is kept his cool, and spun a special emphasis on the calling out of "Graduate Toussaint." Dizzy as much from the occasion as the wheelchair spin, I mouthed, "I owe you one." We went past the rest of the dance faculty on the stage, their lips taut, their eyes glued to my every move. I was having a ball. Fine Arts Dean Nohema Fernandez wrapped her arms around me, kissed me on the cheek and handed me the mock diploma. I stiffened a tad, recalling how hard the department had worked to make sure this day wouldn't happen. But that was all water under the bridge. I smiled up at her, secure that she knew this was right and, indeed, wonderful.

I heard the cheers from my family rise above the pomp and circumstance and saw them at the back of the balcony. They were on their feet, screaming, "Go Cynthia!" Above it all, I heard Mom's signature, steel-piercing whistle. I blew them my best *Dating Game* kiss, my arm sweeping wide. And then it was over.

Somehow we found each other amongst the thousands pouring out of the auditorium. Mom and I fell into an embrace. I felt almost as thrilled for her as I did for myself, knowing how she'd dreamed of this day finally happening for her ballerina daughter. I couldn't stop beaming as I showed everyone the campus, *my* campus. We cruised all the old haunts, including the fine arts plaza with its rolling grassy hillock, the dance studios and the theater where John had done his infamous nude scene from Sam Shepard's *The Curse of the Starving Class.*

As usual, Tess insisted on pushing my wheelchair, her head still barely peeking over the back. She stayed proudly by my side all afternoon as we attended the reception where my family surprised me with presents and party crackers, spraying me with confetti and hot-pink streamers.

Though I'm mercilessly kidded that I *never* stop talking, miracles do happen. I was speechless when I opened my mom's gift. She had given me her most beautiful pen and ink drawing, for which I'd posed years before at Grandma's house in Minnesota. I remembered squirming, trying to end the modeling session to get to that chocolate malt with my name on it waiting at Bacon's Drugs. But, boy, am I glad I stuck around. She'd never given anyone an original before. It's the gift of my lifetime.

Near the end of the celebration, a tall, handsome man walked up. He reminded me of my favorite dance instructor at UCI, Larry Rosenberg, whose class I'd been injured in. The man, who I later learned had taken Larry's place on the dance faculty, crouched, bringing us eye to eye, and squeezed my hand firmly. "You did a wonderful thing, Cynthia," he said softly. "You never gave up and you beat us all. I'll never forget you."

Nor will I ever forget this stranger, who in that moment became a friend and placed a beautiful capper on my day.

John's Take

The emotional impact of Cynthia's graduation truly blows me away. As I roll her into that arena with some 4,000 onlookers, the power of my feelings shocks me. I knew this was her day and thought I was just along for the ride. But no, this is my rebirth, too. I get a shot at playing 1983 all over again. The feeling of accomplishment, the hope for the future, the sizzle of expectation. All the things that ebbed away as the pain grew in Reno and Vegas and finally leveled us a few months later.

When we return to Irvine to pick up the actual diploma, something primal stirs in me, something familiar, a fear that they'll snap it away at the last moment. "Nope," the young clerk will say. "No diploma here. NEXT!" But there it is. I slip it out of its manila envelope, and see Cynthia smile. When I look at it, the Governor's name scrawled across its bottom, a tear falls onto the diploma. I start sobbing, unable to hold back. Cynthia puts her arms around me, rocking me back and forth in UCI's Hall of Administration.

Some of the pain of 23 years flows out of me. I feel an elation I haven't felt since I can't remember when. Triumph. It's a heady brew. I'm drinking it up like someone lost in the desert. Its sweet taste fills every part of me.

Back home, I dust off my diploma tucked away deep in the bottom drawer of my dresser. Edges yellowed, cheap faux wood frame I snapped up from Aaron Brothers for a five spot. Never on display because we didn't have hers. Now on the wall we'd left bare for so long, we hang our diplomas side by side.

We're finally celebrating our graduation together, with her diploma proudly trumpeting 2005, mine 1983. I love the symbolism of it. Right there on the wall. Together. Cynthia and John. Just like always.

TWENTY

THE LUCKY ONE

My life did not take me where I longed to go. Not to the lights, the glitter, the thrill of it all. If I could have chosen to live pain-free, I would have grabbed that option by the throat. But I would have been the lesser for it. By a long shot. My years of struggle not only redefined my dreams, they taught me that when we're unflinching and true to our hearts, we can realize the most unlikely dreams of all.

The year after my graduation, filmmaker Don Schroeder invited me to do an on-camera interview to support California's single-payer universal healthcare bill, SB 840. I was honored because this legislation, sponsored by Senator Kuehl, backed my deepest desire for healthcare reform, a single-payer system that puts the government in charge and takes Big Pharma and the insurance moguls out of the picture. Don was using a *60 Minutes* crew to shoot our film and brought them to our downtown office. Wow, did we ever talk about how healthcare is flat out busted in this country and how it can be fixed. I must have gotten plenty heated. "Watch it, Cynthia, you're gonna bust a vein," the cameraman joked at one point. While I sputtered back how I was always like this, John howled his agreement from across the room.

In the middle of the interview, Don started making tongue-ticking sounds, imitating the famous *60 Minutes* intro. "Ooh, gorgeous," he exclaimed. "That sound bite knocked it out of the park."

"We're the great United States of America," I said cynically, then paused. "And we don't even have *healthcare* for our people. What's *wrong* with this picture?" That quote would elicit the biggest response from the audience at the documentary's premiere screening.

During my political run, I had become ever more passionate about fighting for a single-payer plan. It would replace the profit-over-people insurance and pharmaceutical companies with governmental oversight. Equally important, I knew firsthand how our current system was hurting the women I worked with at For Grace. "I have no insurance" were the words I heard most often. There are no uglier words for a disease like CRPS, whose treatment demands early diagnosis and care. This doomed countless good people to a life of pain and, far too often, to suicide.

This contrasts dramatically with a single-payer plan that would control costs while giving health insurance to everyone. Hey, we've been doing this just beautifully with Medicare since the mid-'60s. Greed is the only reason we don't have this basic human right in place. It's going to be a long, hard fight, and I'm committed to being one of the noisiest, get-in-your-face voices on that firing line.

When I spoke out about universal healthcare in my HMO reform days, I was chided on TV as being a "naïve young woman," someone who "didn't look to the future." Now, because of President Obama's healthcare reform, this topic is on the tip of most everyone's tongue. For me, the Affordable Care Act is a significant step in the right direction, but I'm extremely disappointed that it doesn't include a single-payer plan.

In the summer of 2007, I began to recognize the depth of my involvement in this effort. Then I was invited by Sheila to speak for her bill at what would be the largest healthcare rally in U.S. history. She was enough of a hell-raiser to battle the world on this one, even though she knew the insurance industry and Governor Schwarzenegger would stand in the way—which is exactly what happened when he ultimately vetoed her bill. But like the sports teams often say, I keep telling myself, "wait till next year!"

The Great L.A. Healthcare Rally was held outdoors on a sunny August day at the Los Angeles City Hall. I wore a bright orange velvet blazer with jeans and my new Skechers. The moment we arrived, the electricity generated from the crowd of about 6,000 lifted me to the nearby mountaintops. This energy seemed even stronger than the anti-war rallies John and I marched in regularly. Michael Moore's *Sicko* had just premiered that summer and people were fired up for healthcare reform. I loved reading all of the homemade signs—everything from "Healthcare, Not Warfare!" to "No Compromise, Arnie, Sign SB 840 Now!"

The day's speakers included Lily Tomlin, Presidential candidate Dennis Kucinich, Lt. Governor John Garamendi, civil rights legend Delores Huerta, Sheila and, of course, me. Media vans lined Spring Street, their antennas snaking into the sky.

I rehearsed my speech in a tented room for maybe the billionth time. I drive myself nuts as I always insist on memorizing every damn word. Meanwhile, John networked and took pictures. Excitedly, he peeked his head into my tent and blurted, "I met Tomlin. She's running her speech just like you. You're gonna love her!" Then Tomlin was up there talking, with me just behind the main stage curtain poised to go on after her and still going over my lines. I was eager to nail this one.

My ribs ached from Tomlin's priceless Ernestine-as-HMO-administrator routine when John and another gentleman picked up my wheelchair and set me down front and center stage. The crowd instantly erupted into cheers and whistles. Their hoots and hollers got louder and louder. *What the hell is going on?* I wondered. *Are they cheering for somebody behind me?* But I was alone on the stage. Tingling, I gave them two thumbs up. They went nuts.

I started to speak, feeding off their energy. As I talked, the crowd's cheers continued to interrupt. I projected over them, stirred with emotion. When their voices became louder than mine, I stopped mid speech, pausing long enough to smile from ear to ear, my eyes brimming with tears.

I was still waving as they whisked me off stage. A flurry of people, their hands outstretched, greeted me, starting with the various speakers and politicians around the stage. Then nurses and patients from the crowd rushed up, mentioning where they'd seen me and heard my interviews, thanking me for the work I was doing.

It was finally sinking in. These people actually knew me and my work. I was astonished and overwhelmed.

The rest of the day passed in a blur. As an activist, it's not easy to accept applause and thank yous because we're all in this together. But my standing up (figuratively) for the cause had stirred appreciation in them. Deeply satisfied and more than a little healed, I stayed close to John and held his hand.

I could feel his pride. He later told me that he felt his love for me—his "lightning bolt disguised as an earthly being"—flow out from every pore as he listened to me speak before those thousands. And now, after watching this show for nearly three decades, he wanted to tell everyone at the rally, "You ain't seen nothing yet."

I may have been his lightning bolt, but he was the force from which the lightning originated. Without him, I'd never have gotten anywhere near that stage. Hell, I wouldn't have survived.

The year I sustained the injury, 1982, feels like the Dark Ages now. No one had any notion about pain as a disease back then, let alone about the gender divide. No one was talking about either in the media. Today, cover stories about pain constantly pop up in national magazines. Weeklong exposés air on major network news programs. This surge of awareness has greatly eased the suffering of millions. I'm proud of the role I've played in making this happen. My soul is rich with the power of it. A power that remains undiminished by the increased harassment at our condo, something we've now made peace with.

I've received other gifts from my advocacy work. I have come to believe that all living things are interconnected. This collective consciousness, which is built on love and care, has the power to bring about goodness and beat back the evil that tries to overwhelm it. My spirit has grown because of this, and I'm humbled by the realization that my voice is one of those helping to bring about something better for our planet. I feel grateful for the task. The ego-drive that originally propelled me is ebbing away—and an unexpected wholeness is filling me.

One of my favorite quotes is "the strongest souls are forged by the hottest fires." As much as this applies to my life and evolution, I haven't always believed it. My change was triggered by a woman I hold dear.

In the early '90s, after moving to Los Angeles, I hooked up with an old college buddy, Terri Navarra, one of the few friends left from my pre-CRPS days. Terri's an amazingly talented and bright comic to whom I sometimes turn for advice. Her career was impeded when she developed fibromyalgia as a young adult, but she pushed on with her dreams.

When my hopes for the *Playboy* feature, which I thought of as my last chance, were crushed, her response stunned me.

"I don't feel sorry for you," Terri said. "I know what you can do. Screw *Playboy*. You don't need them." And then she said it. "The work you'll do will ultimately be much more important than the work you would have done."

Her words cut deeply, engulfing me in anger. I shouted out, "No, Terri. You're not getting it. I want the life I planned, the career in show business I worked my ass off to get. I can't believe you just said that."

"Someday you'll see it, Cynthia," she said, her tone softening.

Hallelujah! She was right.

The fire within burns differently now. I still get a charge from work in and about the entertainment business, but something's missing. When I get an acting audition or modeling job, I notice

I'm distracted, wondering what's going on at For Grace. *Who did I really help today?*

I didn't fully experience all of Terri's "rightness" until early 2008 when *People* magazine threw a Hollywood bash for my brother-in-law Jack's 50th birthday. The elegant invitation specified a '50s theme. It sounded like a gas.

That day, I had a ball getting dolled up for the party. I was in my element. Getting ready felt a bit like slipping on a sequined G-string and fishnets in Vegas, like donning the lacy white ballet skirt and wings before *Les Sylphides*, like dressing up to put on a show for Mom and my siblings when I was a kid. I adored having my make-up and hair done à la Marilyn Monroe and then putting on my black cocktail dress, long velvet gloves and the gorgeous mink stole that had belonged to John's grandmother. *Who'd ever have thought I'd get a chance to wear that classic?* I went all out, right down to the perfect '50s purse and shoes, costume jewelry and red manicured nails. My date for this soirée, Mister John, looked simply fab in his black suit, white handkerchief and slicked-back hair.

The bash was held at a swanky Hollywood Hills home with lots of trendy polished cement, an infinity pool, an actual movie theater and a post-modern art collection all fronted by a million dollar view of Los Angeles. The place was packed with upward of 200 people, including the casts of *Dynasty* and *Heroes*, the two series Jack had starred in. I recognized Joan Collins upon entering and smiled up at her from my chair. Her surprisingly indifferent glance tipped me to the vibe churning in the room.

Looking for something warmer, I got out of my chair and camped on the high marble fireplace hearth in the living room. I felt more like a curious observer than a participant as I listened in on conversations about new swimming pools, upcoming career moves that would propel the speakers to bigger stardom, family vacation in the Maldives and disappointing plastic surgeries.

Twice, my focus was broken. A talent manager walked up and shook my hand, mistaking me for Scarlett Johansson (*so sorry, just li'l ol' me*) and then abruptly turned on his heel. Then Tess shot out of nowhere, hugging me tight, not letting go. In a moment, her generous love swept aside the pomp and pretense. Adorned in a tight-waisted, powder blue dress with full petticoat and bows in her long, strawberry blonde hair, she quietly sang "Frère Jacques" in my ear, the perfect balm for what was turning out to be an evening of disconnect.

I didn't understand why I felt so far out of the loop here. Why wasn't I having fun? I love being loud and silly with people, especially show people, cracking jokes, stirring up a ruckus, always the last to leave. But I wasn't feeling that way now.

Midway into the party, it struck me. I was watching a picture of what my life might have been. I was talking to people I had little ability to relate to anymore, people who found it just as difficult to wrap their heads around my experience. A Grand Canyon of separation had been forged by my challenges and their apparent ease of life. This night was giving me a remarkable gift. A front row seat that showed, quite dramatically, how much my values had changed. I had become quite different from my dream. And now, on this night, I had a much better one.

Theirs was a fine life. God, how I respect that talent and drive, that ability to entertain. It was the life I thought I couldn't live without. But I didn't need it anymore. And in that moment, with peace in my heart, I said goodbye to what might have been.

I have found a wondrous new stage, one where it's no longer only about me. It's about millions of others, about alleviating their suffering and, indeed, about saving lives.

Oddly, my life is not *so* different from the one I wanted. I had planned to live on the high wire, to not know what was coming next, to be in front of an audience, to make the impossible happen and to always, always reach for the highest star. And this is, in fact, my life today. Despite unrelenting pain that can still force me, after just a few steps, to sit like a bird on a perch before I can continue, I have found a way to give my suffering meaning. Sitting in that party, surrounded by the Hollywood elite, I realized that I'd lucked out.

I was deep in this reverie when John walked up to wheel me out. Our eyes connected and I felt his heart reach out to mine. He nodded with an "I get it, Cynth" smile that told me he felt it, too. When we got out into the cool night air, we shared a soft, gentle kiss, and I knew I would never go back. Terri's words echoed in my head, and I realized that at age 47, I'd come full circle. I had been given the opportunity to travel to a place most haven't. I had survived the hottest of fires and emerged renewed. I had found gratitude for a love that had been challenged and remained solid. I had chosen a dream that I never knew was possible.

And I had found grace.

I am a victim no more.

EPILOGUE

The most important word in this book has not yet been mentioned.

Remission.

It's a place that for almost 30 years I never thought possible. A place of normalcy. Of peace. Of singing, swimming and playing the piano again. Of doing a ballet floor barre and returning to Pilates, which is probably why I don't dream about dance anymore. It's like being reborn. A transcendence.

A place I experience as sacred space where I live more fully with the love of my life and pursue the changing passions of my life. I nurture my family relationships more deeply. I've returned to my life as an athlete and musician. And I continue my mission to help women in pain live, grow and receive equal treatment from medical professionals.

Being in remission does not mean I live pain free. Not even close. I still have CRPS, but the flare-ups are less frequent and less severe. I also have serious pain that isn't CRPS. Simply put, it's *normal* pain caused by normal body movement. Tendonitis, for example, has been triggered by playing the piano for about two hours each day, using muscles that have been idle since the mid-'80s. In my joy at being able to play again, I've overextended. I've done much the same with swimming, which has caused a painful knee problem. Clearly, my remission is a work in progress.

We've never been sure what caused this remarkable recovery, but John and I believe that the writing of this book triggered most—if not all—of it. Baring our souls to you—and more importantly, to ourselves—washed away much of the angst, pain and trauma we dumped on each other. We needed to tell it true. To relive *all* the anger and hurt. This brought back the chaos and pain almost full force, but it also helped rebuild my emotional well-being, freeing my body's natural healing powers. I strongly recommend daily journal writing to everyone, especially women in pain. I believe it had the power to heal me.

There was also that night at Jack's party when we experienced our enormous gift—the realization that we were leading lives more meaningful than any we'd hoped for. That reality lives with us to this day.

I've grown in ways I never imagined. Top of the list, I learned to befriend my pain after years of demonizing it. I also learned to stop hating, judging and blaming. And to forgive. Most of all, I learned to listen to my body and inner voice. And to appreciate all my blessings, especially my John of Arc.

I've been asked if this change was spiritual. It feels that way to us. Things like resisting suicide, again and again. And not following doctors' advice to have breast surgery. And our trip to Paris, which I knew might increase my pain—it did so, fiercely—but became an emotional and spiritual building block for much of my growth. These choices and many others came from the belief in myself and are an integral part of my spirituality.

Probably most spiritual of all was our refusal to let the physical and emotional violence end us.

People often say my remission is a miracle. I believe each of us can tap into powers we're unaware of. New wisdom and choices that can free us. If that's a miracle, how wonderful.

My wellness and emotional strength was impacted strongly by Dr. Brodsky who introduced me to integrative medicine and a new kind of hope. I'm now in control of my well-being. It took patience, time and a doctor who believed in the power of self-care.

My "sisters in pain," as I call them, have provided another blessing. There are six of us, including me. We talk often. About our lives. Our pain. Our love for each other and all our other sisters. We often work together. There's already a power here, a backbone for more grace. I feel certain this group will grow.

There's more. John and I, being adventurers at heart, will continue to travel widely. Like our trips to Paris, Australia, Italy and Tahiti. Our last jaunt took us to Africa to celebrate my 50th birthday. It posed significant health risks, but my doctors endorse our journeys and we thrive on them.

I also carry with me, every day, the spirit of John's brother David. His passing taught me so much about life and dying.

I've come to believe everything happens just as it's supposed to. Everything I do and whatever everyone else does affects everything on the planet. And, in a way almost beyond my power to imagine, opens the door for peace. This profoundly raises my hope for all of us everywhere.

I base this on my own life. I know that I, in microcosm, represent everyone. And having experienced the emotional, physical and spiritual transformation born from the depths I lived in, I can see a day when we could all be on the path to global healing.

Let's make this planet our sacred space.

ACKNOWLEDGEMENTS

With love and appreciation, I thank you from the bottom of my heart, Irene Jursyzk, for being the conscience of our book. I can truly never thank you enough for listening so lovingly to my many tape recordings of pain and joy. Your homework assignment for me to write my entire life as an outline began this process with a flurry of passion. It opened my eyes to the reality that I could write. Thank you also, Irene, for coming up with the loving, brilliant idea of having John write "takes" as my partner, caregiver and witness.

Many thanks to you, sweet friend, Tony Westbrook, for giving *Battle for Grace* its title. You're forever masterful, Tony, at capturing the essence of a story and putting it into a few potent words. In fact, you're so good at it, you don't remember coming up with this title. But the moment you shared those three words, I knew they said it all.

Ron Kovic, I'm indebted for your challenge that I write my story exactly the way it happened. You, by proxy, were the deciding vote when John and I sometimes disagreed about being completely open and leaving nothing out. I agree with you, Ron, that one can only shake up the world by writing the entire truth.

For the late Jill Kinmont Boothe, I thank you for being such an inspiring force in my life since I saw your movie *The Other Side of the Mountain* when I was 13. Your strength and grit in the face of adversity gave me a rock to hold on to in my darkest days, and, later, someone to emulate. Getting to know and work with you was a blessing I didn't expect. Your support of this book never wavered. Thank you, sweet Jill, for emboldening me and millions of others. Your spirit lives on.

I grin as I thank you, Morgan Grether, for telling me at our Board meeting the idea that came to you while shaving that fateful morning in June 2005. You shared your strong feeling that I had an important story and should write a book about it. John is correct, my dear. You are one of my enablers and I thank you for continuing to stir the pot.

For the story our front cover photo tells, I thank you, the amazing Coral von Zumwalt. I loved our shoot for *Woman's Day*, and your release of this photo to me is one of the greatest gifts I've ever received. I could have shot with a hundred other people and never gotten the essence of my struggle and spirit. You crystalized it, Coral. And the day of the shoot was the only time I again wore the ballet garb I was wearing when I injured my leg. I'm moved every time I look at it.

To the phenomenally talented Dana Patrick, I thank you for our back photo, one that captures the sparks and joy John and I feel when we're together. This photo is especially meaningful as it was at the end of our shoot and my broken arm was giving me some pretty fierce pain. In three shots, you nailed it!

A gigantic thank you to Hugh Milstein and Michael McHugh at Digital Fusion for spinning your design magic on our book jacket. I deeply appreciate your connection with my story and wrapping it up with such a beautiful bow.

My sincere gratitude to Sarah Stegemoeller at Public Counsel for working with John to find the best attorneys for this book's legal review: David Halberstadter and Susan Grode at Katten Muchin Rosenman LLP. In my wildest dreams, I couldn't have hoped for a more skilled and caring team to guide me through *Battle for Grace's* legal maze. Thank you for the considerable gift of your great wisdom and compassion for this project.

To my agents, Alan Shafer and Mike Hamilburg, you have my utmost love and respect for never wavering in your confidence about the power of this project. Year after year, you've encouraged me beyond belief. I've been told that one isn't supposed to love their agents, a Hollywood ritual you both compelled me to break. As we move this book into movie adaptation, I am forever indebted to your exquisite teamwork to give this story its furthest reach.

Wow! Thank you, Linden Gross, for coaching me through the writing of my life. No easy task! Your weaving of my over-abundant first draft writings was phenomenal. You made clear what this book was, whittling and shaving to its core. You taught me how to use all of my senses, and I learned to smell and taste each experience. You gently guided me into insights about pieces of my life that needed clarity. I deeply respect you using your considerable talents to aid other women in the telling of their stories, Linden; you've been an empowering partner in this dance.

Thanks, Mom, for always being there through the dark and light of this enormous project. I can't count the times I phoned to ask you to remind me of a detail. No matter what you were in the middle of, you dropped everything and took me back, sparking my memory. It was so much fun, Mom, to relive the joys and the warmth of our family's early life together. And the pain, as always, made more sense once we talked it through. Your love and goodness shines through these pages. I love you.

For the love of my life, John, I'm in my usual state of awe because you were there every moment. From dictating to you my overflowing words when I was unable to see due to that glaucoma test spreading the CRPS to the five years of writing and remembering together to being there to help me make the thousands of decisions that this work demanded, you kept me on course and constantly reminded me that this book would someday be a reality. Mostly, sweetie, thank you for going to therapy to find the strength and courage to "open your Grand Canyon of pain," to be vulnerable enough to bleed your heart out onto these pages. Your writings and perspectives are what make this story so powerful. You are my hero.

And most of all, I thank you, Mr. Dick Freed. Without your brilliant edits and the way you understood my feelings and the heart of our story—plus your love, care, sacrifice and unflinching belief in our book, there would be no *Battle for Grace*. And dare I say, there might be no John and Cynthia. I know your sweet modesty will want to brush this sentiment aside, but it is the truth and I ask that you wrap your loving arms around it. You re-lived my life with me, Dick, and you helped me make sense of it as you fine-tuned every word, and maddeningly (at points!) every letter of the numerous versions of this book. When I saw your beautiful movie, *Wildflower*, two decades ago, I immediately knew that I *had* to work with you. I pitched my story soon afterward and you've been my mentor in writing, producing and, yes, life ever since. Despite the endless obstacles and trials that conspired to stop this story from being told, you always refused to quit—a strength that continues to mystify me. Your ever-affirming spirit is boundless; your heart reminds me there are angels walking this earth. To you and your bride of 56 years, Kathy, who stood by us every step of the way, I send unending love. Bless us all.

ABOUT THE AUTHORS

Cynthia Toussaint founded the organization For Grace in 2002 to raise awareness about the chronic pain disease Complex Regional Pain Syndrome, and five years later expanded the organization's mission to ensure the ethical and equal treatment of all women in pain. She currently serves as spokesperson, and has had CRPS for 30 years. Before becoming ill, she was an accomplished ballerina and worked professionally as a dancer, actor and singer.

Since 1997, Toussaint has been a leading advocate for women in pain, raising awareness through local, national and worldwide media as well as public speaking. Toussaint championed and gave key testimony at two California Senate informational hearings. The first, in 2001, was dedicated to CRPS awareness, and the second, in 2004, explored the under-treatment of chronic pain and gender bias toward women in pain. Both of these efforts were the first of their kind in the nation.

Toussaint has been featured on *ABC World News with Diane Sawyer*, PBS, Discovery Health, The Learning Channel, *AARP The Magazine, Newsweek, Woman's Day* and *The New York Times*, among others. She is a consultant for ABC News, FOX News and *PainPathways*, the official magazine of the World Institute of Pain.

In 2006, Toussaint ran for the California State Assembly to bring attention to her CRPS Education Bill that Governor Schwarzenegger vetoed after it got to his desk in its first year. Her current Step Therapy bill will reform an unethical prescription practice used by the health insurance industry to save money in a way that increases the suffering of California pain patients.

Toussaint continues to be a leading advocate for healthcare reform in California and beyond. She was instrumental in changing public opinion that sparked sweeping HMO reform legislation that was signed by California Governor Gray Davis in 1999. Her focus has now shifted to creating a single-payer, universal health-care plan in California that would provide a model for the rest of the country.

Toussaint is currently experiencing her second partial CRPS remission (first in 27 years!) However, in 2011, she sustained a broken right elbow at the hands of an overly aggressive physical therapist, leading to a year of misdiagnosis, harmful therapies and an upcoming surgery. Her interest in upgrading healthcare in America will continue to be a focus for her and For Grace in the future.

Cynthia currently resides in Los Angeles with her life-partner John Garrett and their two Siamese cats, Zanzibar Stone and Haydée Grace.

Linden Gross is a best-selling writer. She ghostwrote Julia "Butterfly" Hill's national bestseller *The Legacy of Luna* (HarperCollins, 2000). *Publishers Weekly* called the book "a remarkable inspirational document."

Gross is also the co-author and writer of *Raising Boys without Men* (Rodale, 2005) and *Son of a Preacher Man* (HarperCollins, 2001), which led to the TV series about Jay Bakker. Her collaboration on *Ms. Cahill for Congress* (Ballantine, 2008) was one of Random House's main releases that year. The book is slated to be made into a film starring Halle Berry.

Most recently, Gross helped Olympic champion and BBC commentator Michael Johnson write *Gold Rush* (HarperSport, 2011), a compelling analysis of the fascinating combination of psychological and personal qualities that go to create an Olympic champion.

She is the sole author of *Surviving a Stalker: Everything You Need to Know to Keep Yourself Safe* (Marlowe & Company, 2000) and *To Have Or To Harm* (Warner Books, 1994), the first book written about the stalking of ordinary people. She is the founder of www.stalkingvictims.com and the Stalking Survivors' Sanctuary & Solutions, a nonprofit organization.

Formerly Special Features Editor for the *Los Angeles Times Magazine* and associate editor for *Ladies' Home Journal,* she has written freelance articles for many publications including *Reader's Digest, Cosmopolitan, Ms., Self, Redbook, Parents, Us* and *TV Guide.*

CPSIA information can be obtained
at www.ICGtesting.com
Printed in the USA
LVOW10s1734050418
572436LV00012B/1376/P